ACCENTS ON SHAKESPEARE

General editor: TERENCE HAWKES

# Green Shakespeare

Ecocriticism, a theoretical movement examining cultural construc-tions of Nature in their social and political contexts, is making an increasingly important contribution to our understanding of Shake-speare's plays.

*Green Shakespeare* offers:

- an overview of the concept of ecocriticism;
- detailed ecocritical readings of *Henry 5, Macbeth, As You Like It, Antony and Cleopatra, King Lear, Coriolanus, Pericles, Cymbeline, The Winter's Tale,* and *The Tempest*;
- analysis of themes such as nature and human society; food and biological nature; the supernatural and the weather;
- a bold argument for a contemporary 'EcoShakespeare', taking into account the environmental and political implications of globalization and twenty-first century science.

Crossing the boundaries of literary and cultural studies to draw in politics, philosophy, and ecology, this volume not only introduces one of the most lively areas of contemporary Shakespeare studies, but also offers a convincing case for Shakespeare's continuing rele-vance to contemporary theory.

**Gabriel Egan** is a Senior Lecturer in English at Loughborough University. He is the author of *Shakespeare and Marx*, and edits the journals *Theatre Notebook* and *Shakespeare*.

# ACCENTS ON SHAKESPEARE
## General editor: TERENCE HAWKES

It is more than twenty years since the New Accents series helped to establish 'theory' as a fundamental and continuing feature of the study of literature at the undergraduate level. Since then, the need for short, powerful 'cutting edge' accounts of and comments on new developments has increased sharply. In the case of Shakespeare, books with this sort of focus have not been readily available. **Accents on Shakespeare** aims to supply them.

**Accents on Shakespeare** volumes will either 'apply' theory, or broaden and adapt it in order to connect with concrete teaching concerns. In the process, they will also reflect and engage with the major developments in Shakespeare studies of the last ten years.

The series will lead as well as follow. In pursuit of this goal it will be a two-tiered series. In addition to affordable, 'adoptable' titles aimed at modular undergraduate courses, it will include a number of research-based books. Spirited and committed, these second-tier volumes advocate radical change rather than stolidly reinforcing the status quo.

## IN THE SAME SERIES

# Green Shakespeare

## From ecopolitics
## to ecocriticism

GABRIEL EGAN

Routledge
Taylor & Francis Group

LONDON AND NEW YORK

First published 2006
by Routledge
2 Park Square, Milton Park,
Abingdon, Oxon OX14 4RN

Simultaneously published in
the USA and Canada
by Routledge
270 Madison Avenue,
New York, NY 10016

Routledge is an imprint of the
Taylor & Francis Group,
an informa business

Typeset in Baskerville by
Florence Production Ltd,
Stoodleigh, Devon
Printed and bound in Great Britain
by TJ International Ltd,
Padstow, Cornwall

British Library Cataloguing in
Publication Data

A catalogue record for this book is
available from the British Library

Library of Congress Cataloging in
Publication Data

Egan, Gabriel.
Green Shakespeare: from ecopolitics to
ecocriticism / Gabriel Egan.
    p. cm. – (Accents on Shakespeare)
Includes bibliographical references and index.
1. Shakespeare, William, 1564–1616 –
Knowledge – Natural history. 2. Ecology –
Political aspects. 3. Human ecology in
literature. 4. Nature in literature.
5. Ecocriticism. I. Title. II. Series.

PR3039.E35 2006
822.3′3–dc22                    2005030248

ISBN10: 0–415–32295–2 (hbk)
ISBN10: 0–415–32296–0 (pbk)
ISBN10: 0–203–30077–7 (ebk)

ISBN13: 978–0–415–32295–9 (hbk)
ISBN13: 978–0–415–32296–6 (pbk)
ISBN13: 978–0–203–30077–0 (ebk)

For reading so much that was not
good enough and for saying so without malice,
this book is dedicated to my wife, Joan Fitzpatrick.

# Contents

# Figures

# General editor's preface

In our time, the field of literary studies has rarely been a settled, tranquil place. Indeed, for over two decades, the clash of opposed theories, prejudices, and points of view has made it more of a battle-field. Echoing across its most beleaguered terrain, the student's weary complaint 'Why can't I just pick up Shakespeare's plays and read them?' seems to demand a sympathetic response.

Nevertheless, we know that modern spectacles will always impose their own particular characteristics on the vision of those who unthinkingly don them. This must mean, at the very least, that an apparently simple confrontation with, or pious contem-plation of, the text of a 400-year-old play can scarcely supply the grounding for an adequate response to its complex demands. For this reason, a transfer of emphasis from 'text' towards 'context' has increasingly been the concern of critics and scholars since the Second World War: a tendency that has perhaps reached its climax in more recent movements such as New Historicism, Cultural Materialism, or Presentism.

A consideration of the conditions – social, political, or economic – within which the play came to exist, from which it derives, and to which it speaks will certainly make legitimate demands on the attention of any well-prepared student nowadays. Of course, the serious pursuit of those interests will also inevitably start to undermine ancient and inherited prejudices, such as the supposed distinction between 'foreground' and 'background' in literary studies. And even the slightest awareness of the pressures of gender or of race, or the most cursory glance at the role played by that strange creature 'Shakespeare' in our cultural politics, will reinforce a similar turn towards questions that sometimes appear scandalously 'non-literary'. It seems clear that very different and unsettling notions of the ways in which literature might be addressed can hardly be avoided. The worrying truth is that nobody can just pick up Shakespeare's plays and read them. Perhaps – even more worrying – they never could.

The aim of *Accents on Shakespeare* is to encourage students and teachers to explore the implications of this situation by means of an engagement with the major developments in Shakespeare studies over recent years. It will offer a continuing and challenging reflection on those ideas through a series of multi- and single-author books which will also supply the basis for adapting or augmenting them in the light of changing concerns.

*Accents on Shakespeare* also intends to lead as well as follow. In pursuit of this goal, the series will operate on more than one level. In addition to titles aimed at modular undergraduate courses, it will include a number of books embodying polemical, strongly argued cases aimed at expanding the horizons of a specific aspect of the subject and at challenging the preconceptions on which it is based. These volumes will not be learned 'monographs' in any traditional sense. They will, it is hoped, offer a platform for the work of the liveliest younger scholars and teachers at their most outspoken and provocative. Committed and contentious, they will be reporting from the forefront of current critical activity and will have something new to say. The fact that each book in the series promises a Shakespeare inflected in terms of a specific urgency should ensure that, in the present as in the recent past, the accent will be on change.

Terence Hawkes

# Acknowledgements

Several people read drafts of this book in different forms, but the two sharpest readers whose comments have helped most are my wife, Joan Fitzpatrick, and the general editor of the *Accents on Shakespeare* series, Terence Hawkes. If only I had listened to the former sooner, I could have saved myself embarrassment with the latter. Both were endlessly patient and generous with their suggestions. The work was begun in the spring of 2004 at the Huntington Library and Garden in San Marino, California, after discussions about railroads with Gary Taylor and about gardening with John Jowett. We were there to give papers at a theatre history conference organized by Peter Holland, Stephen Orgel, and Robert C. Ritchie, to whom I am grateful for the trip. My long-time friend, the atmospheric chemist Martyn Chipperfield, advised on the Gaia hypothesis (cautioning its present unverifiability), chemical feedback loops, and computer modelling of weather, and the relevance of these to ecology. If I have misrepresented these subtleties, it is not for want of his trying to prevent me. Kevin de Ornellas and Lynn Gajowski kindly sent me cuttings and hints for reading about matters ecocritical, for which favours I am their debtor. It was helpful to attend the 33rd meeting of the Shakespeare Association of America in Bermuda in April 2005 and I am grateful to the British Academy for paying my air fare and to my employers, Loughborough University, for paying the other expenses incurred on that trip. At that meeting Shankar Raman made comments on Lucretius' Epicurean poem *De rerum natura* that greatly helped me write Chapter 4. My citations of his work indicate debts to my undergraduate Shakespeare tutor Jerry Sokol, and here I would like to acknowledge more general debts arising from his tuition and also specifically the story of Friedrich A. Kekulé's dream used in the Conclusion. Almost all of this book was written in the library of the Shakespeare Institute in Stratford-upon-Avon with the assistance of its custodians Jim Shaw and Kate Welch, whose expertise turns an excellent collection of books into a working environment of unrivalled comfort and efficiency. Finally, I am deeply grateful to Dr Sue Knott of the Open University for the drawings used as Figures 1, 2, 3, and 5.

## A note on references and style

References are given by parenthetical author and date, followed by page numbers where relevant, keyed to the single list of works given on pages 182–94. Unless otherwise stated, all quotations of Shakespeare are from the *Oxford Complete Works* edited by Stanley Wells and Gary Taylor (Oxford 1986). Where a year alone appears in brackets after a book's title, this is the year of first publication and is given to evoke the historical context in which the work appeared, although quotations may well be drawn from a subsequent edition cited, as always, by author-date. Most of the world reckons its dates in relation to the birth of Jesus Christ, from which we count backward (BC = before Christ) and forward (AD = *Anno Domini*, Latin for 'in the year of our lord'). In recognition of the fact that many people do not consider Jesus Christ to be their 'lord', historians have settled upon a pair of labels that I will use: BCE (before Common Era, equivalent to BC) and CE (Common Era, equivalent to AD). In the same spirit, I avoid the use of the masculine pronouns 'he' and 'his' where gender is unimportant to the sense. English is notably deficient in gender-neutral pronouns and, since many years of conventional usage have established that one of the genders may stand for both, I have elected to use 'she' and 'her' in this way.

# Introduction
## Babbling of green fields

In the years that this book was written, 2004 and 2005, stories in the Western news media about climate change went from occurring once or twice a month to occurring once or twice a week. To those following the inexorable trend of global warming this is a predictable change in quantity, but in media circles this is a change in quality, for the repetitions are frequent enough to close the gap of forgetting. Once events are reported weekly, in the minds of consumers of news media they become continuous rather than sporadic, and so they represent an ongoing crisis not isolated events. Climate change became a crisis in 2005, long after its most damaging effects had become irreversible. At least, they did for most people. The first draft of this book was completed in March 2005 at the 33rd meeting of the Shakespeare Association of America in Bermuda, and the programme for the conference showed an extraordinarily wide range of interests: romance, sex, war, religion, history, cinema, and many more topics were covered from a Shakespearian angle. The impending ecological disaster facing humankind did not, however, make it onto the agenda. It is an ambition of this book to place it there and to show that our understanding of Shakespeare and our understanding of Green politics have overlapping concerns and can be mutually sustaining.

Green matters were once before treated in the media as a crisis, during the early 1990s when the British Broadcasting Corporation, like many of its rivals, hired its first environment correspondent. The immediate cause of concern then was mounting scientific evidence of environmental degradation, but what made this a media topic was the collapse of the Berlin Wall, and the subsequent demise of the Soviet Union and of Eastern Bloc communist rule in 1990 and 1991. As the only remaining superpower, the United States of America won the Cold War by default, and at a stroke the possibility of a nuclear world war receded to the point where almost no one worried about it any more. In 1983 Terry Eagleton had concluded a landmark study on literary theory by observing that all the complex ideas surveyed in his previous chapters, and indeed all the literature upon which the ideas were supposed to shed light, seemed insignificant once these were considered in the setting of likely nuclear annihilation (Eagleton 1983, 194). He pointed out that much teaching of literature studiously avoids this context and asserted that political criticism – the only kind he declared support for – could at its simplest be defined as the refusal to ignore it. After 1990, the prospect of nuclear annihilation disappeared and was replaced by an equally apocalyptic vision of the world's end brought about by human action, not in a big bang but in a slow asphyxiation.

This book aims to reread Shakespeare in this new situation, which it argues is fundamental. Global nuclear disaster did not occur in the 1980s, but this should not be seen as a lucky escape, only as a postponement. Many states retain possession of nuclear weapons and there are scientists who propose that nuclear power generation not only has a viable future but is a Green alternative to the burning of fossil fuels. Compared to the almost instantaneous destruction of nuclear annihilation, the Green crisis may be slow but it is already far advanced, so the problem is not how to prevent it from happening but how to retard and then reverse what has already happened. For some creatures it is too late. The polar bears, for example, have no long-term future: we have passed the point where their habitats on Arctic ice floes might be saved. This was announced the same day that the Shell oil company reported the largest ever yearly profits for a British company, £9,700,000,000, and Exxon Mobil reported the largest ever yearly profits for a company anywhere, £13,400,000,000, or $40,000 a minute, 24 hours a day. The ever-increasing combustion of fossil fuels that generates these profits is changing the weather in ways that even the most sceptical cannot deny: the four hurricanes that hit America and the ten typhoons that hit Japan in 2004 were both new records. Most starkly of all, as this book was going into production America suffered its worst ever natural disaster when Hurricane Katrina flooded New Orleans.

The bear who, in the first Globe performances, chased Antigonus off the stage at the moment Nevill Coghill calls the 'dramaturgical hinge' of *The Winter's Tale* (Coghill 1958, 35) was fictionally reversing the cruelty of the real animal torture that went on in nearby baiting rings. The bears in Ben Jonson's masque *Oberon* (performed 1 January 1611) and in the anonymous play *Mucedorus* performed at court by the King's Men in 1610 or 1611 were white, and the one who dines on Antigonus might well have been white too. As the polar bears start to make their exit from historical reality, we must consider the distinct possibility that humankind will shortly after follow them offstage. In the midst of the ecological crisis, a rapidly growing number of people have changed their attitudes towards animals and now see an assumption of human superiority to be as irrational and oppressive as assumed male superiority and assumed white superiority. By Peter Singer's analogy with sexism and racism, this assumed superiority is speciesism (Singer 1973). During the 1980s and 1990s the rise of the Green movement was accompanied by the raising of consciousness about animal exploitation and by demands for animal rights on the model of human rights.

This book treats such concern for animals as a part of a growing coalition of grass-roots politics that unites socialists and anarchists with environmentalists, anti-capitalists, their cousins the anti-globalizationists, and animal rights activists. In curious ways, the new ideas about nature and animals have analogues in old ideas expressed in Shakespeare's plays, and for the New Age fringe of ecopolitics this suggests that the entire eighteenth-century Enlightenment was a mistake of hyper-rationality. From their perspective, the solution is to backtrack and recover the organic nature of human relations with plants and animals enjoyed by Shakespeare's contemporaries. However, we do not have to adopt such an irrationalist stance in order to think and act ecopolitically and eco-critically, because the latest developments in science and philosophy (representing the height of rationality) also return us to the same fundamental problems of human existence regarding our relations one with another, and with nature and the animals, that the plays dramatize. Play characters have ways of thinking about these things

that speak to us with surprising urgency if we discard certain prejudices that recent Shakespeare criticism has fostered. One such
prejudice is that analogies between the natural world and human
society, and between different levels of human society, are reductive
and politically conservative. The claim that a monarch's proper relation to his people is like a father's relation to his family is indeed
politically conservative as an argument against democracy, but it is
moderate and potentially sophisticated when expressed within an
argument against absolutism. Moreover, a number of seemingly
naive old ideas about our relations with the natural world – for
example, that the Earth itself is alive and that what we do can change
the weather – have turned out to be true. The plays cannot answer
our questions about how to prevent ecological disaster, any more
than 30 years ago could they answer feminists' questions about how
to fight sexism and undermine patriarchy. But, then as now, the
plays are useful (and indeed infinitely pleasing) as interrogations of
our ideas about our relations one to another and to the world around
us. As such they help us think clearly about what is at stake in those
relations. To that extent, Shakespeare is indeed already Green.

## 'One touch of nature makes the whole world kin' (Troilus and Cressida 3.3.169)

According to Jean Jules Jusserand in an address delivered to the
American Philosophical Society at Philadelphia in 1913, Horace
Howard Furness used a modified version of the above aphorism,
'One touch of *Shakespeare* makes the whole world kin', to signal
camaraderie between men of letters (Jusserand 1916, 319). Furness
knew a great deal about Shakespeare, and undoubtedly understood
that what Shakespeare's Ulysses meant by a 'touch of nature' was
far from the pleasant sense understood by such as the designers of
decorative prints who borrow this phrase. The original lines use
'touch' in its pejorative sense of blemish or taint – still common
until recently in the description of the mentally disabled as touched
– and the speech from which it comes describes the universal
human weakness for novelty:

> [ULYSSES]
> One touch of nature makes the whole world kin –
> That all with one consent praise new-born gauds,
> Though they are made and moulded of things past,

And give to dust that is a little gilt
More laud than gilt o'er-dusted.
The present eye praises the present object.
                    (*Troilus and Cressida* 3.3.169–74)

Far from being the source of goodness that unites diverse human
cultures, Ulysses speaks of nature as though it were the root of an
ineluctable flaw rather like original sin. The implicit contrast is
between human nature – necessarily debased – and human culture
that might in part overcome this fundamental weakness.

How did Shakespeare come to stand in for nature in Furness's
version of common humanity? In their address to 'The Great
Variety of Readers', the editors of the 1623 First Folio, John
Heminges and Henry Condell, call Shakespeare 'a happie imitator
of Nature' and 'a most gentle expresser of it' (Shakespeare 1623,
A3r). In his poem that follows this address, Ben Jonson characterizes Shakespeare as relatively unlearned ('thou hadst small
Latine, and lesse Greeke') and hence little indebted to the classical
model that was 'not of Natures family'. As though making a conces-
sion, Jonson adds:

> Yet must I not giue Nature all: Thy Art,
> My gentle Shakespeare, must enjoy a part.
>                     (Shakespeare 1623, A4v)

As Margreta De Grazia observes, the Jonson Folio of 1616
needed classical imagery to justify presenting plays in this lavish
print format, and the Shakespearian Folio of 1623 needed to be
distinguished from the Jonsonian, creating the polarity of Jonson
(intellectual, classical, artful) and Shakespeare (emotional, demotic,
natural) that persisted through the seventeenth and eighteenth
centuries (De Grazia 1991, 45–8). Mick Jardine traces the history
of this as an opposition between Jonson's constructivism – the
self as made by outside forces – and Shakespeare's humanism,
his selfhood as essentially given (Jardine 1999). The same sense
of Shakespeare as a natural rather than a bookish talent underlies
Stephen Greenblatt's claim that 'no one who responds intensely
to Shakespeare's art can believe that the plays and poems came
exclusively from his reading' (Greenblatt 2004, 13). Shakespeare
had at least partly to live the lives in order to write the characters.

Alexander Pope spotted this polarization, and thought that it
'proceeded originally from the zeal of the Partizans of our Author

and Ben Johnson; as they endeavoured to exalt the one at the expence of the other' (Shakespeare 1725, xi). Yet Pope too insists that Shakespeare's characters were 'so much Nature her self, that 'tis a sort of injury to call them by so distant a name as Copies of her', claiming that he could identify them by their characteristic language even if the speech prefixes were removed (Shakespeare 1725, ii–iii). In a foundational essay of early twentieth-century Shakespeare criticism, L. C. Knights points out that to understand the eighteenth-century fixation on Shakespeare's characters – treated as though there were persons with lives before and after the events shown in the performance – we have to acknowledge 'the variations of meaning covered by the term "nature"' (Knights 1933, 22).

Raymond Williams's book *Keywords* attends to such variations for a selection of essential words in literary and historical studies, and writing on 'nature' (Williams 1976, 184–9) he detects three central strands of meaning: (1) the essential quality of something; (2) the inherent force that directs the world; (3) the material world itself. In *King Lear*, Williams claims, we can see them all:

> Allow not nature more than nature needs,
> Man's life's as cheap as beast's . . .
>
> . . . one daughter
> Who redeems nature from the general curse
> Which twain have brought her to.
>
> That nature, which contemns its origin,
> Cannot be border'd certain in itself . . .
>
> . . . All shaking thunder
> Crack nature's moulds, all germens spill at once,
> That make ungrateful man . . .
>
> . . . Hear, nature hear; dear goddess, hear . . .

In these examples there is a range of meanings: from nature as the primitive condition before human society; through the sense of an original innocence from which there has been a fall and a curse, requiring redemption; through the special sense of a quality of birth, as in the rootword; through again a sense of the forms and moulds of nature which can yet, paradoxically, be destroyed by the natural force of thunder; to that simple and persistent form of the goddess, Nature herself.

(Williams 1976, 186–7)

What Williams identifies as changing in the eighteenth century was the attitude towards enquiry into nature. Were nature a kind of deity, human enquiry would be impertinent, but understood as a set of principles manifested in the world, enquiry can be understood as a form of praise: learning of the creation, one would better appreciate the creator. As a set of creative principles, nature could be emulated and learnt from, and hence a creative genius might, as Pope has it, not merely copy nature but *be* nature.

It is from within this tradition that Furness felt able to rewrite Ulysses' comment as 'one touch of Shakespeare' (like 'a little touch of Harry', *Henry 5* 4.0.47), to express a principle about how the world is. Furness might have got the expression from an associate, the forgotten American Shakespearian Joseph Crosby who used it in a letter to F. G. Fleay in 1876 or 1877. Crosby wanted to dispel the 'sentimental twaddle' of mistaken explications of Ulysses' line (Crosby 1986, 3, 202, 223–4), but there was for these men no contradiction between getting Ulysses' meaning right and adapting the wrong meaning to make a larger point about their intellectual community: for them Shakespeare was like nature. Paradoxically, the origin of the word 'culture' lies in cultivation, the tending of what grows naturally, and to this extent culture/nature is not really a polarity at all. Equally paradoxically, for this dominant line of criticism from the early nineteenth century – for example, in Hazlitt (1817) – to the end of that century, Shakespeare's art lay in his naturalistic characterization.

As Knights complained, an approach to drama based on characterization is in danger of simply mistaking the made object for reality. The trouble started with Thomas Rymer in the late seventeenth century and spread throughout the discipline within 100 years, so that by 1777 Maurice Morgann could write that

> those characters in *Shakespeare*, which are seen only in part, are yet capable of being unfolded and understood in the whole; every part being in fact relative, and inferring all the rest. . . . And very frequently, when no particular point presses, he boldly makes a character act and speak from those parts of the composition which are *inferred* only, and not distinctly shewn. This produces a wonderful effect; it seems to carry us beyond the poet to nature itself . . . it may be fit to consider them rather as Historic than Dramatic beings.
>
> (Morgann 1777, 61n–62n)

Knights saw this as only narrowly missing the mark, for Morgann was right about the effect but wrong about the cause: it comes from the use of words, not from some imagined independence of the characters (Knights 1933, 21). Wholeness and integrity, Knights agreed, were in Shakespeare, but as qualities of poetic art not of imaginary people.

Knights's point about keeping the art/nature polarity always in mind remains pertinent. As Howard Felperin shows, it is all too easy to assume that certain things about the plays' stories are certain – that Desdemona did not sleep with Cassio and Hermione did not sleep with Polixenes – yet these are simply inferences about offstage actions. How far, Felperin asked, are we to judge what is not represented? How far should we treat characters like our next-door neighbours, whom we do not assume cease to exist just because they go inside (Felperin 1990, 36)? The assertion that we should respond only to what is presented on the stage is unhelpful when, as so often happens, what is presented is itself predicated on what the characters tell us happened offstage, about which they do not agree. In this respect, plays are necessarily fragmentary.

However, this insight about the fragmentary basis of dramatic art must itself be re-examined in the light of modern science's revelations of the essentially mechanical processes underlying what was formerly veiled as mysterious nature. An opposing traffic is also pertinent: increasingly, organic nature's processes are emulated in our mechanical systems. The developments present a challenge to our familiar distinctions between art and nature and between parts and wholes, so that, for example, the ancient superstition of regarding the Earth as a single organism of which we are but a part can come to seem the height of reason. The wholeness and integrity that Morgann found in Shakespeare's characters and that Knights found in Shakespeare's poetic construction have lately been undervalued qualities in criticism; the discontinuous and the juxtaposed are fashionably supposed to be more inherently interesting than the coherent and the organically unified. However, developments in genetics and physics are paring away at long-held certainties about wholeness and organic nature, and these will be briefly sketched as needed in this book because they return us to neglected philosophical questions about existence that the plays attend to, and they form part of the context in which Shakespeare can be read ecologically.

To see the kinds of criticism the new insights can enable, it is revealing to trace what has been lost to recent criticism's almost instinctive rejection of artistic organic wholeness. Knights's influential model of how to read a Shakespeare play (Knights 1933, 31–3) is now recognizable as a strand within what came be to called the New Criticism, concerned with minute attention to the words on the page and carefully avoiding bringing in 'extraneous elements' such as biographical knowledge of the author's life and historical knowledge of the author's times. The central principle is one of microcosm/macrocosm relation: a phrase or scene is taken to stand as a miniaturized version of the larger whole. *Macbeth* begins with the First Witch's 'When shall we three meet again? | In thunder, lightning, or in rain?', about which Knights wrote:

> the scene opens with a question, and the second line suggests a region where the elements are disintegrated as they never are in nature; thunder and lightning are disjoined, and offered as alternatives. We should notice also that the scene expresses the same rhythm as the play as a whole: the general crystallizes into the immediate particular ('Where the place?' – 'Upon the Heath.' – 'There to meet with Macbeth.') and then dissolves again in to the general presentment of hideous gloom.
>
> (Knights 1933, 35)

Nature here is the weather, but Knights also wants to include human society among the natural things of the world:

> Act I, Scene IV suggests that natural order which is shortly to be violated. It stresses: natural relationships – 'children', 'servants', 'sons' and 'kinsmen'; honourable bonds and the political order – 'liege', 'thanes', 'service', 'duty', 'loyalty', 'throne', 'state' and 'honour'; and the human 'love' is linked to the more purely natural by images of husbandry.
>
> (Knights 1933, 39)

Realizing that this might seem an odd way to think about natural order, Knights explicitly asserts that, in this play at least, order 'comprehends both "wild nature" – birds, beasts and reptiles – and humankind', and a principle of mirroring between the two: 'society in harmony with nature, bound by love and friendship, and ordered by law and duty' (Knights 1933, 39–40).

Not everyone will agree that thrones and servants are human manifestations of natural order and perhaps Knights here performs the familiar critical and political manoeuvre of presenting particular social arrangements as ahistorical and acultural. This allows him to explain the Macbeths' actions as a rebellion not merely against other humans but also against a principle of non-human order that human society is allegedly modelled upon. By way of contrast we have only to think of Terry Eagleton's assertion that the witches are the true heroines of *Macbeth* who, by exploiting its own contradictions, take revenge on the Scottish state that oppresses them (Eagleton 1990, 1–2). Eagleton's response expresses a deep-seated scepticism about critical analogies from nature that is widespread among left-leaning literary critics and which has prevented them from seeing the radical potential of an ecological approach to Shakespeare.

One might reasonably respond to Eagleton's characterization of the witches' role in *Macbeth* by saying that it expresses how the story would go were it written by Eagleton (an accomplished creative writer) but that Shakespeare's version is better represented by Knights's claims, even if we dislike the fact. It is certainly true that the play's microcosmic/macrocosmic correspondences pointed out by Knights are hard to deny. A good example would be the connections between sickness in the individual (the Macbeths' neurotic behaviour) and sickness in the state (Knights 1933, 57–60). Assertions about natural order of the kind made by Knights have so affronted critics with radical political agendas (feminists and Marxists especially) that reasonable assertions about metaphor and analogy in the drama – for example, the macrocosm/microcosm correspondence – have been rejected as well. Or, to be more precise, the correspondences have been passed over in silence and countervailing examples of non-correspondence adduced in their place. This critical approach has fostered partiality regarding the evidence, as parts of the plays that support the radical agenda are promoted and the rest discarded.

Of course, discarding a certain proportion of a play is an operation already familiar to theatre and cinema practitioners, for whom cutting the text to create an individual production is an enabling artistic task that informs, and is informed by, parallel decisions about design and setting. For Knights, however, this shows just why criticism should not treat the plays as simply drama. As A. C. Bradley saw it, Macbeth's speech to his assassins about the various classes of dog – 'hounds and greyhounds, mongrels, spaniels, curs, | Shoughs, water-rugs, and demi-wolves' (3.1.94–5)

– is dispensable, but for Knights this shows a critic blinded by 'preconceptions about "drama"', who would lose one of the play's essential images, 'an image of order, each one in his degree' (Knights 1933, 44), just the kind of thing to contrast with the disorderliness of the lords' exits after Macbeth spoils the banquet in 3.4 (Knights 1933, 47).

The theatricalists, whose disintegrating impulses and fixation on character were to be resisted, could only see parts of the picture, and criticism since the early eighteenth century had been engaged in

> that process of splitting up the indivisible unity of a Shakespeare play into various elements abstracted from the whole. If a play of Shakespeare's could not be appreciated as a whole, it was still possible to admire and discuss his moral sentiments, his humour, his poetic descriptions and the life-likeness of his characters.
>
> (Knights 1933, 18)

Knights was right to see theatrical thinking as contributing to the disintegration he deplored. In his edition of 1723–5, Pope demoted to the bottom of the page lines he thought unworthy of Shakespeare and highlighted with marginal commas the particularly good bits, which critical distinction he saw as a necessary corollary of the inherited textual situation. Whatever Shakespeare wrote, some inferior non-Shakespearian matter had, Pope insisted, got mixed with it.

Knights's insistence upon the 'undivisibility' of a single play was in tune with an inter-war British insistence of the indivisibility of the received canon of Shakespeare: all the plays were by him alone, as E. K. Chambers set out to prove in the face of the statistical evidence to the contrary marshalled by F. G. Fleay and others in the New Shakspere Society (Chambers 1924–5). Understandably, a generation that fought trench warfare involving devastating fragmentation in which more than half the combatants became casualties had a deeply seated desire for wholeness. Winston Churchill's metaphor of the 'theatre of war' (OED theatre n. 6c) was coined in the 1914–18 conflict and suggests an unreality that many of those involved reported themselves feeling. The events were scarcely believable. They were tragic in the Bradleyan sense of seeming to fulfil an unfathomable, inscrutable destiny.

Knights disagreed with Bradley over where to find the unity in Shakespeare (Knights located it in the language, especially imagery, rather than the characters and the plot) but not over the value of unity itself. Much Shakespeare criticism of the last two decades (essentially since publication of Jonathan Dollimore's *Radical Tragedy* in 1985) can without too great crudity be characterized as a rejection of the desire for unity and a celebration of the dispersed, the indefinite, the self-contradictory, the de-centred. The recent revival of interest in the differences between early printings of Shakespeare is, in some quarters at least, an extension of this process into the textual domain. Textually as well as thematically, the present aversion to wholeness is intellectually disabling and, one suspects, also a convenient excuse for leaving difficult work undone. It certainly was for Pope who, lacking the editorial skills of his rivals, declared that the passage of time meant that there could be no restoring the body of Shakespearian text to wholeness – the organic metaphor used repeatedly in the preliminaries to the 1623 Folio – and that the best one could do was to cut out the parts that did not belong.

Thus, when in the Folio *Henry 5* the Hostess says of the dying Falstaff that 'his Nose was as sharpe as a Pen, and a Table of greene fields. How now Sir *Iohn* (quoth I?)' (Shakespeare 1623, H4r) Pope simply removed the meaningless phrase in the middle to give 'his nose was as sharp as a pen. How now, Sir *John*, quoth I'. Pope explained:

> †*his nose was as sharp as a pen, and a table of green fields.* These words and a table of green fields are not to be found in the old editions of 1600 and 1608. This nonsense got into all the following editions by a pleasant mistake of the Stage-editors, who printed from the common piecemeal-written Parts in the Play-house. A Table was here directed to be brought in, (it being a scene in a tavern where they drink at parting) and this direction crept into the text from the margin. Greenfield was the name of the Property man in that time who furnish'd implements &c. for the actors. A Table of Greenfield's.
>
> (Shakespeare 1723, 422n)

The theatre, then, explains the offensive intrusion.

Pope's arch-rival Lewis Theobald came up with an alternative explanation that has found universal editorial favour. It changes 'A Table' to 'a' babled' so that Falstaff was simply said by the Hostess to have talked nonsense about green fields. Theobald's was

not a rejection of the theatrical per se, for he paid attention to the
fact that this is reported offstage action:

> It has certainly been observ'd (in particular, by the Superstition
> of Women;) of People near Death, when they are delirious by
> a Fever, that they talk of removing: as it has of Those in a
> Calenture, that they have their heads run on green Fields. – To
> bable, or babble, is to mutter, or speak indiscriminately; like
> Children, that cannot yet talk; or like dying Persons, when they
> are losing the Use of Speech.
>
> (Shakespeare 1733a, 30n)[1]

Eighteenth-century editors argued at length over Theobald's
emendation. William Warburton took Pope's view and complained
that Falstaff was 'in no babling humour: and so far from wanting
cooling in green fields, that his feet were cold, and he just expiring'
(Shakespeare 1747a, 349). Samuel Johnson followed Theobald and
included Pope's and Warburton's comments because their specu-
lation 'excited merriment' (Shakespeare 1765, 396n). George
Steevens went for Theobald's explanation, but footnoted Pope,
Warburton, and Johnson's comments and yet another suggestion
that the true line was 'for his nose was as sharp as a pen upon a
table of green fells' (Shakespeare 1778a, 53n). Mockingly, Steevens
added a quotation from Mary Herbert's translation of Robert
Garnier's play *The Tragedie of Antonie* about the Tyrian dye adding
'a purple glosse' (Garnier 1595, F8v), ostensibly to support Smith's
assertion that 'fells' could become 'fields' but transparently to mock
the tone and length of his predecessors' efforts.

Late eighteenth- and early nineteenth-century editions grew in
size to accommodate these ongoing critical and editorial debates:
Steevens's had 12 volumes and in 1821 Edmond Malone's had
21. Malone himself added a new suggestion to the accumulated
gloss: 'his nose was as sharp as a pen [i.e. pinfold stake] in a table
[i. e. picture] of green fields' (Shakespeare 1821, 318n). The logical
consequence of this haphazard inflation of editions was to produce
a set of 36 volumes, one per play, to record the various important editorial notes, which is what Horace Howard Furness's *New
Variorum Shakespeare* set out to do. The organic wholeness of
Shakespeare could, within such a project, extend to the preservation of every significant gloss that had been made upon his text.
This is at once an act of containment – expanding the container
to keep everything Shakespearian within it – and an act of dispersal

because in registering the validity of debate about his meanings it acknowledges the works' semantic porosity. Expanded thus, the category 'Shakespeare' does indeed take on shades of the self-contradictoriness of the category 'nature', marked off from the non-Shakespearian and yet of such a broad compass that almost every possible meaning is available within. Equally, in ordinary use the category nature marks off those things not attributable to human artifice, yet we know that as humans we are products of nature.

Why should green fields be something to babble about? A long-standing critical prejudice of both left and right wings has been the characterization of anything to do with the countryside as feminine, sentimental, and childish. The dying Falstaff reverts to childish babbling about nature because, as Peter Topglass in the novel *The Bell* imagines, 'all children naturally live in the country' (Murdoch 1973, 125). As we shall see in Chapter 1 (pp. 39–41 below) Falstaff's babbling is a step on what Raymond Williams calls the 'escalator' of Edenic yearning – each generation of writers feeling that since its youth the world has become urbanized – and from the opposite perspective this could be said to validate the sense of a loss of nature as one of the incremental stages in human maturity. By such unstated logic, Falstaff's loss of his childhood in the country – and our collective loss of natural environments – is as necessary as Hal's break from the fat knight. In historical reality, Topglass's assumption was literally correct in respect of many in Shakespeare's London, for the great increase in its population during the late sixteenth century was largely due to new arrivals from outside. Part of the appeal of Theobald's gloss is undoubtedly the feeling it gives that we have made sense of the text's own babbling, as if we were present at the offstage scene and privy to the childish ravings that the Hostess has misheard, just as 15 lines later she mishears 'carnate' as 'carnation'. In such a case, nature is not so much given as actively constructed by the play's ideological work of having 'green fields' come to the mind of childlike Falstaff in his dying moments.

The idea that such talk must be frivolous babble has a long and broad history. In his poem 'To posterity' (1939) Bertolt Brecht writes about the need for artistic relevance and laments that in a crisis 'to speak of trees is almost a crime' because other more pressing matters (such as fighting fascism) should take precedence. The implication is that we can get back to the matter of natural beauty once the crisis is over. Elsewhere Brecht took the standard Marxist line that production of all kinds, enhanced by technology and embodying the dominance of the natural world, is the beneficial aspect of capitalism that socialism would free for the enjoyment of all. Thus in his 'Short organum for the theatre' he asks:

> What is that productive attitude in the face of nature and of society which we children of a scientific age would like to take up pleasurably in our theatre? . . . Faced with a river, it consists in regulating the river; faced with a fruit tree, in spraying the fruit tree; faced with movement, in constructing vehicles and aeroplanes; faced with society, in turning society upside down.
>
> (Brecht 1964, 185)

In one sense it is quite easy to agree with Brecht, for the technological advances (steam power, mass production, mass communication) are prerequisites for general human well-being, and as Marx observed (and as the Soviet disaster proved) until the productive forces have developed sufficiently to produce an abundance of what we all need to live, communism can only create universal want (Marx and Engels 1940, 24).

The naivety of Brecht's view of nature and technology, however, lies in treating the Earth as an inexhaustible supply of raw materials and an infinitely capacious receptacle for waste. There are, at present rates of consumption (and these are rising), only a few decades worth of fossil fuel left in the Earth, and the increasing toxicity of landfill sites and of the oceans shows that, in classic environmentalist terminology, there exists no such place as 'away' to which waste can be thrown. In the face of these opposing forces – our need to exploit the Earth's resources while acknowledging their finitude – it can seem naive to speak of a singular nature that must be protected. However, an analogous ontological problem in relation to ourselves shows a way forward. Marxists rightly assert that are no such things as rights, for example human rights, that inhere in things by virtue of their being what they are. Rather, there are only struggles over how things get used, which in the case of human rights means local victories won against particular oppressors. Nonetheless, the fiction of inalienable rights is enabling if, for example, one is trying to end the torture of political prisoners. So it is with an imaginary unified nature, another self-deluding abstraction that, to those of us with pleasant places to live and work, can seem to take insufficient account of the complexities and contingencies in the history of human production. The abstraction 'nature' suddenly becomes an all too real and all too easily lost physical reality, however, when a government wants to put a nuclear reactor, a landfill site, a highway, or a strip-mine near one's home.

At times, then, we may want to dismiss 'nature' altogether as a metaphysical category of no value to progressive political thought and action and, indeed, one constructed to trivialize as effeminate or childish concerns about human productive capacities. At other times, however, it is valuable to deploy just this category in distinguishing wise actions from rash ones that threaten to destroy the Earth. The readings of Shakespeare offered here do not attempt to reconcile these opposing views; indeed, they insist that these positions are irreconcilable. In revisiting the plays in the light of recent debates about humanity's relations with nature, it will emerge that at times nature is irreducibly ideological in construction and the point is then to examine the ends to which this construct is being put. Frequently, the plays dramatize the contesting notions of nature and invite us to consider why the antagonists choose to articulate their positions in relation to them. At other times, however, the plays seem to draw upon the audience's sense of what truly is natural and to characterize behaviours and relationships as violations of nature's principles. Shakespeare's analogies between human society and the wider cosmic order should not embarrass us, as they seem to have embarrassed late twentieth-century criticism that chose to avert its gaze. The latest ideas from science offer us ways to understand these analogies as politically progressive.

# 1
# Ecopolitics/ecocriticism

To see how ecopolitical insights can inform critical readings of Shakespeare, it is necessary to survey briefly the origins of the Green movement and in particular the twentieth-century scientific and industrial developments that it defined itself in opposing. In the summer of 1942 Edward Teller, one of J. Robert Oppenheimer's team building the first atomic bomb, calculated what would happen in the first few millionths of a second after detonation. Enrico Fermi was worried that the new weapon might disastrously replicate the conditions inside the Sun, and Teller's new calculations started to convince Oppenheimer's team that merely testing the bomb 'might ignite the earth's oceans or its atmosphere' (Rhodes 1986, 418). Unknown to the Americans, in June 1942, the theoretical physicist Werner Heisenberg expressed to Hitler, via Albert Speer, the same fear about Germany's atomic programme (Rhodes 1986, 404–5). The night before the first Manhattan Project test, Fermi offered to take bets on whether the atmosphere would catch fire, and Teller wondered if he was right (Rhodes 1986, 664–5). Stunned by the brightness of the flash, Oppenheimer's colleague Emilio Segrè feared that the worst had indeed happened (Segrè 1970, 147). The scientists who performed the first atomic test believed it carried a small, but quite real, chance (about one-in-fifty, some of them thought) of instantly igniting the world, and they decided to risk it.

Among other things, the international Green movement is a response to the rapid increase in the power of human technologies and the hubris of the scientists and technocrats in charge of them. All life on Earth is a direct expression of the energy released by thermonuclear reactions inside the Sun and, ironically, the means to initiate such reactions on Earth made Oppenheimer's the first generation capable of ending all life. Over the succeeding decades, the nuclear states developed the technologies with which to threaten doing this, each fearing another gaining a technical advantage that would upset the balance of terror. This fear was acute in the 1960s when intercontinental ballistic missiles (ICBMs) became too fast for the available computers to track reliably, raising the possibility that a sneak attack might overwhelm an opponent before retaliation could be mounted.

One of the breakthroughs that restored the balance came from, of all places, the technique of lithography used in commercial book publishing and refined into a fine art by Henri de Toulouse-Lautrec and Paul Gauguin. Rather than wire individual components together, transistors, diodes, capacitors, and resistors of microscopic size could be lithographically printed directly onto semiconductor material, to make an integrated circuit, or microchip. Computing devices shrank in size and cost, and rose exponentially in power. A second breakthrough was the distributed networking of computers invented by Paul Baran of the Rand Corporation, which showed that 'highly survivable system structures can be built, even in the thermonuclear era' (Baran 1964, 4). The Advanced Research Projects Agency Network (ARPANET) embodying this technology first connected four university computer sites in 1969, and in 1972 it explicitly acquired the adjective 'defense' to become DARPANET, which became the Internet. Epitomizing the beauty of the swords-into-ploughshares principle, the Internet is now the primary means by which Green activism communicates with itself and the wider political domain.

A certain kind of political idealism and activism driven by global thinking came to an end in 1968 as within a few months Martin Luther King and Robert Kennedy were assassinated, anti-Vietnam demonstrations were suppressed, the French uprising collapsed and Charles de Gaulle won a landslide victory, the Civil Rights movement in Northern Ireland was violently crushed, and Warsaw Pact forces invaded Czechoslovakia and stayed there to ensure that Alexander Dubček's political and social reforms were cancelled. One strand of activism turned from the global to the local, producing the communes and self-help groups of the early 1970s, but at the same time a new kind of global thinking emerged to replace the old. In September 1969, Friends of the Earth was formed by David Brower in San Francisco and the following year it was transformed into an international organization with affiliated groups forming first in France (1970) and the United Kingdom (1971). In 1970, Friends of the Earth began to publish the journal *Not Man Apart* that outlined its core campaign topics: the fur trade, preservation of rivers, pollution from supersonic flight, and whaling.

The international organization Greenpeace arose from protests against American underground nuclear bomb tests. In 1970 three Canadian activists, Jim Bohlen, Irving Stowes, and Paul Cote, formed the Don't Make a Wave committee to prevent nuclear testing on the island of Amchitka, one of the Aleutian Islands off the west coast of Alaska. The name alluded to the danger of triggering a tsunami, for Amchitka is a few miles from a geological weakness that leads to the Californian San Andreas Fault. The youngest member of the committee, Bill Darnell, suggested that 'Green Peace' captured the group's philosophy and should be the name of their boat. In the event the trip failed to prevent the test, but brought extensive media coverage, following which the future, bigger tests at Amchitka were cancelled (Hunter 1979, 11–118; Brown and May 1989, 7–15).

Yet another strand of the new movement arose within the academy. The phrase 'animal liberation' – with an exclamation mark to indicate the novelty – first appeared in print on the cover of the 5 April 1973 issue of the *New York Review of Books* to advertise that within was Peter Singer's review of a collection of essays on the maltreatment of 'non-humans' (Godlovitch, *et al.* 1971; Singer 1973). Singer, a philosopher of the preference utilitarian school, approvingly quoted Jeremy Bentham's assertion that what mattered when deciding how much value to place on individuals' interests was not 'Can they *reason?* nor, Can they *talk?* but, Can they *suffer?*' (Bentham 1789, 309n). Singer coined the expression 'speciesism' to liken the unthinking assumption of human superiority to the long-standing but recently challenged assumption of racial superiority by whites and of gender superiority by men. Singer developed his review into a full-blown utilitarian argument for the capacity to suffer, rather than membership of a particular species, being the primary criterion by which to weigh the good or harm of any of our interactions with humans and other animals (Singer 1975). Looked at this way, a severely mentally disabled person incapable of preferences and protected from pain has less right to life than a healthy chimpanzee with rudimentary sign-language skills, a well-developed social network, and a degree of self-consciousness, as Singer argues in his book *Practical Ethics* (Singer 1979, 93–105, 127–57).

These roots of the Green movement are worth tracing because they counter the common misconception that ecopolitical thinking arose only after the collapse of communism. In truth, it was an active force in the extraordinary events of 1989–90. The final decline of the Soviet Union was triggered by Mikhail Gorbachev's refusal to assist Erich Honecker's government in suppressing the fledgling ecology-and-peace movement in the German Democratic Republic. This movement was inspired by the West German Green Party founded by Herbert Gruhl and Petra Kelly in 1979, whose programme called for the demilitarization of Europe by dissolving the NATO and Warsaw Pact agreements, the closure of nuclear power plants, rigorous state control of polluting industries, and economic advantages being given to small-scale businesses over large corporations. The connection between nuclear power and pollution was especially urgent after the explosion of the Ukrainian nuclear electricity generator at Chernobyl in April 1986 spread radiation clouds across Western Europe as far as Ireland. This outcome contrasted with the narrow escape from a similar reactor core meltdown at the Pennsylvanian Three Mile Island nuclear electricity generator in 1979, strengthening a perception of communist technological inferiority rooted in political and economic inferiority. Chernobyl bolstered the nascent Ukrainian independence movement which achieved its goal when Gorbachev's government in Moscow collapsed in August 1991.

It is clear, then, that ecopolitics has operated strategically at key moments in recent world history. What are the consequences of this for literary criticism? By analogy with the politics of class, race, and gender, it would seem that ecopolitics will necessarily have things to teach us about literary criticism, but it is far from clear what those lessons might be. Virtually every dramatic character, like every reader and theatre spectator, has an identifiable class, a race, and a gender and it is abundantly clear that politicized criticism can investigate how these classifications arise, how they are figured in oppression, and how they might be transfigured in the future. By analogy with these, ecocriticism would seem to lack an oppressed subject, unless it take up something as potentially risible as the Earth's point of view, or the animals'. I will suggest some means by which ecopolitical concerns can be projected into the domain of criticism, despite the absence of an oppressed subject on whose behalf a political struggle could be mounted. For this, a little more popular science must be essayed before we return to the literary and the dramatic.

The Earth is effectively a sealed system, bombarded by energy from the Sun but closed in the sense that (barring a few trivial exceptions) we and our products cannot leave. Whatever we make here stays here, and the only replenishment of spent energy is in the form of sunlight. This insight is largely absent from mainstream Marxist analysis, which treats the Earth as an infinitely rich supplier of raw materials and an infinitely capacious sink for wastes. This is a surprising oversight, since one of the central principles of Marx's analysis of capitalism was that the extraction of surplus value from producing workers leaves them too poor to buy back what they have made, so capitalism is forced to scour the world for new markets and new workforces (Marx 1954, 713–15; Marx and Engels 1974, 58) and must eventually come up hard against the Earth's finitude: at some point it will exhaust the last market and the last free worker. Since this is a central principle, acknowledging the finite ought really to be habitual for Marxists. The ever-increasing productive forces of humankind cannot go on indefinitely even if the systems of production and exchange are revolutionized, since the Earth's resources are finite. Marx, however, chose to focus on the vast and as-yet untapped resources of the Earth and the fact that individual productivity has always increased more quickly than population, which is why humankind's capacity to feed itself has never faltered. (As is well known, distribution rather than production is the cause of majority world hunger: more than enough food is produced each year to feed the world's population.) Engels was explicit about what keeps productivity ahead of consumption: 'science – whose progress is as unlimited and at least as rapid as that of population' (Marx 1977, 176).

The rapidly expanding production of the Industrial Revolution, also enabled by a mistaken sense of the Earth's infinitude, was undergirded by a new conception of nature that arose in the second half of the seventeenth century. It was, in essence, the replacement of a vitalistic model with a mechanistic model. Instead of the natural state of things being movement, as Aristotle articulated in his *Physics* (Aristotle 1930, 184a–267b), it was inertia, as Isaac Newton proved; the transition is neatly summarized by R. G. Collingwood in *The Idea of Nature*. Throughout the drama of Shakespeare, characters speak of the world around them as though it is alive, and this view is put into conflict with the emergent mechanistic view, as we shall see. As Collingwood points out, 'The naturalistic philosophies of the fifteenth and sixteenth centuries attributed to nature reason and sense, love and hate, pleasure and pain, and found in these faculties and passions the causes of natural process' (Collingwood 1945, 95). In an essentially clockwork universe, on the other hand, the Earth is merely an instrument of human self-fulfilment.

The twentieth-century field of cybernetics bridges these different conceptions of the world in its concern with communication and control systems in living organisms and machines, and its origins can be traced to the eighteenth-century invention of mechanical self-regulation modelled on living organisms. The key notion is feedback: the connection of the outcome of an event or process with the originating conditions. Contrary to everyday use of the term, positive feedback is often a bad thing and negative feedback often a good one. In positive feedback, the outcome of a process reinforces the originating conditions so that the system accelerates, as when a snowball rolls downhill, a debt accumulates compound interest, or the subatomic particles ejected in a chain reaction excite yet more particles. Exponential growth is the characteristic outcome of positive feedback. In negative feedback, however, the outcome diminishes the originating conditions so that the system achieves a dynamic equilibrium, and if perturbed by an external force (so long as it is not too great) the system is able to restore its equilibrium.

The ecological processes with which Green politics are concerned are chiefly examples of either of these two conditions: explosive growths (bombs, populations, atmospheric gases) and the countervailing systems of self-regulation. The ozone layer problem identified in the 1980s has been solved by banning chlorofluoro-carbons. A zone of partial ozone depletion over the Antarctic remains, but will disappear in about 50 years because of what atmospheric chemists – a group not given to excessive anthropo-morphism – call the self-healing effect, a classic negative-feedback loop. The ozone layer is created in the upper atmosphere by the bombardment of solar ultraviolet radiation that turns $O_2$ (oxygen) molecules into $O_3$ (ozone) molecules that block the radiation from reaching the Earth's surface. Where ozone depletion occurs, solar radiation penetrates further, but in doing so it creates fresh ozone at the lower level and backfills the hole.

On the other hand, the accumulation of greenhouse gases from human activity starts a positive-feedback reaction. The northern polar ice cap floats on an ocean, so as it melts it occupies the volume it formerly displaced, leaving the sea-level unchanged. The southern ice cap, however, rests on land and as it melts it exposes dark soil where there was previously white ice, lowering the Earth's capacity to reflect sunlight and thereby accelerating the absorption of heat and the melting. The key determinate of whether human-kind survives the next 100 years is whether our perturbations of the Earth's self-regulating systems have exceeded its capacity to restore an equilibrium, or, to be more precise, whether the new equilibrium state that emerges can support human life. In these debates, distinctions between organic and inorganic processes begin to break down, as we shall see.

The most famous early example of a machine emulating organic self-regulation was James Watt's steam engine governor of 1769, which made an engine run at a constant speed irrespective of the load applied to it (Figure 1). The collar (C) is connected to the engine's throttle, so if the speed rises, the balls (M) rise under centrifugal force and pull the throttle closed, thus lowering the speed; if the speed falls, the balls descend and so open the throttle to raise the speed.

For Charles Dickens, such regulatory devices made for fearful hybrid creatures, animal yet robotic, that mocked human labour in the fictional Coketown of *Hard Times*:

> But no temperature made the melancholy mad elephants more mad or more sane. Their wearisome heads went up and down at the same rate, in hot weather and cold, wet weather and dry, fair weather and foul. The measured motion of their shadows

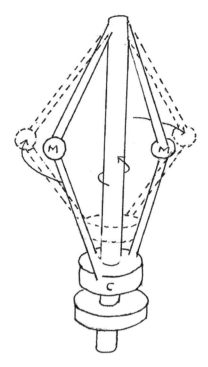

*Figure 1* James Watt's steam engine governor.

on the walls, was the substitute Coketown had to show for the
shadows of rustling woods; while, for the summer hum of insects,
it could offer, all the year round, from the dawn of Monday to
the night of Saturday, the whirr of shafts and wheels.

(Dickens 1854, 132–3)

Positive and negative feedback loops are common to organic and
inorganic systems, and a full understanding of them is a key difference between our times and Shakespeare's. They nonetheless appear
in the plays and are treated as paradoxical situations that might
be understood mystically, although particular characters attempt
to offer materialist accounts of them and rightly perceive negative
feedback to be one of the reasons that the world is, in important
respects, essentially unchanging. In teasing out the range of ideas
about feedback presented in the plays, and the characters' efforts

to make sense of them as vitalistic or mechanical phenomena, we are exploring their capacity to understand the world around them.

This project of mapping how Elizabethans made sense of the world takes us to the second specific insight that ecological thinking can bring to criticism. In his model of what he called the Elizabethan World Picture, E. M. W. Tillyard characterizes the set of beliefs, assumptions, and habits of mind that a typical educated person might hold as a cobbled-together patchwork of medieval commonplaces and newly minted explanations (Tillyard 1943, 1–6). The Picture itself has been widely criticized by historians of science and philosophy for its oversimplification of belief systems, its understatement of scepticism and dissent, and most of all for its claim that despite the obvious disorderliness of Elizabethan drama, 'the conception of order is so taken for granted, so much part of the collective mind of the people, that it is hardly mentioned except in explicitly didactic passages' (Tillyard 1943, 7). A central element of Tillyard's Picture is a system of alleged correspondences between the celestial bodies, social relations, and human biology (Tillyard 1943, 77–93), which Elizabethan prose and verse art endlessly returned to for analogies.

The focus of the attack on Tillyard has been that Elizabethans did not actually believe the picture he outlined, but for our purposes that question may be somewhat beside the point. Like witchcraft or alien-abduction for us, the account of the universe that the Picture embodied was available for use in plays and poems. Characters in Shakespeare speak meaningfully about comets presaging disaster and about the music of the spheres, and unless we suppose that these lines elicited derisive laughter from the theatre audiences we have to accept that such things were within the realm of the believable even if not widely believed. This alone gives us cause enough to study Tillyard's Picture, but in fact (and unlike witchcraft and alien-abduction) his model of reality might also in some surprising ways be objectively true. A macrocosm/microcosm correspondence need not of itself run counter to the particularities of life as it is lived on Earth and events in the wider universe.

To see why, we should recall that Newton's great discovery, announced in *Philosophiae Naturalis Principia Mathematica* (1687), was that what happens to the largest heavenly bodies is governed by the same mechanics that control what happens on Earth. This development could easily be taken as confirming macrocosm/

microcosm correspondence rather than displacing it: the universe's condition, Newton proved, really was the earthly condition writ large. The telescope had shown that the planets were imperfect, like the Earth, and the microscope showed that processes occurring within organisms invisible to the naked eye were the same as the processes occurring in larger creatures. The corresponding phenomena on different scales were to a considerable degree real, not superstition, nor mere analogy.

The twentieth-century sciences of holograms and fractals have advanced this principle of correspondences between phenomena on different scales to an extraordinary degree.[2] When a glass hologram is smashed, each resulting shard contains the full image rather than a fraction of it, and this image can be shattered again to produce yet smaller versions. A fractal is a mathematically defined curve that also exhibits this principle of diminishing self-similarities: any part of it, when enlarged, is the same shape as the original. These curves occur in non-organic and organic nature, such as the snowflake (Figure 2) and the fern leaf (Figure 3).[3]

From the new perspectives provided by holograms, fractals, and genetics, Tillyard's version of an alleged Elizabethan concern for macrocosmic/microcosmic correspondences looks considerably less naive than critics have given him (and, indeed, the Elizabethans) credit for. Such correspondences are how the world is, and as we shall see, they are the bases for sophisticated analogical thinking that we must not dismiss out of hand.

Previous generations of critics had a firmer grasp of this point than recent ones. For all their differences over the proper approach to literature, old historicists such as Tillyard and Lily B. Campbell shared with their contemporary New Critics the principle that a fragment of a literary work might operate as a miniaturized version of the whole. Writing about *Macbeth*, for example, the founding father of New Criticism Cleanth Brooks considers the images of the naked babe (1.7.21–2) and clothed ('breeched') daggers (2.3.115–16) to be 'two of the great symbols which run throughout the play' and 'so used as to encompass an astonishingly large area of the total situation' (Brooks 1947, 49). For the New Critics, the compression of meaning in, for example, an image was the essential quality of literary writing, and it was this forcing of so much into so little that made the words on the page (as opposed to the collateral knowledge about the writer's biography and historical context) all one needed to do criticism.

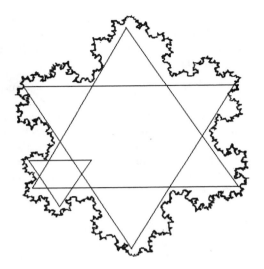

*Figure 2* Fractal snowflake.

*Figure 3* Fractal fern leaf.

The compression need not happen via imagery; according to the English New Critic William Empson[4] it could be a matter of surprisingly awkward syntax or diction. However achieved, it was the compression that made the text literary:

> When you are holding a variety of things in your mind, or using for a single matter a variety of intellectual machinery, the only way of applying all your criteria is to apply them simultaneously; the only way of forcing the reader to grasp your total meaning is to arrange that he can only feel satisfied if he is bearing all the elements in mind at the moment of conviction; the only way of not giving something heterogeneous is to give something which is at every point a compound.
>
> (Empson 1930, 302)

Approaching literature from entirely the opposite angle – 'I do not believe that a poet exists in a vacuum, or even that he exists solely in the minds and hearts of his interpreters' – Lily B. Campbell nonetheless shares the New Critics' convictions that the poet, because a poet, relates the microcosm to the macrocosm:

> He is inevitably a man of feeling. If, however, he is not merely a poet but a great poet, the particulars of his experience are linked in meaning to the universal of which they are a representative part. ... the greatest poets ... have seen life as a whole, not in fragments.
>
> (Campbell 1947, 6–7)

Hugh Grady observes that uniting the disparate modernist approaches to Shakespeare was a faith in the organic unity of art and a respect for hierarchy, both of which he hopes can be swept away by postmodernism:

> The relevant characteristics are the abandonment of organic unity as an aesthetic value and practice and the overthrow of a series of formerly privileged hierarchical oppositions through a Postmodernist anti-hierarchical impulse (as, for example in the collapse of the High Modernist distinction between 'art' and 'popular culture' or in the championing of the various Others of Western rationality like women and Third World peoples).
>
> (Grady 1991, 207)

Understandably, Grady worries that any new mode of literary analysis might become just as easily professionalized, and hence made safe for mass dissemination in English studies, as the old ones have (Grady 1991, 213–14); indeed, some deconstruction can seem remarkably like New Criticism. However, I wish to argue that the abandonment of 'organic unity as an aesthetic value' is a mistake and that ecopolitics shows why. Insisting on the value of various kinds of unity can be a powerful solvent of the fracturing impulses of late industrial capitalism, not least of all in the case of the unitary Earth.

Drawing on the principle of feedback, the final example of what ecological thinking can bring to criticism is the notion of a unitary Earth, or Gaia. In essence, this holds that the Earth is a single organism comprised of the obviously alive biota (the life forms we recognize) and the parts that we have previously treated as inorganic, the background environment such as the rocks, oceans, and atmosphere – that is, the latter parts are, in a sense, as alive as the former. The hypothesis was first formally presented by the chemist James E. Lovelock (Lovelock 1972), subsequently expanded upon in collaboration with a biologist (Lovelock and Margulis 1974a; Lovelock and Margulis 1974b), and finally submitted as a cybernetic proof using fundamental principles of physics and natural selection (Lovelock 1983). Lovelock's simplified DaisyWorld model illustrates that regulation of an entire planet's temperature can occur merely from competition between two kinds of plants, one dark and hence absorptive of heat and the other light and hence reflective of heat; over time their population ratios alter to keep their planet comfortable. The details of Gaia need not detain us, and the essential point is Lovelock's demonstration that the entire Earth exhibits a characteristic (temperature regulation) that we have, since the Enlightenment, attributed only to individual living creatures. It is a disturbing thought for us, but if Tillyard's model of the Elizabethan World Picture is even faintly close to the habits of minds of Shakespeare's first audiences and readers, that is to say, if it was thinkable as a model of the world even as it was dismissed as official propaganda, then the Gaia hypothesis would have appeared unremarkable to them.

A belief in the connection between the affairs of human beings in the sublunary sphere and occurrences among the higher layers (the sky, planets, and beyond) was firmly, and it seemed at the time irrevocably, ruptured in the eighteenth century. Modern science seems to be restoring this belief, and there are two ways we may respond to this development. One is to accept that aspects of

Enlightenment thinking were excessively particularizing and, in ways that suited the Industrial Revolution, overlooked connectivities that we find obvious. Had factory owners been forced to site their fresh water intake pipes downstream of their waste-water discharge pipes, for example, the idea that inputs come from an unlimited pure source and that outputs can be sent to an infinitely capacious 'sink' would not so easily have persisted. That is to say, certain rational responses to the practices that flowed from Enlightenment habits of mind might quickly have identified the discrepancies between theory and reality.

An alternative response to the new sciences is to find in them cause to reject reason, rationality, and the Enlightenment *tout court*. One of the most noticeable cultural developments in the Western world in the past 30 years has been the rise of an anti-rationalistic, alternative culture that embraces the New Age movement, complementary medicine, and forms of holistic spiritualism, and which links these to the broader anarchist and animal rights movements. For an apparently rising number of people the Enlightenment itself should be dismissed as an illusory detour into hyper-rationality. For such people, the cosmic connectedness voiced in Elizabethan drama and poetry offers a sociable spirituality already packaged within a rich supply of artistic works that are central to Western culture.

This latter response is, of course, delusional and riven by contradiction: the new sciences themselves are founded on reason and cannot simply be co-opted to irrationality. This Alan Sokal and Jean Bricmont brilliantly demonstrate in their book *Intellectual Impostures* about certain postmodernists' exploitation of the myth that science is coming around to accept irrationality (Sokal and Bricmont 1998). The proper way to understand the new sciences in relation to artistic culture is to respect their counter-intuitive claims while exploring how these throw light on past works of art. This can be illustrated by considering Shakespeare's characters' understanding of why black people are black, which is essentially correct (the sun makes them black) but for the wrong reason.

An early modern conception of racial blackness is expressed by characters such as the prince of Morocco in Shakespeare's *The Merchant of Venice* who assumes (correctly, it turns out) that Portia is racist:

MOROCCO (*to Portia*)
Mislike me not for my complexion,
The shadowed livery of the burnished sun,
To whom I am a neighbour and near bred.
(*The Merchant of Venice* 2.1.1–3)

On the inside, he insists, his blood is as red as anyone else's, even though he is coated with blackness (a 'shadowed livery') caused by living in a sunny country. Desdemona's father uses the same idea of a burnt coating that should have revolted his daughter, and that hence magic must have been used to make her 'Run from her guardage to the sooty bosom | Of such a thing as thou' (*Othello* 1.2.71–2). Othello comes to share this sense of his blackness as a coating: convinced that Desdemona is unfaithful he says 'My name, that was as fresh | As Dian's visage, is now begrimed and black | As mine own face' (3.3.391–3).

Likewise, in the very act of denying that blackness can wash off, Aaron in *Titus Andronicus* imagines it not as an innate colour but a coating:

[AARON]
Coal-black is better than another hue
In that it scorns to bear another hue;
For all the water in the ocean
Can never turn the swan's black legs to white,
Although she lave them hourly in the flood.
(*Titus Andronicus* 4.2.98–102)

Washing the Ethiop (or blackamoor) white was, of course, proverbial in Shakespeare's time (Dent 1981, Appendix A, E186). What conceptions about the world gave rise to the idea that blackness is a coating? For a white actor playing Morocco, Othello, or Aaron the character's sense of his blackness as a coating is, of course, literally true: excluding the unlikely possibility that a black actor worked in Shakespeare's company (about which we would expect there to be some record), a white actor would have 'blacked up' as preparation for the performance. The part, then, with its references to blackness as a coating, suits the particulars of the theatre's impersonation of blackness, which is far from real blackness, and this adds support to the argument made by the Ghanaian actor Hugh Quarshie that black actors should not play Othello, or at least not without major reworking of the play (Quarshie 1999).

Elizabethans noticed that black people live in hot countries and since skin darkens in the sun it was reasonable to suppose that they simply had deep tans. Certainly, the melanin pigment that tanning brings to the surface is the same in all humans, but colour differences between races are an effect not of any one person's tanning but a phenomenon operating across whole populations. In countries where sunshine is strongest, humans whose melanocyte cells produce much melanin are less likely to get skin cancers than those whose cells produce little because the pigment absorbs harmful ultraviolet light before it penetrates too far into the body, and hence natural selection favours dark skins. If humans first evolved in Africa, as seems likely, then those who migrated to colder northerly climates no longer needed to make so much melanin, and indeed making too much would carry an evolutionary penalty since it costs energy that were better spent elsewhere in the body. Hence, over evolutionary time, people in the cold climates turned white. Sunshine is the explanation of blackness (and indeed whiteness) in humans, just as it is – and by precisely the same genetic pressures – in Lovelock's model of light and dark daisies changing the face of DaisyWorld. Disturbing as it is to our post-Enlightenment sensibilities to acknowledge, the Elizabethans, while not exactly right about blackness, had a fair inkling of what was going on.

There is, of course, no simple continuity between Renaissance habits of mind and our own. We might nonetheless share ideas with the Renaissance by the indirect route: we may find ourselves returning to consider their commonplaces in the light of new science and philosophy that rational study has made possible. Large-scale systems thinking and correspondences between processes at the micro- and macro-levels are not to be ruled out as archaisms. This is one of the fundamental insights of ecological thinking and it has practical, political, consequences. The Internet, the cellular telephone network, franchised corporations, and indeed terrorist networks share design principles from nature that humankind has not hitherto emulated. The topologies of such networks make for peculiar (frequently, counter-intuitive) relationships between the part and the whole, and although we encounter them in structures we have made, Shakespeare's contemporaries encountered them in the natural world. For example, we know from genetics that in response to the human migration from its birthplace in Africa to colder climates, no individual got paler or shorter or rounder (the physical attributes better suited to cooler climates), but, considered collectively, human beings did.

In the twentieth century several of the central mysteries of life ceased to be mysteries, as the mechanical processes of sexual reproduction and its relation to heredity became explicable in terms of interactions among proteins. Although there remains considerable ignorance of the detail, organic processes, it seems, can be understood in mechanical terms. A corollary of this dissolving of the organic/mechanical binary, and one that criticism has yet to fully encompass, is that organic explanations for mechanical processes can be perfectly valid too: it is reasonable to say that DaisyWorld, treated as a singularity, cools itself down by changing colour just as humankind, treated collectively, changed skin colour to suit local climates. Post-Enlightenment science has long treated such metaphors as intentionalist errors deriving ultimately from Aristotle's personification of matter in his *Physics*, which explained things coming to rest because getting tired is the way of the world. Virtually all Shakespeare criticism has been written according to the Enlightenment's scientific principles, and these are currently being revised. It is worth taking notice of the revision.

*

> A generation ago, the first academic refuge of the intellectual out of touch with his times was the Department of the Classics. It is now above all the Department of English.
>
> (Wiener 1950, 158–9)

Norbert Wiener's complaint that English is a subject out of touch with life and recent history made perfect sense when written in 1950, in the heyday of New Criticism, and it makes perfect sense now at the tail end of post-structuralism. It would, however, have seemed itself acutely out-of-touch with the subject between the late 1960s and the late 1980s when the relevance of the subject *was*, for the most part, the subject. I share with Wiener the conviction that not engaging with 'the main facts concerning science and machinery' (Wiener 1950, 163) is a dereliction of critical duty. At the start of the twenty-first century, that engagement is ecocriticism.

The term ecocriticism was first used in the essay 'Literature and ecology: An experiment in ecocriticism' (Rueckert 1978) and most simply it expresses a desire to bring to the study of literature the

concerns of ecopolitics. Ecocriticism is not yet codified or institu-
tionalized sufficiently to prescribe how this might be done. Those
who object to the destruction of forests, animals, and waterways
might well find themselves attracted to literary works about those
things, as opposed to, say, Fyodor Dostoyevsky's novels of life in
nineteenth-century Saint Petersburg. Much ecocriticism has been
concerned with nature writing – prose and poems about walks
in remote and beautiful places – by English Romantics such
as William Wordsworth and Samuel Taylor Coleridge and the
American Transcendentalists such as Ralph Waldo Emerson and
Henry David Thoreau and their followers. There are at least two
good reasons not to confine ecocriticism within these bounds,
however.

The first is that the history of politicized criticism teaches us
to move from the obvious cases to the not so obvious. Feminist
criticism began with analysis of female characters in novels, poems,
and drama, and with female writers, but produced its most
compelling work when it moved from this marginal position to
look at male characters and writers, from which perspective it could
discover the concealed sexism that made female desires, experiences, and creativity marginal in the first place. In Shakespeare
studies this involved a move from harping on daughters, as Lisa
Jardine's landmark book of the first kind called it (Jardine 1983),
to Catherine Belsey's analysis of how Shakespeare's comedies call
into question 'that set of relations between terms which proposes
as inevitable an antithesis between masculine and feminine, men
and women' (Belsey 1985, 167). By analogy, ecocriticism could
concern itself with the relations that propose an inevitable antithesis
between nature and culture.

Similarly, gay studies (later subsumed into queer theory) began
its critique of canonical heterosexism first with a purchase on
writers and characters whose homoeroticism was fairly obvious
(say, Oscar Wilde or Patroclus in Shakespeare's *Troilus and Cressida*)
and moved from there to an analysis of how far sexual orientation itself might be a category of human personality that emerged
under particular historical circumstances (Bray 1982). By these
models, ecocriticism could attend to positive representations of
nature but should not confine itself to these, for its proper purview
is all that happens in literary culture that tends to create or sustain
the political, social, and cultural conditions that ecopolitics seeks
to change.

A second reason why ecocriticism should not confine itself to nature writing is that the English Romantics and American Transcendentalists themselves did not do so, unless we exclude such obvious members as William Blake from the first group and Margaret Fuller, historian of the Italian revolution, from the second (Mehren 1994). When Blake writes what seems to be a paean to the pastoral life, the activities of the city enter as a means of communicating the life:

> Piper sit thee down and write
> In a book that all may read –
> So he vanish'd from my sight.
> And I pluck'd a hollow reed.
>
> And I made a rural pen,
> And I stain'd the water clear,
> And I wrote my happy songs
> (Blake 1789, 'Introduction')

For all that it is a 'rural' pen, the clear stream water has to be stained to make ink and the book of paper must have been manufactured somewhere other than the countryside.

In a similarly worldly-wise vein, Blake's questions about the origins of tigers are as much metallurgical as biological:

> What the hammer? what the chain,
> In what furnace was thy brain?
> What the anvil? what dread grasp,
> Dare its deadly terrors clasp!
> (Blake 1789, 'The Tyger')

The Romantic poets' own representation of nature as a domain of solace and respite from the depredations of industrialization has long been understood as subjected to critique from within that movement itself: Blake's tiger is more fashioned (by 'hammer', 'furnace', and 'anvil') than reared.

Such critique of romanticizing about nature and the countryside can also be found in Wordsworth and Coleridge's *Lyrical Ballads*, whose oxymoronic title was as self-contradictory as the literary manifesto, the second edition's preface, which was produced two years after the poems it sought to introduce (Wordsworth and Coleridge 1800, v–xlvi). Wordsworth opposes the natural, unmannered life of the country to 'encreasing accumulation of men in cities' that coarsens appetites so that Shakespeare and Milton are neglected in favour of 'frantic novels, sickly and stupid German Tragedies, and deluges of idle and extravagant stories in verse' (Wordsworth and Coleridge 1800, xviii–xix). The city is the place of artifice and the country the place of emotional and linguistic origins and hence Wordsworth concerns himself with the latter (Wordsworth and Coleridge 1800, xvi–xvii).

This assertion that rural people and behaviours have an inherent dignity was a radical statement at the time, but the obvious question that follows from such a digging below artifice in search of natural purity is why, then, use verse at all? Wordsworth did not shy away from that question and gave an answer which might have surprised himself as much as it does us:

> The end of Poetry is to produce excitement in coexistence with an over-balance of pleasure. . . . But if the words by which this excitement is produced are in themselves powerful, or the images and feelings have an undue proportion of pain connected with them, there is some danger that the excitement may be carried beyond its proper bounds. Now the co-presence of something regular [that is, metre], something to which the mind has been accustomed when in an unexcited or a less excited state, cannot but have great efficacy in tempering and restraining the passion by an intertexture of ordinary feeling.
>
> (Wordsworth and Coleridge 1800, xxx–xxxi)

The value of verse, then, is to restrain the over-excitement the readers might suffer if the poet immoderately exploited the power of everyday language. As well as clipping the peaks of excitement, metre can ameliorate the boredom 'if the Poet's words should be incommensurate with the passion' (Wordsworth and Coleridge 1800, xxxi), and thereby it evens out the readerly experience. Thus artifice retains its place as the necessary mediator within a literary manifesto of the man who has been most widely received, and by this manifesto promoted himself, as the poet of simple nature.

The Romantic poets are a good place to start thinking about the relationship between ecological politics and art, not only because their poems so often invoke the natural world but also because as poets they (conveniently for our purposes) took pains to explain themselves in political terms. Percy Bysshe Shelley's *Defence of Poetry* was among other things a politicized response to Philip Sidney's book of the same name of 230 years earlier that had patiently refuted Plato's dismissal of fiction-makers as liars and made a modest claim for the good poets do. Contrary to Plato's view that poets copy objects from nature, which are themselves only copies of Ideas, Sidney characterizes as poetic mimesis the relationship between the Idea and its natural manifestation. This manoeuvre disables the objection to poetic copying of reality with the insistence that since reality is a copy, poets are something like makers of reality (Sidney 1595, B4v–C1r; Egan 2005, 69–71). Alexander Pope makes precisely this case in relation to Shakespeare:

> His *Characters* are so much Nature her self, that 'tis a sort of injury to call them by so distant a name as Copies of her. . . . every single character in Shakespear is as much an Individual, as those in Life itself.
>
> (Shakespeare 1725, ii–iii)

No such half measures suited Shelley, whose extraordinary closing assertion is that, as mouthpieces of the best thoughts of an age, poets are the 'unacknowledged legislators' of the world.

Before reaching this point, Shelley argues that poetry is merely one aspect of the general human love of order and beauty that makes us arrange the things at our disposal in pleasure-giving ways. Like Wordsworth, Shelley claims that the capacity to be poetic is shared by everyone, albeit to different degrees, and is manifested in a capacity to create language that 'marks the before unapprehended relations of things and perpetuates their apprehension' (Shelley 1840, 5). This, rather than any arbitrary distinction between verse and prose, was for Shelley the essence of poetry, and in this mind-expanding role it finds its true power:

> It awakens and enlarges the mind itself by rendering it the receptacle of a thousand unapprehended combinations of thought. Poetry lifts the veil from the hidden beauty of the world, and makes familiar objects be as if they were not familiar; it reproduces all this it represents, and the impersonations clothed in its Elysian light stand thence-forward in the minds of those who have once contemplated them, as memorials of that gentle and exalted content which extends itself over all thoughts and actions with which it coexists.
>
> (Shelley 1840, 16–17)

Thus poetry is necessarily social, not individualistic, for it enables a man to 'put himself in the place of another and of many others;

the pains and pleasures of his species must become his own' (Shelley 1840, 17).

Raymond Williams observes that in redefining the artist as a person with a special sensibility and special powers of expression rather than just special manufacturing skills (the earlier meaning of 'artist'), the Romantics enabled a one-way traffic between art and life. The dehumanizing effects of increasing industrialization and the degradation of the urban and rural poor, it was imagined, could be ameliorated by literature expressing repugnance at this and revealing the finer thoughts that even ordinary people speaking ordinary language are capable of. This humanizing impulse should not be confined to art, Williams argues, else art becomes an isolated mode of resistance; rather the resistance to dehumanization has to be part of a full social response (Williams 1958, 43–6). That is to say, for Williams it is not enough to find comfort, as Wordsworth allegedly did, in country walks that inspire eulogies to the daffodil, nor in encouraging the masses to take such walks when they can get them and to obtain the same pleasure vicariously when they could not. Yet such a view of the value of literature is offered by the most widely read modern critic of Romanticism and ecology, Jonathan Bate:

> This book is dedicated to the proposition that the way in which William Wordsworth sought to enable his readers better to enjoy or endure life was by teaching them to look at and dwell in the natural world. . . . most people know two facts about Words-worth, that he wrote about daffodils and that he lived in the Lake District, and these two facts would seem to suggest that he was a 'nature poet'. . . . this book will argue that, unfashion-able as that way [of seeing him] is in literary circles, it might just be the most useful way of approaching Wordsworth in the 1990s and the early twenty-first century.
>
> (Bate 1991, 4)

For Bate the English proto-socialism of John Ruskin and William Morris stands at odds with Marxist theory, for it recognized that the real basis of 'political economy was not money, labour, and production, but "Pure Air, Water, and Earth"' (Bate 1991, 59). We should not, Bate argues, deconstruct out of existence the differ-ence between human artifices such as class and city and the non-human given of nature – as Cultural Materialism in particular is apt to do – because 'Whatever our class, nature can do something for us' (Bate 1991, 56).

Bate's opposition between politics and nature is false because class struggle is in fact concerned with the enjoyment of those things that nature can do for us, and it is only class (the category that Marxism seeks to do away with) that keeps nature's bounty from the majority of the world. Bate rightly points to an important political consequence of industrialization in eastern Europe – 'Where capitalism has its Three Mile Island, Marxist-Leninism has its Chernobyl' (Bate 1991, 57) – but seems to think that this was because capitalist industrialization was somehow inherently cleaner, brighter, and more safety-conscious than communist industrialization. The truth is that governmental restraints on capitalist rapacity were won by campaigning workers, not beneficently granted by self-restraining energy companies, so that we have the workers not the bosses to thank for the marginally safer conditions in American nuclear power plants.

In his landmark publication of ecocriticism *avant la lettre*, *The Country and the City*, Williams points out that the sense of a bucolic paradise lost in the recent past can be detected in the literary work of each generation, reaching back through Edwardian, Victorian, Romantic, Augustan, Restoration, Renaissance, and late medieval writers. To avoid mistaking this impulse for a real loss, 'we must get off the escalator' of Edenic yearning and consider its general movement (Williams 1973, 12). For Williams the only way to make sense of this is within the phases of capitalism:

> I am then very willing to see the city as capitalism, as many now do, if I can say also that this mode of production began, specifically, in the English rural economy, and produced, there, many of the characteristic effects – increases of production, physical reordering of a totally available world, displacements of customary settlements, a human remnant and force which became a proletariat – which have since been seen, in many extending forms, in cities and colonies and in an international system as a whole. . . . What the oil companies do, what the mining companies do, is what the landlords did, what plantation owners did and do.
>
> (Williams 1973, 292–3)

The shared sense of lost innocence comes from the shared experience of increasing forces of production, and hence, as a way of understanding change, historical materialism – the explanation of the world that posits the increasing forces of production as the engine of everything else (Egan 2004, 25–6, 38–9, 54–7) – dissolves all hard distinctions between country and the city, and specifically between 'the country as cooperation with nature, and city and industry as overriding and transforming it' (Williams 1973, 293). From this point of view, Shakespeare's works are particularly of interest because they appeared during a crucial transition from nascent to full-blown early capitalism, as joint-stock companies of players as well as buccaneers and merchant traders gained royal monopolies that enabled them to accumulate capital at rates quite impossible within guild regulation. There will be more to say about this shortly.

Even ecocritics such as Bate who are familiar with and apparently approving of Williams's work tend to reinforce the false distinction between urban capitalization and rural pastoralism in its literary form, thinking of country walks as a balm to soothe the troubled mind. Of course, country walks *are* such a balm and in Britain the right to use public footpaths formerly (illegally) closed by landowners was established by a series of mass trespasses organized by the founders of the Ramblers' Association, which itself arose out of informal workers' walking clubs (Stephenson 1989). To see Wordsworth as an early popularizer of the pleasures of walking, however, it is not necessary to hold that an arbitrary division of time between work and leisure is inevitable. Those who are able to afford to live in the country because they like it, while working in a city because they need to, can easily come to see ' "the state" or "the planners" as their essential enemy, when it is quite evident that what the state is administering and the planners serving is an economic system which is capitalist in all its main intentions, procedures and criteria' (Williams 1973, 294).

Norbert Wiener, the founder of cybernetics and writer of this section's epigraph, saw this too and observed of his New Hampshire farmhouse:

> it is all very well for me to wish to enjoy the amenities of life which still remain in a country community of this sort. I must, however, realize that whereas in the old days the New England cities were tributary to this community and to communities like it, nowadays these communities represent nothing more than economic extensions of our cities. The *Saturday Evening*

*Post* cover is not an adequate representation of the facts of modern life.

(Wiener 1950, 57) [5]

Williams observes that Wordsworth had been aware of retreat into 'deep subjectivity' as one of the responses to our modern way of living among strangers whose behaviour, for all its anonymity, affects us. Alternatively, we

> look around us for social pictures, social signs, social messages, to which, characteristically, we try to relate as individuals but so as to discover, in some form, community. Much of the content of modern communications is this kind of substitute for directly discoverable and transitive relations to the world.
>
> (Williams 1973, 295)

Shakespeare wrote nothing that we can directly call a city comedy, but he wrote of people leaving cities and constructing alternative communities elsewhere, and he wrote of people confronting the paradoxical isolation of city life. Indeed, the impulse to create communities impinged on his professional life. It is well known that there was no city guild for early modern actors, but Roslyn Knutson suggests that they formed their own guild-like communities in response to this economic isolation (Knutson 2001). That is to say, rival playing companies might not have been as competitively cut-throat as we have imagined. On the other side of the equation, it is easy to overstate the sense of community among those in a guild. As Zachary Lesser has shown, within the Stationers' Company the printers were greatly inferior to the booksellers and publishers, and from 1603 the leading stationers created a joint-stock company within the guild, operating with royal monopoly just like the theatre troupes and the buccaneers (Lesser 2004, 26–51).

In his second work of ecocriticism, Jonathan Bate develops his thesis, contra Williams, that reading about wandering as lonely as a cloud might fruitfully offer a recreational escape from urban life, that poems 'may create for the mind the same kind of re-creational space that a park creates for the body' (Bate 2000, 64). This kind of thinking easily descends into risible sentimentality – 'Nature is calling to us in a voice like that of our primal mother' (Bate 2000, 67) – and it does not even make for convincing criticism of Bate's favourite neglected poet, John Clare. Bate reproduces Clare's poem

'The Pettichap's Nest', which ostensibly describes the finding of a nest with 'scarce a clump of grass to keep it warm | . . . Or prickly bush to shield it', and 'Built like an oven with a little hole' (Bate 2000, 158–60). Unencumbered by a post-Freudian suspicion that Clare's choice of words might speak of concerns of which the poet was unaware, Bate does not connect this vaginal imagery to the little-man phallus of the title, even when the poet speaks of the nest being concealed, its entrance 'Scarcely admitting e'en two fingers', and the wider space inside being 'full of eggs'. Bate appreciates in Clare his ability to just be in the countryside, soaking it up rather than thinking too hard about it. Despite Bate's claim to theoretical sophistication in this book (Jensen 2003–4, 113), it offers little more than the dumbstruck peasant awe that Terry Eagleton pointed out was the logical conclusion of the ideas of Bate's favourite philosopher, Martin Heidegger (Eagleton 1983, 62–6).

In a final programmatic chapter called 'What are poets for?' Bate uses the idea from Heidegger (and, indeed, Hans-Georg Gadamer, although Bate does not credit him) of a reader's and a writer's horizons of experience meeting in the text (Bate 2000, 243–83). The idea is that a poem gives us an experience of another's way of being in the world, another's attitude towards it, that we share when we read it, and that this experience can be a dwelling 'at home', as it were, in the work. Bate thinks that Heidegger's writings about the nature of technology and the storing of energy showed why windmills are safe but large dams are not, but this is of course nonsense. No one would object to nuclear power if it were in fact clean.[6] It is not the particular means of generating power that people object to in principle, it is the real danger they present and the damage that they cause in their processes. An exception to this point might be made for those extraordinary country-dwellers who oppose the construction of on-shore windfarms, for whom the obvious solution to the nation's rising energy needs is not they should put up with living near wind-mills but that someone else, somewhere else, should put up with living near a coal mine or a nuclear power station.

A guiding theme of Bate's book is that language is our means to reconnect with nature, and yet language is the acme of human artifice, the triumph of the cultural over the natural. This presents an ecocritical dilemma: the poetry and the criticism are at a remove from the pure experience of nature that they seek to articulate. Bate's tackling of, and solution to, this dilemma are reminiscent of

Wordsworth's wrestling in the preface to *Lyrical Ballads* with the related problem of complex and artificial verse being in the service of plain speaking. For Bate, the solution comes in a kind of low-impact poetry that does as little reasoning and exhorting as possible and seeks instead to emulate the natural world in itself.

Such poetry should be read in a gentle, awestruck, and non-political, way:

> The poet's way of articulating the relationship between human-kind and environment, person and place, is peculiar because it is experiential, not descriptive. Whereas the biologist, the geographer and the Green activist have *narratives* of dwelling, a poem may be a *revelation* of dwelling. Such a claim is phenomenological before it is political, and for this reason ecopoetics may properly be regarded as pre-political. . . . Marxist, feminist and multiculturalist critics bring explicit or implicit political manifestos to the texts about which they write. They regard their work as contributing towards social change. Green critics have a difficulty in this respect: it would be quixotic to suppose that a work of literary criticism might be an appropriate place in which to spell out a practical programme for better environmental management. . . . Ecopoetics must concern itself with consciousness. When it comes to practice, we have to speak in other discourses.
>
> (Bate 2000, 266)

This is simply a new way to formulate the old cry that politics should stay out of literary studies, which plea the Romantic poets would scarcely have credited as arising from their work.

In the latest literary scholarship too, such a split between consciousness and social practice has been discredited. On principle, a feminist critic must be in favour of equal pay for women (since a founding principle is that sex discrimination is unfair) and there is no conflict between this pragmatic concern and the feminist analysis of the kinds of consciousness evident in the poems under discussion. Indeed, the greatest critical dividends occur when one can show how the two discourses, the literary and political, are mutually reinforcing: low social status has long degraded women and the internalizing of this degradation (including its literary versions) has added to women's reluctance to fight their employers, which is why raising consciousness has been part of the feminists' political struggle.

Bate's claim that ecocriticism should necessarily be non- (or in his phrase, pre-) political is as absurd as it would be in the fields of Marxist, feminist, postcolonial, and queer criticism. Having kicked away the political leg upon which ecocriticism might stand, one could expect Bate to lean rather more heavily upon the other leg, science, but his grasp of neo-Darwinism is shaky too:

> There is no such thing in nature as what Thoreau in the section of *Walden* entitled 'Shelter' calls 'superfluous property'. The savage has his shelter, writes Thoreau, the birds their nests and the foxes their holes, but 'in modern civilized society not more than half the families own a shelter'. 'Civilization' creates laws which prevent the 'natural' process whereby shelter superfluous to the necessities of one individual animal or animal-family is swiftly occupied by others. . . . In the natural world, different species fight for territory between each other and among themselves, but each must share its ecosystem with other species.
>
> (Bate 2000, 279)

It is tempting to respond that urban squatters fill the gap in civilization that Bate has identified, but more importantly his model of natural sharing is entirely sentimental. Genes are in competition with one another and this causes the organisms they create to share nothing with other individuals in the same species, let alone other species, except inasmuch as doing so furthers their own chances of replication. As we shall see in Chapter 2 (pp. 52–4 below), the proper use of the analogy of human cooperation with cooperation elsewhere in the natural world is that altruism can nonetheless emerge from competition between genes.

In a book-closing swipe at the latest manifestations of the modern, Bate complains about the insidious 'susurrus of cyberspace' that threatens to drown the grasshopper and the cricket (Bate 2000, 282). This is a remarkable objection to a technology that has put means for the dissemination of writing into the hands of millions who otherwise would never have learned to type, and irony is piled upon irony when we reflect that the Internet, far from silencing insects, achieves mass dissemination of words without cutting down trees to make the sheets of compressed woodpulp upon which, regrettably, Bate's words (and my own) have to appear.

*

Let us retreat from the blind alley of treating of ecocriticism as the study of nature writing and consider again Williams's deconstruction of the distinction between country and city. The word 'ecology' was coined in the late nineteenth century to mean 'that branch of biology which deals with the relations of living organisms to their surroundings' (OED ecology 1), from the Greek word 'οἶκ-ος' (house) and the Greek suffix '-logy', which had by then come to be used for 'departments of study' (OED -logy). The model for this formation was 'economy', the sixteenth-century meaning of which was the art of managing a household (OED economy 1a), and which by analogy between the domestic and the social came in the seventeenth century to mean the management of a community's affairs (OED economy 2a). Economics and ecology are not antithetical but cognate. An ecocriticism that drew on this shared origin in 'home' would have a wide remit indeed, for that word has always meant not just one's particular dwellings but also the collection of dwellings of which it is a part, and the native land (country) where that collection is located (OED home n.[1] 1, 2, 6).

In relation to Renaissance drama, a concern for place has lately driven attempts to connect the plays to their first home, the cultural phenomenon of London theatre that arose in a particular location at a particular time. Drawn on a map of early modern London such as Steven Mullaney provides (Mullaney 1988, 28–9), the open-air amphitheatres encircle but do not encroach upon the central area, the city, controlled by the London corporation; this central area, like its analogues in New York and Tokyo, is now one of the vital organs of international capitalism.

In Mullaney's analysis, the liminal zone around the central area was special because it was not quite within nor was it without the privileged centre:

> the ideological and topological structure of the walled medieval and Renaissance city was a tertiary rather than a binary one; long before the emergence of popular drama, the Liberties of London had served as a transitional zone between the city and the country, various powers and their limits, this life and the next – as a culturally maintained domain of ideological ambivalence and contradiction, where established authority reached and manifested, in spectacular form, the limits of its power to control or contain what exceeded it.

(Mullaney 1988, viii-ix)

Approaching London from the countryside, this outer zone of suburbs might be as far as many would-be immigrants could reach. Conversely, viewed from within, it was the place to which the city expelled what was unwanted: lepers (for hospitalization), felons (for incarceration or execution), and actors (for whatever it is they do).

The last group, at least, could exploit their marginality:

> Secular drama in the city often played with the festive inversion of cultural norms, but rituals of misrule, dramatic and otherwise, are precisely what their name implies: misrule, defined against and delimited by proper rule, its reigning antithesis. The public playhouses were born, however, at a time when traditional hierarchies were breaking down, and neither they nor the plays they fostered were thus contained by the customary antithesis of rule and misrule, order and disorder, everyday and holiday. With their advent we are no longer concerned with an interstitial stage, but with what we might can an *incontinent* one.
>
> (Mullaney 1988, 49)

Playhouses were physically dangerous because of thieves and morally (as well as physically) dangerous because of prostitutes, but they were also socially dangerous because on their stages ordinary men broke the dress codes that applied everywhere else (the sumptuary laws) by appearing as aristocrats, princes, and monarchs (Hunt 1996, 295–324), and because within them gathered thousands of workers who should, at 2 p.m. on a weekday afternoon when the performances began, be at their jobs.

In Mullaney's view, the plays are self-consciously concerned with their liminal powers and use them to explore the basis of every aspect of Elizabethan ideology, including the right to govern others, the differences between men and women, and the lessons to be drawn from the past for deciding how things should happen in the future. As such, they were inherently political:

> The public playhouses were not a minor irritation to London: they represented a threat to the political well-being and stability of the city. Their rise and continued existence marked a radical shift in the delicate balance between the city and the Court – a balance that had been graphically enacted in the past at the point where civic and royal authorities met and in a sense

combined, to display their mutual limits and limitations through the vehicle of marginal spectacle.

(Mullaney 1988, 53)

The radical shift referred to here was the granting of royal monopolies to joint-stock companies such as the acting troupes and the East India Company that, this dispensation notwithstanding, operated as free-enterprise rather than guild-regulated industries.

Granted the epitome of control – royal patronage – the Shakespearian drama paradoxically gained a licence to reflect upon wider society as well as upon its own conditions of possibility. Being based in the liminal environment of the Liberties, traditional places of licence, 'The stage decentered itself, and its displacement provided it with something approaching an exterior vantage point upon the culture it was both a part of, yet set apart from' (Mullaney 1988, 54).

Attractive as Mullaney's hypothesis is, and however appealing its relation of the drama's ideological interrogations to the geographical situation of the playhouses, there are important qualifications to be made. Throughout *The Place of the Stage* Mullaney calls the marginal zone beyond city authority the Liberties, as though the mere fact of being outside made for freedom of expression. In fact, a Liberty meant any place that would normally be subject to city authority were it not exempted by special licence. The freedoms enjoyed by the theatres of London's South Bank were not due to the city's authority ending at the water's edge on the northern shore (it did not), but because they were within specific places, the Liberties of the Clink and Paris Garden, that were (because Liberties) exempt from city control despite where they stood.

This matters because Liberties were not necessarily geographically marginal at all: the indoors Blackfriars theatre was in the heart of the city, on the site of a former Dominican monastery that had Liberty status. Far from relishing their marginal status in demotic open-air amphitheatres in the suburbs, the players always wanted to play indoors to rich patrons in the city and did so whenever they could, for example in the city inns before the ban of 1594. In 1596 James Burbage purchased the Blackfriars building as a new home for his son Richard's troupe, but they were prevented from using it by a petition raised by the residents of this select district.

Until 1608 most of the opportunities to play indoors were in temporarily adapted halls rather than permanent structures. When the boy players who were using the Blackfriars once a week for semi-public performances were forced to cease in 1608, Shakespeare's company took possession of the building and achieved their goal of playing indoors to rich patrons. They kept their open-air Globe amphitheatre going too, in the summer, probably not because they could afford to be profligate nor, as Andrew Gurr suggests, because they had a nostalgia for the pre-1594 habit of touring the suburban amphitheatres in the summer and then moving into the warm city inns in the winter (Gurr 1988, 10). A more likely reason for running two theatres at once was that, although their Blackfriars survived on this occasion, the ending of the privileges of the Liberties in 1608 made them wonder if their prized foothold in the city might be lost yet again, as it had been in 1594 and 1596. Only if their royal patronage failed the King's Men would the advantage of being distant from central authority outweigh the cost of being distant from the most lucrative market for playing, which was in the heart of the city. Mullaney's model of a liminal space between country and city is insufficiently attentive to the dynamic equilibrium by which are balanced these changeable centripetal and centrifugal forces.

In *Theatre, Court and City, 1595–1610*, Janette Dillon gives Mullaney's geopolitical domain a finer reticulation by using Henri Lefebvre's theory of place (Lefebvre 1991), tying locations to their effects on the psyche:

> The concept of 'place' . . . needs to be understood as both topographical and conceptual. Particular locations in London may emblematically represent particular activities (the Royal Exchange, for example, may stand for commercial transaction), but the inhabitants of the city who do not experience those aspects of city life only within those special locations. They carry their experience of the city in all its aspects with them, experiencing their own subjectivities as the sum (and conflict) of those various locations and activities.
>
> (Dillon 2000, 6–7)

In London a new kind of space opened up in the early seventeenth century when buildings appeared on the Strand running between the city of London and the courtly centre in Whitehall, forming a new district called 'the town' as a shopping location, especially once Robert Cecil's New Exchange was opened there in 1609 with a performance written by Ben Jonson (Dillon 2000, 9–10). More complex than Mullaney's model of centricity, Dillon's account helps us see that the city's boundaries were not clearly marked – its power had long extended beyond the walls – and the word 'court' too embodied a slippery notion of place, for it meant (and still means) wherever the monarch happens to be residing. In Marxist theoretical terms, one of capitalism's abiding characteristics is reification, the turning of the immaterial into something material (Egan 2004, 28–38), but it can also accomplish the opposite transformation, which we might call virtualization. The word 'market' had, in medieval times, denoted the place where transactions took place, but in Shakespeare's time it came to acquire its modern sense of the placeless domain within which exchange occurs. The theatre came to see itself as a market, 'a place where values may be tested in relation to one another' (Dillon 2000, 11).

These ideas about how early moderns experienced the city provide a useful bridge between ideas about urban alienation (from Lefebvre) and Edenic yearning (from Williams) and our present concerns with destruction of the natural environment. Late sixteenth- and early seventeenth-century London underwent a population explosion despite the death rate outstripping the birth rate, because thousands of immigrants came from the rest of the country and from abroad (Dillon 2000, 23–5). Most Londoners were born in the countryside, so naturally their ideas of it were bound up with thoughts of their own childhoods. Dillon rightly insists that although they seldom represent city life directly, Shakespeare's plays show urban concerns, as when in *Love's Labour's Lost* the young men form what is effectively a new city: their academy is bound by oaths, statutes, and signatures, it requires surveillance, and it is subject to intrusion and disruption. Even the oath they take is effectively that of an apprentice: stay put for a fixed term, live-in, work hard, and do not marry (Dillon 2000, 67). Characters in Shakespeare seek, construct, fly from, and attempt to destroy formal and informal communal structures, and they do these things in the countryside and in the cities.

The readings that follow draw nothing from such sentimentalities as the idea that there exists, among certain people who tend not to inhabit the cities of the industrialized world, something called ecological wisdom, nor that 'poetry is the place where we save the earth' (Bate 2000, 283), to which Bate's flight from politics leads him. Political action is where we save the Earth, and analysis of poetry can be where we wield ecopolitical insights to re-examine past representations of analogous situations, and indeed to see how past understandings of the world gave rise to the conditions of the present. Although he would not, of course, have used these terms, Shakespeare's plays show an abiding interest in what we now identify as positive- and negative-feedback loops, cellular structures, the uses and abuses of analogies between natural and social order, and in the available models for community. Characters in Shakespeare display an interest in aspects of this natural world that are relevant for us, and if we take that interest seriously we find that there is nothing childlike or naive about their concerns.

# 2

# Nature and human society
## *Coriolanus, Henry 5,* and *Macbeth*

## *Coriolanus*

Reading and watching *Coriolanus* and *Henry 5* from the perspective of the early twenty-first century, we have a particular advantage over the first readers and audiences: we know much more about how the human body works than they did. From the science of genetics, we are possessed of knowledge about how individual cells relate to the bodily whole that throws new light on the plays' use of analogies between cooperation in the natural world and social organization. To see how, let us start with the most famous body/politics analogy in the drama. Faced with a rebellion of mutinous citizens in the opening scene of *Coriolanus*, Menenius rehearses well-known nautical and familial analogies for class relations in order to reproach the hungry crowd: 'you slander | The helms o' th' state, who care for you like fathers' (*Coriolanus* 1.1.74–5). No more convinced by these images of proper social relations than the rebels are, Menenius tries something altogether more intimate, the Fable of the Belly:

> MENENIUS
> There was a time when all the body's members,
> Rebelled against the belly, thus accused it:
> That only like a gulf it did remain
> I' th' midst o' th' body, idle and unactive,

> Still cupboarding the viand, never bearing
> Like labour with the rest; where th' other instruments
> Did see and hear, devise, instruct, walk, feel,
> And, mutually participate, did minister
> Unto the appetite and affection common
> Of the whole body. The belly answered –
>
> *(Coriolanus* 1.1.94–103)

The answer is easily guessed at, that the belly distributes the viands throughout the whole body and that all parts benefit from what it receives. Whether this part of the fable had an analogy in recent Roman events is not the point, and indeed the play never reveals whether the rich are guilty as accused of hoarding grain. More fundamental is the bodily metaphor itself, for were the Roman state truly incorporate, rebellion by the citizens would be as absurd as one part of a human individual rebelling against another.

The analogy between cooperation among the parts of an individual's body (belly, mouth, limbs) and cooperation in the state is a familiar microcosm/macrocosm correspondence described in E. M. W. Tillyard's model (Tillyard 1943, 87–91) and it has been widely understood as a manipulative ideological manoeuvre that the original audiences would have treated with scepticism. Even such a conservative critic as E. K. Chambers was moved to call it 'the ordinary sophistry by which the middlemen and unproductive classes generally justify to themselves their own appropriation of nine-tenths of the profits of industry' (Shakespeare 1898, 122). As a false analogy, it would seem, the fable is deceptive because there is no reason to suppose that what applies in the single body applies also to the collective body politic. But the analogy can be run the other way with disturbing consequences, for the cooperation of the components of a single person is itself in need of explanation. Surprisingly, the explanation itself involves a kind of biological democracy at the heart of genetic replication, and one that runs parallel to a terrifying genetic fascism.

Until the 1960s, geneticists shared Menenius' sense of the singularity and wholeness of the human or animal body, and sought to explain certain puzzling behaviours (such as altruism) in relation to their benefit to the individual. Drawing on the work of W. D. Hamilton, Richard Dawkins showed that a model of competing genes, not competing individuals or groups, makes sense of animal behaviour that a model of competing individuals or groups cannot explain (Dawkins 1976). Related individuals share many of the same genes (50 per cent of them, in the case of mammalian siblings) so a gene that makes an individual help its relatives runs of a good chance of helping a copy of itself inside another individual. When the cost of helping is low and the benefit to the recipient is high – as when, being sated, one shares the remains of a meal with a hungry sibling – then even a small chance that the relative has the same gene is worth taking. Once we realize that genes effectively 'seek' to replicate themselves – in the sense that those that do not so 'seek' tend to die out – and that they have no investment in particular individuals other than as means to achieve this end, what was seemingly altruistic (from the individual's point of view) is revealed as selfishness.

This changed perspective on the individual raises a new problem, however. Each cell in a body contains a set of the genes, but only those genes in the sex cells have a chance of being reproduced in the next generation. Why do the genes trapped inside cells in one's leg muscles or one's liver promote cooperation among the parts of the body if they are doomed to die with the individual? The answer is that sex is a lottery: the genes do not know whether they (or rather, copies of themselves) will end up in the testes or ovaries of the infant being made (and so get a ticket to the future), but, because there is a chance they will, anything that promotes the overall well-being of the infant (so that it reaches maturity and reproduces) is a way of raising their own chances of replication. Moreover, since the cells of a body are all identical clones (sharing 100 per cent of one another's genes), from the cell's point of view helping one's neighbour is identical to helping oneself. As Daniel Dennett relates (Dennett 1995, 455–60; Dennett 2003, 150–5), the philosopher Brian Skymes spotted that the lottery of sex provides close analogies of the problems of ethics and social organization explored by John Rawls in his book *Theory of Justice* (Rawls 1971). In particular, not knowing what place in a social structure one is going to have (the so-called 'veil of ignorance') makes an individual's best interest lie in fairness for all. Cooperation by genes can be an expression of selfishness, which paradox of course takes us to the conflicting accounts of the social contract in Thomas Hobbes's masterpiece *Leviathan* (1651) and Jean-Jacques Rousseau's *Discourse on the Origin of Inequality* (1755) and *The Social Contract* (1762). The essential points, however, are that genes got there first and that Shakespeare dramatizes the consequences.

Menenius' understanding of the cooperation between cells in the body makes the mistake that until recently biologists had made concerning the unit of Darwinian selection. Genes, not people, are what get selected, but the extreme interdependency of cells inside a multicellular individual ensures that the individual succeeds or fails as a whole, either surviving to reproduce and raise descendants, or dying first. Much more successfully than post-structuralist philosophy and social science, genetics has decentred the human individual by putting genes at the centre of attention and explication. Whereas for Menenius the question is why individuals do not work together in perfect harmony like the parts of the body, for us the question is why the parts of the body work in harmony as though in emulation of social organization. The answer to our version of the question is that what counts as cooperation and what as competition depends upon what one takes to be the unit of replication: the individual or the gene. Human history is full of mistaken identifications of the object of replication and ideological structures based on these misidentifications abound. The Nazi ideology of *Volksgemeinschaft* (folk community) treated races as though they were individuals in competition with one another, and drew on the Social Darwinism of Herbert Spencer (who coined the phrase 'survival of the fittest' often misattributed to Darwin) that justified laissez-faire capitalism as a natural process of weeding out the weak.

The Roman republic of *Coriolanus* has a nascent ideology of collective identity manifested in the Fourth Citizen's description of Martius Caius as an enemy to the 'commonalty' (1.1.27) and in Menenius' characterization of the First Citizen as the 'big toe' of the rebellion. The sense of collective identity among Romans that we see emerging in *Coriolanus* would make the city a kind of individual in competition with other city states, and much of this play – indeed much of Shakespeare's political drama in general – is concerned with the degree to which such collective ideology is compatible with individual freedoms and with the Christian ideas that were to emerge five centuries after Coriolanus' time in the Roman empire. Early Christianity, it must be remembered, was politically revolutionary in its insistence that each human being, regardless of station in life, was individually and equally in possession of a soul and hence of special interest to God. Notions of a united city or a united country may seem merely analogies based on the natural unity of a human body, but that unity of the human body is itself only the manifestation of the combined imperatives of human genes; biologically it has no special status other than as a gene-vehicle. Moreover, human houses, weapons, and social systems are also manifestations of human genes (albeit more indirectly than human bodies) so that at no level is it possible to assert that particular unities of cooperation are natural and others artificial. Indeed, a view of life based on the singularity of the individual is likely to mistake parts for wholes and vice versa, a failing that will appear more clearly when we consider the Commonwealth of Bees analogy in *Henry 5*.

For Martius at the start of the play, the city is the singularity of interest and like a body it can be regulated by the letting of blood:

> MESSENGER
> The news is, sir, the Volsces are in arms.
>
> MARTIUS
> I am glad on 't. Then we shall ha' means to vent
> Our musty superfluity.
> *(Coriolanus* 1.1.224–6)

Martius applies the principle to himself ('The blood I drop is rather physical | Than dangerous to me' 1.6.18–19) and instinctively extrapolates this personal good to a social good:

> [MARTIUS]                         If any such be here –
> As it were sin to doubt – that love this painting
> Wherein you see me smeared; if any fear
> Lesser his person than an ill report;
> If any think brave death outweighs bad life,
> And that his country's dearer than himself,
> Let him alone, or so many so minded, *He waves his sword*
> Wave thus to express his disposition,
> And follow Martius. *They all shout and wave their swords,* [*then
> some*] *take him up in their arms and they cast up their caps*
> *(Coriolanus* 1.7.67–75)

To put the group first in this way is to treat the individual as though he were a cell in a body, and the likelihood of dying in war forces the soldier to address the matter of what he wishes to impart to the future. Martius' answer, of course, is that reputation (avoiding an 'ill report') is all, and at particular times in the play he seems to convince others to share this desideratum. Mostly, of course,

characters express the wish to impart their genes to the future, and
the play is careful to show the absurdity that ensues when soldierly
concern for reputation overrides this genetic imperative, as when
Cominius exclaims of an unnamed (and unnameable) poor man
of Corioles, 'Were he the butcher of my son he should | Be free
as is the wind' (1.10.87–8).

Martius' own genetic (or, in contemporary terminology, dyn-
astic) ambitions are ambiguous, as are his mother's. Volumnia's
insistence on the martial ethic of honour is meant to strike audiences as excessive and unnatural, as in her first speech bragging
about the dangers she put her son through at an early age. 'But
had he died in the business, madam, how then?' asks Virgilia,
and Volumnia's answer makes plain that she would gladly accept
an intangible substitute: 'Then his good report should have been
my son. I therein would have found issue' (1.3.18–21). This first
speech raises thoughts of the genetic danger of incest, as the mother
imagines herself the wife: 'If my son were my husband, I should
freelier rejoice in that absence wherein he won honour than in the
embracements of his bed where he would show most love' (1.3.2–5).
The image of self-consuming sexuality – by which blood lines,
instead of fanning out, re-converge – is paralleled in Volumnia's
image of self-harm used to persuade Martius not to attack Rome:

> [VOLUMNIA]                          Think with thyself
> How more unfortunate than all living women
> Are we come hither, since that thy sight, which should
> Make our eyes flow with joy, hearts dance with comforts,
> Constrains them weep and shake with fear and sorrow,
> Making the mother, wife, and child to see
> The son, the husband, and the father tearing
> His country's bowels out; and to poor we
> Thine enmity's most capital.
>
> (*Coriolanus* 5.3.97–105)

Although Volumnia here separates out lineal components (she is
merely the mother, and there are the wife and son to consider),
she nonetheless reprises, in the idea of ripping out bowels,
Menenius' rhetoric of bodily integration as a metaphor for social
cohesion. This is, in effect, a re-run of the opening scene's attempt
to talk down a rebellion by use of a body metaphor, only this time
it works.

Volumnia's rhetoric throughout the play is more supple and effective than Menenius', but it is no less class-bound. Successfully persuading Martius to apologize to the Tribunes, Volumnia makes clear where she sees the real dividing line in Roman society even as she counsels her son to pretend it does not exist:

> [VOLUMNIA]       I am in this [persuading you]
> Your wife, your son, these senators, the nobles;
> And you will rather show our general louts
> How you can frown than spend a fawn upon 'em
> For the inheritance of their loves and safeguard
> Of what that want might ruin.
>
> MENENIUS                    Noble lady!
> (*Coriolanus* 3.2.64–9)

In other words, the struggle boils down to his family and his social equals on the one side, and the louts on the other. Although the play uses the term citizens, the Roman terms for what Volumnia calls the louts were the plebs and proletarians, the latter name derived from their class function as merely the breeders of workers (*proles* and *prolem* are Latin for offspring) and forming the lowest group in the classification by Servius Tullius, sixth king of Rome. The play subtly shifts ground regarding which Romans oppose Martius – the opening scene shows a rabble but the brief peace at the start of 4.6 seems to be enjoyed by small businessmen – but Menenius (like Volumnia) is clearly thinking of the breeding proles, or as he puts it 'Your multiplying spawn' (2.2.78).

By repeated reference to the recent overthrow of the seventh and final king Tarquin, son-in-law, successor to, and murderer of Servius, the action of the play is tied to the events of the early fifth century BCE. Martius, the play insists (2.1.46–7, 2.2.87–95, 5.4.44), was crucial in transition from monarchy to republic, and the play opens with the democratic impulses that this released. Thus, although the play seems to begin with a natural disaster, crop failure and hunger, the subsequent events make clear that the crisis is essentially political. This is why the citizens' demands for corn are mollified by the granting of political representatives, the Tribunes. As with Slackbridge of United Aggregate Tribunal in Dickens's *Hard Times* (Dickens 1854, 163–71), the political representatives of the people are self-serving and manipulative (the citizens are 'lessoned' by them, 2.3.177), which might make us think this not a progressive work. But the situation is rather more complex than that, for the essential humiliation that Martius cannot bring himself to perform ('Let me o'erleap that custom', 2.2.137) is his obeisance to the ordinary people, which indicates a gap between political reality and customary practice. By a show of submission a consul acquires power, and Martius cannot even bring himself to make the display; he cannot stomach even a gesture towards the equality among disparate parts that Menenius' Fable of the Belly posits as the essential characteristic of Roman society.

To be fair, the citizens are not convinced about their own homo-geneity either, let alone the wider cohesion of all Romans:

> [THIRD CITIZEN]            Ingratitude is monstrous,
> and for the multitude to be ingrateful were to make a
> monster of the multitude, of the which we, being
> members, should bring ourselves to be monstrous
> members.
>
> FIRST CITIZEN And to make us no better thought of, a
> little help will serve; for once we stood up about the
> corn, he himself stuck not to call us the many-headed
> multitude.
>
> THIRD CITIZEN We have been called so of many, not that
> our heads are some brown, some black, some abram,
> some bald, but that our wits are so diversely coloured;
> and truly I think if all our wits were to issue out of
> one skull, they would fly east, west, north, south, and
> their consent of one direct way should be at once to
> all the points o' th' compass.
>
> (*Coriolanus* 2.3.9–24)

Knowing themselves to be unalike, the citizens debate the senses in which it is reasonable to treat them as all of one thing. Full of independent thoughts, the wills could not be held by one head, and in this sense, the third citizen admits, the image of a many-headed multitude captures their directionless yet yoked-together condition. Yet to perform the one custom that acknowledges their rights of self-determination, the ritual of consular obeisance, they must break into smaller groups and encounter the candidate as individuals rather than collectively: '[THIRD CITIZEN] We are not to stay all together, but to come by him where he stands by ones, by twos, and by threes' (2.4.42–4). And yet this is a sham individualism, as the Third Citizen (a Tribune in the making?) indicates when, with heavy irony, he offers a lesson in being an independent: 'Therefore follow me, and I'll direct you how you shall go by him' (2.4.42–4).

Excoriating the citizens for failing to reject Martius' consulship, the Tribune Brutus slides back and forth between individual and collective biological want and bodily self-rebellion: 'Why, had your bodies | No heart among you? Or had you tongues to cry | Against the rectorship of judgement?' (2.3.203–5). The body metaphor is ever-available to the rhetoricians on all sides, and it lies at the heart of representative democracy. The election of consuls (of which there were two) went by majority verdict and was to that degree democratic, but the consuls were virtually heads of state. Moreover, within election there was already a principle of many-in-one (the essence of representation) when the forceful lead the weak:

THIRD CITIZEN
He's not confirmed, we may deny him yet.

SECOND CITIZEN And will deny him.
I'll have five hundred voices of that sound.

FIRST CITIZEN
I twice five hundred, and their friends to piece 'em.
(*Coriolanus* 2.3.209–12)

Such natural leaders scarcely need Tribunes to focus collective energies in one direction.

On both sides, the body metaphor is erected only to be knocked down, and defended as natural law only to be abandoned. These manoeuvres are practised wholly within the metaphor's terms. In the central scene before the Senate, Martius deplores the citizens' refusal to fight 'Even when the navel of the state was touched' (3.1.126), and yet in next breath he mocks the very idea of unity-in-multitude: 'How shall this bosom multiplied digest | The senate's courtesy?' (3.1.134–5). Punctuated by just five words from others, Martius' long breathless speeches revert to the body metaphor to counsel radical surgery on it:

[MARTIUS]                        [If you] wish
To jump a body with a dangerous physic
That's sure of death without it – at once pluck out

> The multitudinous tongue; let them not lick
> The sweet which is their poison.
>
> (*Coriolanus* 3.1.156–60)

Precisely the same rhetoric of bodily health is wielded by his oppo-
nents, only for them Martius himself is the poison to be drawn
out: 'BRUTUS Sir, those cold ways | That seem like prudent helps
are very poisons | Where the disease is violent. Lay hands upon
him, | And bear him to the [Tarpeian] rock' (3.1.219–22). In the
play's first scene Menenius readily accepted that in relation to his
Fable of the Belly, the exegesis is all: 'How apply you this?' asked
the First Citizen, and Menenius told them that the senators are
the belly and the rebels the limbs (1.1.145–7). In the central scene
that leads to Martius' exile, Menenius is prepared to engage in
precisely the same kind of debate, and to switch terms as the need
arises:

> SICINIUS
> He's a disease that must be cut away.
>
> MENENIUS
> O, he's a limb that has but a disease –
> Mortal to cut it off, to cure it easy.
>
> (*Coriolanus* 3.1.296–8)

Saving this particular limb of the Roman state, Menenius argues,
is merely due respect for past service. To this Sicinius has a ready
answer from Menenius' own catalogue of body metaphors: 'The
service of the foot, | Being once gangrened, is not then respected
| For what before it was' (3.1.307–9).

Even more than his class prejudice, Martius stands accused of
harbouring ambition to be king:

> BRUTUS
> In this point charge him home: that he affects
> Tyrannical power. If he evade us there,
> Enforce him with his envy to the people.
>
> (*Coriolanus* 3.3.1–3)

The Tribunes are dishonest inventors of wrongs – their ensuing
claim that Martius kept the spoil of the Antiats is untrue too – but
the claim is, in the play's term, entirely plausible and worth
repeating, as Sicinius does in the play's brief moment of proto-

bourgeois peace (4.6.34–5). Indeed, Aufidius independently hits upon it to justify killing Martius at the end of the play (5.6.135–9). The accusation links this play with *Julius Caesar*, which suggests that across five centuries of history Rome was beset with essentially the same political problem regarding government. Both plays explore what may with justice be done to prevent monarchy, which is characterized as the unreasonable subsuming of diversity under unity. Even in his plan to kill Martius, Aufidius is held in check by a kind of democracy ('We must proceed as we do find the people', 5.6.15) and the final confrontation on the streets of Corioles[7] is, like the scene of Martius' expulsion from Rome, a contest of political rhetoric.

The trouble really started with Cominius bestowing the name Coriolanus upon Martius for his work of subduing Corioles (1.10.62–4). Although the nature of the copy underlying the only substantive text of the play, the 1623 Folio, is uncertain (Wells *et al.* 1987, 593–4), it might be significant that in it Martius' speech-prefixes do not change to reflect his new name until he is officially welcomed back to Rome in triumph at 2.1.158–65 (Shakespeare 1623, aa4r, aa5r). That is to say, we might reasonably conclude that only Roman ritual (not Cominius' fiat) has the power, in Sicinius' words, to reduce a city to one man, who would then 'Be every man himself' (3.1.265) when in fact, rightly considered (so the Citizens agree), 'The people are the city' (3.1.200). This concern with naming the hero links the play's exploration of politics and genetics, for Martius has no apparent patrilineal inheritance; he seems the epitome of the self-made man. Indeed, Menenius' rhetoric of his uniqueness takes the point to an extremity that is bound to produce absurdity:

> [MENENIUS]                    Yet you [Tribunes] must
> be saying 'Martius is proud', who, in a cheap
> estimation, is worth all your predecessors since
> Deucalion, though peradventure some of the best of
> 'em were hereditary hangmen.
>
> (*Coriolanus* 2.1.87–91)

Deucalion is Greek mythology's equivalent of Noah in the Judaeo-Christian-Muslim sacred texts, and there will be more to say about him in relation to *The Winter's Tale* (pp. 130–1 below). For now it suffices to note that, as with the Noah story, Deucalion's survival of a global disaster that destroys the rest of humanity makes him the common ancestor of all subsequent people, so Menenius' claim is self-defeating. Ascending the family trees, Martius' ancestry and the Tribunes' necessarily converge upon Deucalion, so he is hardly a suitable figure by which to distinguish noble from ignoble lineages. Menenius' comment points up Martius' absent male lineage, and the play is much concerned with what stands in its place.

For Aufidius, Martius' superiority over his fellow Romans is best understood by an analogy with hierarchy in the animal kingdom:

> [AUFIDIUS]       I think he'll be to Rome
> As is the osprey to the fish, who takes it
> By sovereignty of nature.
>                                                  (*Coriolanus* 4.7.33–5)

Since the early eighteenth century this has generally been explained via the popular misconception that fish, recognizing in the osprey a superior creature, offer themselves belly-up that it may take its choice of them (Shakespeare 1928, 475–6). The textual evidence to substantiate this belief is compelling, but the explanation must be supplemented to account for this singular capitulation. (After all, if fish do it why do other creatures not sacrifice themselves to their predators?) The full significance of Aufidius' comment emerges in relation to the ascending cosmological hierarchy of earth, water, air, and fire. The osprey hunts by descending out of its natural element (the air) to meet the interface of the airy and watery domains, and so necessarily gets only fish at the top of their element. Thus in the hierarchical cosmological model, the most senior fish are the most vulnerable to predation from above; as an analogy for human society this is potentially subversive. Milton's account of Samson's destruction of the Philistine temple shows a fine sense of the irony of the analogous human phenomenon of the rich putting themselves in danger by asserting their privilege of place:

> He tugged, he shook, till down they came and drew
> The whole roof after them, with burst of thunder
> Upon the heads of all who sat beneath,
> Lords, ladies, captains, counselors, or priests,
> . . .
> The vulgar only scaped who stood without.
>                    (Milton 1966, 555; *Samson Agonistes* lines 1650–9)

The analogy of human and natural hierarchies runs all the way through the political dramas of Shakespeare, and although there is a strong perception that these analogies are available to ideological manipulation (as we shortly see) this is not to say that, on the plays' own terms, the analogies are untrue or conservative. Indeed, the analogies can be used to confound oppression precisely because they assume that the human subject is made of the same materials interacting in the same ways as are found in nature. For this reason, although Menenius is quite capable of manipulative metaphors there is no reason to treat his supplication to Martius as insincere:

> [MENENIUS]                    (*Weeping*) O, my
> son, my son, thou art preparing fire for us. Look thee,
> here's water to quench it. I was hardly moved to come
> to thee, but being assured none but myself could move
> thee, I have been blown out of our gates with sighs,
> and conjure thee to pardon Rome and thy petitionary
> countrymen.
>
> (*Coriolanus* 5.2.71–7)

A man's tears *are* the same as the rains that might quench a fire – operating indirectly via persuasion but nonetheless effective for that – and a city, conceived as a place and as a group of men, *can* exhale like a man does.

Only from the perspective of our modern scepticism about the body politic metaphor do poetic images of mediation through the human body seem calculating and forced. The main purpose to which Shakespeare puts this metaphor is to examine how things that happen on the macrocosmic scale (classes, societies, cities) are related to those that happen on the microcosmic, and attempts to poetically reimagine human collectivities as biologically cohesive unities pervade his work. Inflected tragically, this reimagining animates Martius' sardonic 'The beast | With many heads butts me away', and in a darkly comic mode it powers Iago's brilliant deployment of the proverbial expression for a human sexual coupling known across Europe (Dent 1981, B151) as 'the beast with two backs' (*Othello* 1.1.118–19).[8] Far from being simple minded, the analogies from nature are capable of conveying Shakespeare's favourite paradoxes that recur in the drama, such as the fact that, depending on the force one uses, blowing upon a fire makes it hotter or puts it out. Thus the First Watchman mocks

Menenius' attempted intercession with the question 'Can you think to blow out the intended fire your city is ready to flame in with such weak breath as this?' (5.2.47–8). As we shall see, the human analogy to this principle is explored in depth in *Antony and Cleopatra*, where sexual appetite is something that can be simultaneously sated and whetted.

The climax of *Coriolanus* is the scene of Volumnia's successful intercession that persuades Martius not to reduce Rome to embers, which would, in Menenius' memorable mockery, be a consequence of the proto-bourgeois readiness to commodify everything:

> [MENENIUS]          You have made good work.
> A pair of tribunes that have wracked fair Rome
> To make coals cheap – a noble memory!
> > (*Coriolanus* 5.1.15–17)

The play's images of coal help date the play because Martius' reference to 'coal of fire upon the ice' (1.1.171) seems the sort of thing that might be particularly sayable after the Great Frost of 1607–8 (Shakespeare 1994b, 5). As we shall see in relation to *King Lear*, the climate change underlying this frost was an effect of stellar influence that the play (rightly, it turns out) takes seriously, but which for most of the history of these plays' reception has been dismissed as naive superstition. For us, of course, climate change is again a reality, not because of stellar influence but (ironically) because of human consumption of hydrocarbons such as coal. Shakespeare's poetic concern with the burning of wood and coal, however, frequently invokes a principle of wetness that strikes us as particularly odd: he imagines the fuel extinguishing its own fire with its tears.[9] For Shakespeare, it is in the nature of things that equal and opposite reactions emerge from the transformations of matter, and these provide ready analogues to the human reactions and transformations in the stories he wished to tell.

It might seem that the scene of Martius' family persuading him against the attack on Rome shows the genetic imperative finally asserting itself, and indeed the intense emotional pressure of the moment is made clear in the Folio text's unique call for silence in a mid-scene stage-direction.[10] Significantly, Volumnia explicitly connects Martius' renaming with his lack of familial feeling: 'To his surname "Coriolanus"' longs more pride | Than pity to our prayers' (5.3.171–2). The entire appeal draws on ideas about the proper order of the natural world, but as ever this order is capable of paradoxical inversions of place. Martius initiates the imagery of such transgressions in response to the unnatural scene of his mother kneeling to him:

> [CORIOLANUS]
> Your knees to me? To your corrected son? [*He raises her*]
> Then let the pebbles on the hungry beach
> Fillip the stars; then let the mutinous winds
> Strike the proud cedars 'gainst the fiery sun,
> Murd'ring impossibility to make
> What cannot be slight work.
>                          (*Coriolanus* 5.3.57–62)

Articulating almost hysterically the disorder we would call cognitive dissonance, Martius imagines nature up-ended so that pebbles are thrown to the heavens and trees tossed (as fuel?) into the sun. Abstract and concrete nouns collide in this apocalyptic vision: impossibility is murdered so that anything is possible. Thus 'What cannot be' (that is, the impossible) is made slight work and yet the idea of the impossible has already been destroyed. Martius' speech is magnificently defiant of logic, and in that it embodies the natural turmoil it expresses.

In the face of this hysteria, Volumnia's 'I holp to frame thee' (5.3.63) might, in the contemporary pronunciation of 'hope' – and as the Folio spells it (Shakespeare 1623, cc2r) – indicate a double meaning: I helped make you, and I intend to bring you back to order. Certainly, Volumnia entwines the familial and social order in her extended appeal:

> [VOLUMNIA]          Come, let us go.
> This fellow had a Volscian to his mother.
> His wife is in Corioles, and this child
> Like him by chance. – Yet give us our dispatch.
> I am hushed until our city be afire,
> And then I'll speak a little.
>                          (*Coriolanus* 5.3.178–83)

The little speaking might be some kind of curse or prayer for forgiveness, but the important thing from our point of view is that, as with Menenius' 'weak breath' (5.2.48) mocked by the First Watchman, human breath can inflame a fire or put it out, which dual nature is maddeningly true also of language. What characters say has the same double-edged potential (can persuade or dissuade) that breath itself has, which for Shakespeare is an endlessly fascinating expression of the essential unity (oneness of nature) of human social interaction and our physical beings. Our bodies are structured just like the wider cosmos, which is of course an essential Green insight lost in recent Shakespeare criticism. To reject Menenius' interpretation of the Fable of the Belly it is not necessary to reject such analogies altogether, for as the play shows it is quite possible to construct alternative, democratic foundations to society using the same bodily analogies by which others might construct a defence of autocracy. To argue this is only really to say that analogies do not explicate themselves.

## *Henry 5*

The obvious parallel to Menenius' Fable of the Belly in *Coriolanus* is Canterbury's Commonwealth of Bees speech in *Henry 5* (1.2.183–220), which likens proper order in human society to the orderly division of labour in honeybee colonies. Before considering this speech in detail, it is worth observing that both sides in this play's war agree on one thing about France: it is the best garden in the world. Burgundy describes it so when lamenting the neglect that it has fallen into because of the war (5.2.36), and the Chorus – who surely represents an English point of view throughout – agrees (Epilogue.7). It is, however, a peculiar thing to say about a kingdom and to understand what they mean by it we must consider the extended horticultural and landscape metaphors that the play wields to liken human affairs to natural ones and to explore the impact of the former on the latter.

The play begins, famously, with an apparent apology for the compression of world-size events into the small compass of the open-air amphitheatre, and a plea for imaginative engagement:

> [CHORUS]
> Suppose within the girdle of these walls
> Are now confinèd two mighty monarchies,
> Whose high uprearèd and abutting fronts
> The perilous narrow ocean parts asunder.
> Piece out our imperfections with your thoughts:
> Into a thousand parts divide one man,
> And make imaginary puissance.
> (*Henry 5* Prologue.19–25)

Reference to the scaled-down representation of the wider world would be especially apt were the play presented at the Globe theatre, whose name invokes the idea of encompassing within itself the entire world. The particular place to be imagined here is the English Channel with the chalk cliffs of Dover on the one side and those of Cap Gris-Nez and Cap Blanc-Nez on the other. These names given by the French to their equivalent of the Dover Cliffs indicate that these landscapes seem human, and indeed at the dramatic high-point of the attack upon Harfleur, in the play's most famous speech, King Harry exhorts his men to set their faces like cliffs:

> [KING HARRY]
> Then lend the eye a terrible aspect,
> Let it pry through the portage of the head
> Like the brass cannon, let the brow o'erwhelm it
> As fearfully as doth a gallèd rock
> O'erhang and jutty his confounded base,
> Swilled with the wild and wasteful ocean.
> Now set the teeth and stretch the nostril wide,
> Hold hard the breath, and bend up every spirit
> To his full height. On, on, you noblest English.
>
> (*Henry 5* 3.1.9–17)

The cliffs at Dover and Calais scowling at one another is so powerful an image of opposed soldiers' faces that Shakespeare seems to have rerouted the English army's march to make the most of it. The historically correct London–Southampton–Harfleur route was in his sources, but Shakespeare changed this to London–Dover–Calais (Shakespeare 1982, Figure 5), apparently in order to make the most of the cliff image, to judge by the contradiction between the Chorus's 'Unto Southampton do we shift our scene' and his 'The well-appointed king at Dover pier' (2.0.41, 3.0.4). Calais has a particular historical importance in this regard, as it had been England's last possession on the far side of the Channel and fell to François de Lorraine, second duc de Guise in 1558. Thus when Henry's terms for avoidance of war are presented to the French court, a modern audience is likely to hear in Exeter's 'he is footed in this land already' (2.4.143) a dishonourably pre-emptive attack under the cover of negotiation, while those who recall the contemporary political situation will understand that Henry could be in 'this land' of France while still on English soil.

For the original audiences, however, the fall of Calais was a recent and memorable calamity and it structured the central concerns of Shakespeare's *Richard 2*. Calais was the location of the unsolved murder of Gloucester, and we can register a dramatically proleptic effect of its loss in Gaunt's insistence that the English treat the natural boundary provided by their sea-wall as though it were a divinely appointed limit: 'This fortress built by nature for herself' (*Richard 2* 2.1.43). For a London audience in 1595, this rationalization accommodates the loss of Calais and the failure of the Spanish Armada, and four years later the same audience would presumably hear in Exeter's 'footed in this land' a suggestion of pre-emptive extension, whether or not they recalled the historical status of Calais at the time.

Gaunt's famous image of the island of England as a cohesive organic whole is of course an imagining away of the awkward geopolitical realities of Wales and Scotland. These too, with Ireland thrown in, feature in *Henry 5*'s fictive harmony of British identities manifested in the collective labours of Fluellen, MacMorris, and Jamy. Before these labours are portrayed, the rulers suspected that they would be not harmonious but treacherous:

> KING HARRY
> We must not only arm t' invade the French,
> But lay down our proportions to defend
> Against the Scot, who will make raid upon us
> With all advantages.
> [. . .]
>
> [A LORD]
> But there's a saying very old and true:
> 'If that you will France win,
> Then with Scotland first begin.'
> For once the eagle England being in prey,
> To her unguarded nest the weasel Scot
> Comes sneaking, and so sucks her princely eggs,
>
> (*Henry 5* 1.2.136–71)

This at least gets the fear out into the open and we might approve of Shakespeare dealing with the reality of England's relations with its neighbour kingdom, even though the military cooperation in Act 3 suggests that the fear was always unfounded. (The situation regarding Wales is rather more complex, of course, since its separate national identity had long been subsumed under Englishness, as Henry's former title Prince of Wales indicates.) For our purposes, however, this coming together of the nation has a precise characterological precedent in the transformation of wastrel Hal into the eagle-like Henry.

Several characters struggle to find natural-world metaphors for this transformation, and the Bishop of Ely has his own:

> ELY
> The strawberry grows underneath the nettle,
> And wholesome berries thrive and ripen best
> Neighboured by fruit of baser quality;
> And so the Prince obscured his contemplation
> Under the veil of wildness – which, no doubt,
> Grew like the summer grass, fastest by night,
> Unseen, yet crescive in his faculty.
>
> (*Henry 5* 1.1.61–7)

In this view, Hal was changing all the time that he was wild and his goodness was able to grow amidst foulness. Generally plants were imagined suffering from their neighbours' foulness, hence Prospero's image of a usurping brother as ivy sucking the verdure of his 'princely trunk' (*The Tempest* 1.2.86) and the gardeners in *Richard 2* talking of 'fairest flowers choked' and weeds that 'seemed in eating him [Richard] to hold him up' (*Richard 2* 3.4.45, 52). The strawberry, Gary Taylor records, was the exception to this principle: it was thought to be unaffected by its neighbours (Shakespeare 1982, 1.1.61n). Some such explanation must hold, Canterbury agrees, or else Hal's transformation were a miracle, and those 'are ceased' (1.1.68). Anyone in the first audiences who knew of the historical John Oldcastle's Lollardism would doubtless hear this as prolepsis: time spent with Falstaff (= Oldcastle) has turned Hal into a monastery sacker ('temporal lands ... Would they strip from us', 1.1.9–11) and Protestant doctrine about miracles already prevails.

Another way to explain Hal's transformation is to see his former life as a kind of slumming to learn the ways of the poor to better oppress them, as Stephen Greenblatt suggests (Greenblatt 1985, 36). Certainly the Constable of France sees deception in the former state:

[CONSTABLE]
And you shall find his vanities forespent
Were but the outside of the Roman Brutus,
Covering discretion with a coat of folly,
As gardeners do with ordure hide those roots
That shall first spring and be most delicate.

(*Henry 5* 2.4.36–40)

This Brutus is the Lucius Junius Brutus who feigned stupidity so as not to appear dangerous and who led the rebellion (in which Caius Martius is supposed to have distinguished himself, see p. 57 above) to eject the Tarquins after Lucretia was raped. The Constable switches rapidly from this 'coat of folly' pretence to a gardening simile about dung, presumably because, to use Caroline Spurgeon's brilliant insight about image clusters, there is a missing third term, 'weeds', that links clothing to horticulture (Spurgeon 1931). The point here, though, is not about nature-in-itself (as was Ely's claim about strawberries) but about human interaction with nature: cultivation not wilderness. As an image of Hal's transformation, this suggests that he cultivated himself rather than simply grew out of his childish ways. And yet, as Exeter put it, those were his 'greener days' (2.4.136).

As Hal pulls himself together, so do the British Isles, the play seems to be saying. Initial fears about internal strife Exeter dismisses with a likening of the division of labour in the body to the division of labour in the body politic:

[EXETER]
While that the armèd hand doth fight abroad,
Th' advisèd head defends itself at home.
For government, though high and low and lower,
Put into parts, doth keep in one consent,
Congreeing in a full and natural close,
Like music.

(*Henry 5* 1.2.178–83)

Canterbury says he agrees – the military forces can be split to serve differing purposes at home and abroad – and to illustrate this he makes the play's famous argument from nature about the division of labour:

[CANTERBURY] For so work the honey-bees,
Creatures that by a rule in nature teach

The act of order to a peopled kingdom.
They have a king, and officers of sorts,
Where some like magistrates correct at home;
Others like merchants venture trade abroad;
Others like soldiers, armèd in their stings,
Make boot upon the summer's velvet buds,
Which pillage they with merry march bring home
To the tent royal of their emperor,
Who busied in his majesty surveys
The singing masons building roofs of gold,
The civil citizens lading up the honey,
The poor mechanic porters crowding in
Their heavy burdens at his narrow gate,
The sad-eyed justice with his surly hum
Delivering o'er to executors pale
The lazy yawning drone. I this infer:
That many things, having full reference
To one consent, may work contrariously.
                                    (*Henry 5* 1.2.183–206)

This of course goes far beyond what was known about the division of labour among honey bees, and indeed the central belief that the monarch is male, wrongly repeated since Aristotle (Aristotle 1910, 553a–4b, 623a–7b), was not widely corrected until publication of Charles Butler's *The Feminine Monarchy* (Butler 1609).

Moreover, we can now explain the behaviour of bees in genetic terms unavailable in Shakespeare's time, and it is worth briefly surveying the current explanation because it returns us to old philosophical and political questions about governance that have become newly relevant again. The central genetic fact is that worker bees are more closely related one to another than they are to their mother. Because male drones are made from unfertilized eggs the male sperm contains only one set of genes, so the 50 per cent of a worker's genes that come from her father are identical to those in all her sisters, while of the 50 per cent that come from her queen mother (who was born from a fertilized egg) only on average half are common with her sisters. Thus a worker is 75 per cent genetically related to her sisters and only 50 per cent related to her mother, and hence raising a sister is a more effective way of passing on her genes than having a daughter would be. For this reason, a bee colony is really as much like a single organism (in which the cells are 100 per cent genetically related to one another) as it is a family structure (in which individuals are at best 50 per cent related to one another). Menenius' Fable of the Belly in *Coriolanus* would seem to find in the natural coherence of the parts of an organism a model for social relations, and Canterbury's Commonwealth of Bees would seem to find in a naturally occurring social structure the model for division of labour within a coherent national organism. But these distinctions are false: modern genetics dissolves such notions of what constitutes an individual and what a society.

We can find in nature complex organizations that seem to offer analogues for the human social structures, but new knowledge about the material conditions that give rise to them indicates that a system might seem to be a kind of democracy from one point of view (which is how a sex looks from the gene's point of view) and yet can also be a kind of fascist dictatorship when seen from another (which is how a human body seems from a cell's point of view, or a bee colony seems to a bee). This Douglas Hofstadter made the subject of a humorous interlude in his book *Gödel, Escher, Bach* in which an anteater describes himself as a surgeon to his patients, ant colonies, each of which taken as a unitary collective appreciates his interventions (Hofstadter 1980, 311–36). No more than we mind having removed the unhealthy cells that comprise our tonsils or a wart, the ant colonies do not mind losing certain ants to the anteater. This should of course make us very wary indeed of analogies from nature, but it also indicates the radical variability of perception when we move between different scales of existence, and this movement is precisely what Tillyard's Elizabethan World Picture would encourage in us. It is here that we find the true limitation of the macrocosmic/microcosmic analogy, and happily it is one that Shakespeare seems to have preceded us to.

A puzzling aspect of Shakespeare's analogizing is a curious tendency to imagine something or someone serving as a model to its or her self. If we players had the right setting, says the Chorus in *Henry 5*, 'Then should the warlike Harry, like himself, | Assume the port of Mars' (Prologue.5–6), as though Harry could be anything but like himself. Shakespeare's uses of the word 'model' have a double sense of miniature representation and equal likeness, the former active in such uses as 'one that draws the model of an house' more grand than he can afford to build (*2 Henry 4*

1.3.58) and the latter in Hamlet's claim that by possession of a ring 'Which was the model of that Danish seal' he was able to put a wax impression upon his fake instruction to the English king (*Hamlet* 5.2.51). It is hard to know which sense is active when the Chorus introduces the plot to assassinate King Harry:

> [CHORUS]
> O England! – model to thy inward greatness,
> Like little body with a mighty heart,
> What mightst thou do, that honour would thee do,
> Were all thy children kind and natural?
> But see, thy fault France hath in thee found out:
>
> (*Henry 5* 2.0.16–20)

The country is like a person (with a heart) and comprised of persons; the outer person then is a manifestation of the inner persons. But then the 'model' would seem to be the outward greatness that fashions by example the smaller 'inward greatness', rather than being a miniature version that the larger form follows. On the other hand, if 'model' means equal likeness then, as with warlike Harry, England is like itself and the representation collapses into identity.

Here, and in the prologue and epilogue, the Chorus engages with the different scales of human and social life, suggesting self-similarities of the fractal kind in which nature abounds – for example, the fern and the snowflake (see pp. 25–7 above) – and refusing to accept the theatrical as a miniaturizing of history. The epilogue begins with what sounds like a typical apology for the play:

> CHORUS
> Thus far with rough and all-unable pen
> Our bending author hath pursued the story,
> In little room confining mighty men,
> Mangling by starts the full course of their glory.
> Small time, but in that small most greatly lived
> This star of England.
>
> (*Henry 5* Epilogue.1–6)

This apparently straightforward excuse becomes more complicated on close examination. If the 'little room' means the author's study, rather than the space given the 'mighty men' on the stage, then this can be read as an approval of the artistic process of encapsulating greatness in discrete moments. But it need not be the author who is 'mangling by starts', but rather the mighty men themselves who fail to run 'the full course of their glory'. The tone of the rest of the epilogue follows through with the catastrophe of the successive history. As Antony Hammond points out, the Chorus 'criticizes the author, in a vein that goes a good deal beyond the normally self-deprecating tone adopted for epilogues', creating a gap between dramatist and his creation that follows from a doubleness in the central character: 'Henry is a hero, and a cold, conniving bastard' (Hammond 1987, 142, 144). In such a condition King Harry cannot be like himself.

Hammond's 'bastard' is particularly apt, for the play is endlessly obsessed with King Harry's blood-line and its relation to his maturation. Unlike the Dauphin, King Charles takes Henry 5's threats seriously:

> [KING CHARLES]
> . . . he is bred out of that bloody strain
> That haunted us in our familiar paths.
> Witness our too-much-memorable shame
> When Crécy battle fatally was struck,
> And all our princes captived by the hand
> Of that black name, Edward, Black Prince of Wales,
> Whiles that his mountant sire, on mountain standing,
> Up in the air, crowned with the golden sun,
> Saw his heroical seed and smiled to see him
> Mangle the work of nature and deface
> The patterns that by God and by French fathers
> Had twenty years been made. This is a stem
> Of that victorious stock, and let us fear
> The native mightiness and fate of him.
>
> (*Henry 5* 2.4.51–64)

This is an extraordinary image of a good Englishman (Richard 2's father) being as satanic as his name implies (prince of darkness) and mangling nature.[11] Apparently an English audience would enjoy hearing the French think of their enemy as unnatural despoilers, and yet this horticultural imagery of seed and stem would seem contradictory: nature of one kind destroys another. Perhaps an unspoken sense of 'weeds' (the bad nature that good nature must uproot) is again active, for shortly after Exeter enters to impart King Harry's message in terms of taking off stolen clothes:

'divest yourself and lay apart | The borrowed glories' (2.4.78–9).
Likewise, in King Harry's speech the horticultural and sartorial
homonyms collocate: 'we should dress us fairly for our end. | Thus
may we gather honey from the weed' (4.1.10–11).

Certainly, the sack of Harfleur is imagined by King Harry as an
act of horticultural cropping by fiend-like Englishmen:

> [KING HARRY]
> With conscience wide as hell, mowing like grass
> Your fresh fair virgins and your flow'ring infants.
> What is it then to me if impious war
> Arrayed in flames like to the prince of fiends
> Do with his smirched complexion all fell feats
> Enlinked to waste and desolation?
>
> (*Henry 5* 3.3.96–101)

'Impious' here might carry a sense of imp-like, as when Pistol calls
King Harry an 'imp of fame' (4.1.46) and so combines the horticultural sense of scion or shoot (OED imp *n.* 1–3) with that of devil
(OED imp *n.* 4) and also brings in a sense of the soaring fame of
England borne aloft by the feather of Harry engrafted (OED imp
*v.*) into its wing. The avian connection is significant because for
King Harry, masquerading as one of his ordinary soldiers, falconry
supplies the image for the idea that the English of all ranks are in
this together and will soar or descend as one: 'though his affec-
tions are higher mounted than ours, yet when they stoop, they
stoop with the like wing' (4.1.105–7). However, stooping is also the
attack-diving of the falcon on its prey (OED stoop *v.*[1] 6a), so King
Harry's claim is a demotic rebuttal of Aufidius' comment about
descending osprey in *Coriolanus* (4.7.33–5; p. 62 above), which
suggested that hierarchy puts the nobles at greatest risk. Whereas
in Rome the senior nobles (the osprey's prey) get picked off because
they are highest, King Harry's faked common touch gives himself
no greater place in the attack (and hence no greater danger) than
any of his men.

The play's imagery of plants being grafted tends to emphasize what the English and French have in common, which is a
shared ancestry evoked whenever the words 'Britain', 'Breton', or
'Bretagne' are spoken, as for example when the first printing of
Richard 3's oration to his troops calls the opposing army 'A scum
of Brittains' (Shakespeare 1597, M2v). The Dauphin's dismissal of
the English as French offshoots seems to overlook the fact that

grafting is a human horticultural intervention intended to improve upon nature:

> DAUPHIN
> *O Dieu vivant!* Shall a few sprays of us,
> The emptying of our fathers' luxury,
> Our scions, put in wild and savage stock,
> Spirt up so suddenly into the clouds
> And over-look their grafters?
>
> (*Henry 5* 3.5.5–9)

From his own imagery we would expect that the Norman Conquest's splicing of Frenchness onto Anglo-Saxon stock would produce these super-crops that exceed their proper domain and bridge the gap between the earth and the sky. For his part, the Constable of France expresses amazement that such plants could grow in English conditions, and in terms that must recall the Bishop of Ely's talk about where strawberries thrive:

> CONSTABLE
> *Dieu de batailles!* Where have they this mettle?
> Is not their climate foggy, raw, and dull,
> On whom as in despite the sun looks pale,
> Killing their fruit with frowns? Can sodden water,
> A drench for sur-reined jades – their barley-broth –
> Decoct their cold blood to such valiant heat?
>
> (*Henry 5* 3.5.15–20)

So dispirited is the Dauphin that he imagines a kind of reverse Norman Conquest that grafts English (or rather, Anglo-Norman hybridity) back onto the French:

> DAUPHIN By faith and honour,
> Our madams mock at us and plainly say
> Our mettle is bred out, and they will give
> Their bodies to the lust of English youth,
> To new-store France with bastard warriors.
>
> (*Henry 5* 3.5.27–31)

The immediately preceding sexualized scene of Catherine and Alice discussing names for body parts provides a context for this imagined commingling of bloods. Disdaining such pessimism, King Charles summons his men to action with a roll-call that in the

Folio text includes a suspiciously English-sounding 'Faulconbridge' that can at best be emended only to Fauconbridge, which is still half French. Catherine's English lesson sexualizes the human body in the act of translating its parts, which is entirely the point at stake: she too will be translated and sexualized. King Harry makes no bones about this cross-channel grafting when 'wooing' her: 'Shall not thou and I . . . compound a boy, half-French half-English . . . What sayst thou, my fair flower-de-luce?' (5.2.204–8). Likewise, down the social scale, the captured Frenchman's name is translated and sexualized, and the English term correctly expresses what will happen to him: 'BOY He says his name is Master Fer. | PISTOL Master Fer? I'll fer him, and firk [fuck] him' (4.4.26–7).

From the ranks, however, comes a much grimmer view of the body divided into its parts and in need of reintegration:

> WILLIAMS But if the cause be not good, the King himself
> hath a heavy reckoning to make, when all those legs
> and arms and heads chopped off in a battle shall join
> together at the latter day, and cry all, 'We died at such
> a place' – some swearing, some crying for a surgeon,
> some upon their wives left poor behind them, some
> upon the debts they owe, some upon their children
> rawly left.
>
> *(Henry 5 4.1.133–40)*

Animals and plants differ in this fundamental: unlike gardeners, surgeons cannot (or rather could not, until recently) graft living tissue. Even a falconer's implants are prosthetic rather than living grafts. Williams's speech shows that the recurrent horticultural metaphors and similes run counter to the integrity of the human body, even as it explores the possibility of legs, arms, and heads making independent cries. Noticeably, there is no suggestion of the owners of these parts doing the crying. This is the serious and tragic counterpart to the comical dismemberment in Katherine's language lesson. For most or all of Shakespeare's audience the unifying principle of bodily integrity would have been the singular soul, whereas for us such integrity cannot be assumed. Like Hofstadter's comic surgeon-anteater, Shakespeare's version of the Commonwealth of Bees – it was not his invention (Gurr 1977) – and the related analogies of bodily wholeness throughout the play force us to consider just where in our materialist models we wish to pitch our claim for human integrity.

Williams's, however, is not the play's dominant voice. The harm that the war does is, at the close, imaged by Burgundy not through human biology but through horticultural imagery:

[BURGUNDY]
And all her [France's] husbandry doth lie on heaps,
Corrupting in its own fertility.
Her vine, the merry cheerer of the heart,
Unprunèd dies; her hedges even-plashed
Like prisoners wildly overgrown with hair
Put forth disordered twigs; her fallow leas
The darnel, hemlock, and rank fumitory
Doth root upon, while that the coulter rusts
That should deracinate such savagery.
The even mead – that erst brought sweetly forth
The freckled cowslip, burnet, and green clover –
Wanting the scythe, all uncorrected, rank,
Conceives by idleness, and nothing teems
But hateful docks, rough thistles, kecksies, burs,
Losing both beauty and utility.
An all our vineyards, fallows, meads, and hedges,
Defective in their natures, grow to wildness,
Even so our houses and ourselves and children
Have lost, or do not learn for want of time,
The sciences that should become our country
(*Henry 5* 5.2.39–58)

This confirms what was suggested by the imagery of weeding we saw used repeatedly during the war: that proper natural development itself is predicated on human labour. Being busy with war, King Harry agrees, 'gives growth to th' imperfections' cited by Burgundy (5.2.69). This might seem like the post-lapsarian state of nature, to be contrasted with the perfectly ordered garden of Eden that needed no labour, as is found in medieval representations. As Catherine Belsey points out, however, the two biblical stories of humankind's creation (Genesis 1.20–31, 2.7–23) differ in this crucial regard: in the first there is no hint of needing to tend natural growth, while in the second there is so much to do that Adam needs a help-meet. Thus Adam was made incomplete and 'imperfection inhabits God's perfect world' (Belsey 1999, 40). Indeed, in Milton's version of the second account, the need for efficient husbandry forms the essence of Eve's argument for dividing their labour in different places, which parting of their company makes her all the more vulnerable (Milton 1966, 375–6; *Paradise Lost* 9.205–25).

Accepting of the peace between England and France, King Harry worries that he will seem to have been bought off with sex from attacking the remaining cities of France. King Charles turns the transaction into simply another way of looking at the same thing:

> KING CHARLES Yes, my lord, you see them perspectively,
> the cities turned into a maid – for they are all girdled
> with maiden walls that war hath never entered.
>
> [. . .]
>
> KING HARRY I am content, so the maiden cities you talk
> of may wait on her: so the maid that stood in the way
> for my wish shall show me the way to my will.
> (Henry 5 5.2.317–24)

As Catherine is girdled and unpenetrated, so are the cities. Entering her obviates entering the cities. This image necessarily invokes the playhouse girdle spoken of in the prologue, with its 'abutting fronts' of the Dover and Calais cliffs and the natural sea girdles of the two kingdoms. Thus Shakespeare returns at the close to his opening image of opposed faces:

> KING CHARLES
> Take her, fair son, and from her blood raise up
> Issue to me, that the contending kingdoms
> Of France and England, whose very shores look pale
> With envy of each other's happiness,
> May cease their hatred, and this dear conjunction
> Plant neighbourhood and Christian-like accord
> In their sweet bosoms, that never war advance
> His bleeding sword 'twixt England and fair France.
> (Henry 5 5.2.343–50)

The landscape is still understood in relation to human concerns and human scale, only now rather than contending these national faces are merely white for envy. The symmetry of the opening and closing images is possible because only the interpretation of Earth's features changes. That is to say, in this play humankind's impact on the natural world is confined to husbandry, and the culmination of King Harry's maturation is his becoming a husband in both senses of domestic master and cultivator of the soil (OED husband *n.* 1, 3).

What seems permanent and unchanging in the English and French cliffs is, in geological fact, only the long-accumulated detritus of life. The white faces of the Dover and Calais cliffs are organic remains, the deposited shells of millions of marine creatures about 100 million years ago, long before the structural downfolding that formed the English Channel. In Shakespeare's imagery, soft biology replaces hard landscape, but this replacement is in fact (and to the ecocritic, crucially) only a return: the landscape itself is made of past life. Conversely, the building itself whose name laid claim to representative universality and singularity was itself but one in a 'living' dynasty of venues begun by the erection of the Theatre in Shoreditch in 1576 and extinguished with the dismantling of the second Globe in 1644. Across this period the design of the original was passed on, as it were, genetically, inasmuch as the 1599 Globe had to be the same size and shape as the Theatre (Smith 1952) and the second Globe (erected 1613–14) had to have the same ground plan (hence the same size and shape) as the first (Orrell 1980, 147). To that extent, the modern replica Globe in south London stands in a simple genetic relation to the Theatre in Shoreditch; like many of the Shakespeare texts, the venues' replication was essentially monogenetic.

The Globe was erected in 1599 while Shakespeare was writing *Henry 5*, and the partially completed building offered a view not available once the final facings had been applied (Figure 4). A cross-sectional view, available only during construction, shows how the middle and upper spectator galleries each overhang the one below, which feature is described as a 'jutty' in the contract to build the Fortune theatre on the model of the Globe (Foakes and Rickert 1961, 307). King Harry used this word 'jutty' for how the top of a cliff overhangs its base and how the martial forehead should overhang the rest the face (3.1.9–17), so perhaps the partially completed Globe inspired the images of overhanging seacliffs and of helmeted human brows. The completed space enclosed by the structure held 'within the girdle of these walls' (Prologue.19) the two mighty monarchies of the play, but the play itself seems to enact the encirclement, the enclosing of open space, that occurred during the theatre construction.[12] At the beginning the

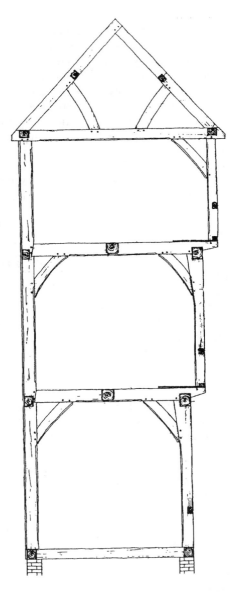

*Figure 4* The Globe playhouse timber frame. Reproduced by kind permission of the London replica Globe's architect, Jon Greenfield.

two monarchies are opposed like cliffs or soldier's abutting fronts, but by the end the girdling brings a feminine resolution (O) of stoutly defended cities 'turned into a maid . . . all girdled with maiden walls' (5.2.318–19). We do not know whether in Shakespeare's time there existed a drawing of the Theatre/Globe walls like the one above – quite possibly the joiner did not need it – but we can recover what Shakespeare must have seen from the pen of the Globe replica architect, Jon Greenfield. Nearly three centuries after Alexander Pope first appealed to the theatrical context – an accidentally interpolated instruction to a property man – to illuminate this play, another table of Greenfield's might take us back to the material context of 1599 in which, as the building went up, aggressive opposition resolved itself into circularity.

## Macbeth

*Coriolanus*, *Henry 5*, and *Macbeth* are in essence all varieties of history play, but the last differs from the first two in the crucial matter of how the Earth relates to the protagonists' actions. We saw nothing in *Coriolanus* or *Henry 5* suggesting earthly sympathy with human affairs, but there are signs of such sympathy in *Richard 2* and *Macbeth*. Returning from Ireland, Richard 2 exhorts the Welsh land of his kingdom to help in his resistance to the rebellion:

> [KING RICHARD]
> Feed not thy sovereign's foe, my gentle earth,
> Nor with thy sweets comfort his ravenous sense;
> But let thy spiders that suck up thy venom
> And heavy-gaited toads lie in their way,
> Doing annoyance to the treacherous feet
> Which with usurping steps do trample thee.
> Yield stinging nettles to mine enemies,
> And when they from thy bosom pluck a flower
> Guard it, I pray thee, with a lurking adder,
> Whose double tongue may with a mortal touch
> Throw death upon thy sovereign's enemies. –
> Mock not my senseless conjuration, lords.
> This earth shall have a feeling, and these stones
> Prove armèd soldiers, ere her native king
> Shall falter under foul rebellion's arms.
> 
> (*Richard 2* 3.2.12–26)

Of course, many of these are things that happen anyway: animals bite, nettles sting, and stones serve as weapons, no matter who is fighting or why. This opens up the possibility that fallible human interpretation of natural occurrences might be the important element in the relationship of human affairs and earthly happening, and indeed that self-confirming superstitions might be at work.

About three minutes of stage time (60 lines) before Richard's return from Ireland, the Welsh captain reports natural phenomena that have convinced his men their cause is hopeless:

> [WELSH CAPTAIN]
> The bay trees in our country are all withered,
> And meteors fright the fixèd stars of heaven.
> The pale-faced moon looks bloody on the earth,
> [. . .]
> These signs forerun the death or fall of kings.
>
> (*Richard 2* 2.4.8–15)

Reading these as signs that Richard is dead, the Welsh disband and so bring about the very defeat that they fear has already occurred. The natural signs, then, truly do 'forerun the death or fall of kings' when mediated through human minds. This goes beyond the familiar Shakespearian mockery of those who see supernatural causes behind ordinary human experience, whom Edmund mocks in *King Lear* (Quarto 2.115–21). In *Richard 2*, belief in Tillyardian correspondence between the human and cosmic planes is right even though wrong: believing makes it so.

There is nothing unambiguously supernatural in *Richard 2*, and indeed its central dramatic fact is the non-materialization of supernatural succour, the armies of angels sent by God, eagerly anticipated by Richard. Rather, the uncanny affects the everyday only via mistaken beliefs about it. In *Macbeth*, on the other hand, the witches could not more clearly signal their supernatural status in words even without their strange appearance (1.3.37–45). At their first meeting, they address Macbeth in terms of the past, present, and future:

> FIRST WITCH
> All hail, Macbeth! Hail to thee, Thane of Glamis.
>
> SECOND WITCH
> All hail, Macbeth! Hail to thee, Thane of Cawdor.

THIRD WITCH
All hail, Macbeth, that shalt be king hereafter!
(*Macbeth* 1.3.46–8)

Macbeth confirms that he has held the first title since his father's death (1.3.69). The second and third hailings sound like prophecies, although strictly only the latter refers to the future: the audience knows that Macbeth is already Thane of Cawdor. For Macbeth, however, the last two hailings are equally prophetic: 'to be king | Stands not within the prospect of belief, | No more than to be Cawdor' (1.3.71–3). The witches have special knowledge, but it is no more than the theatre audience knows. When, a couple of minutes later, Ross tells Macbeth that he is Thane of Cawdor, this apparent confirmation of the prophecy gives Macbeth reason to suppose that the third address ('king hereafter') will come true as well, and having such belief gives him the courage to make it so. As with the Welshmen's superstition in *Richard 2*, the apparent prophecy is self-fulfilling.

Banquo thinks of this capacity to see into the future in organic terms – 'If you can look into the seeds of time | And say which grain will grow and which will not' (1.3.56–7) – but for Duncan the essential component is kingly tending of natural growth:

KING DUNCAN        Welcome hither.
I have begun to plant thee [Macbeth], and will labour
To make thee full of growing. – Noble Banquo,
That hast no less deserved, nor must be known
No less to have done so, let me enfold thee
And hold thee to my heart.

BANQUO                          There if I grow
The harvest is your own.
(*Macbeth* 1.4.27–33)

The horticultural image is common to Macbeth and Banquo, but whereas in *Henry 5* growth (whether good or ill) was an inevitable process, this usage emphasizes the chanciness of it. The imagery is significant because the play is endlessly concerned with what humans and plants have in common, and most particularly in how they differ. It seems that the stage picture of the witches' appearance before Macbeth and Banquo at the Globe seen by Simon Formon on 20 April 1611 might have included trees, since he reported them 'Ridinge thorowe a wod' (Chambers 1930, 337).

The only description of the location in the dialogue is Banquo's 'this blasted heath' (1.3.75), although conceivably Forman was simply remembering the location from Holinshed (Bullough 1973, 494). On a stage dressed with scenic trees, the resonance of horticultural and arboreal imagery would have been amplified.

The human growth with which the play is concerned is, of course, not only the individual's but also the family line's. One of the central contrasts is between Macbeth's personal achievement that cannot be passed on and the future success, despite his personal non-achievement, of Banquo's line. This line presents a horrible spectacle to Macbeth, seeming to 'stretch out to th' crack of doom' (4.1.133) and extended in the mirror held up by the last of the eight kings shown him by the witches. The Macbeths had hoped to cut this line at the source: '[MACBETH] Thou know'st that Banquo and his Fleance lives. | LADY MACBETH But in them nature's copy's not eterne' (3.2.38–9). The root of 'copy' is the Latin *copia*, meaning abundance (OED copy *n.*), and indeed the branching out of reproduction is virtually eternal, leading inexorably to the son of Banquo on the English throne when the play was first performed. Or perhaps not quite inexorably, for as David Scott Kastan remarks, by ending the play with Malcolm on the throne of Scotland, Shakespeare reminds us that yet another disruption of lineal descent lies in the play's future (Kastan 1999, 168–9). There is, then, a sense of inevitability about bounteous reproduction and yet, as we saw with the talk of certain seeds flourishing in the royal bosom, also a distinct chanciness about it.

This combination of the inevitable and the contingent gets verbally presented in the witches' conditional assurances, which appropriately enough are articulated by apparitions of children. The abundant trinities of the play necessarily evoke a supernatural atmosphere, from the opening scene's three witches and their three greetings of Macbeth (on both meetings), to the closing scene's mirroring of this in the three greetings of 'Hail, King!' to Malcolm. Oddly, however, there are only two (not three) conditional assurances given by the witches and one of them comes from a child 'with a tree in his hand' (4.1.102), which Macbeth ought to have taken as a clue that the necessary condition ('until | Great Birnam Wood to high Dunsinane Hill | Shall come against him' 4.1.108–10) could be fulfilled. Macbeth, however, is sure that trees cannot move: 'Who can impress the forest, bid the tree | Unfix his earth-bound root?' (4.1.111–12). He holds this conviction even though his experience of seeing the ghost of Banquo prompted an acknowledgement that peculiar things can happen in the natural world: 'Stones have been known to move, and trees to speak' (3.4.122). Reverse the subjects there (stones to speak and trees to move) and the witches' conditional assurance is much less secure, and Macbeth had already (literally) taken steps to avoid the former condition: 'Thy very stones prate of my whereabout' (2.1.58).

The play's ubiquitous analogies from nature become its dominant tone once the central couple are together and Lady Macbeth counsels her husband to 'look like the innocent flower, | But be the serpent under 't' (1.5.64–5). Nature's threat to humankind is to be emulated, but often the direction of agency is unclear: are the evil things of the Earth sympathetic to the Macbeths' evil, or vice versa? Lady Macbeth's 'The raven himself is hoarse | That croaks the fatal entrance of Duncan | Under my battlements' (1.5.37–9) is supremely ambiguous in that regard, but seems to imply that evil nature corresponds with her evil thoughts, which is quite a different matter from the Welsh captain's prognostication *from* natural signs in *Richard 2*. This correspondence does not exactly mask human agency, but it does tend to make it seem like fate, which is of course the Old English meaning of 'weird', the defining characteristic of the witches (OED weird *n.* 3). Human agency passing itself off as fate is one of the play's concerns and it starts in this scene with Lady Macbeth's conviction that 'fate and metaphysical aid' (1.5.28) favour her husband's attempt at the crown. The mistaken belief that *meta-* means 'beyond' or 'transcending' has coined many new words (meta-chemistry, meta-drama) and it comes from the misreading of the title of Aristotle's *Meta-physics*, which just means the books after the *Physics*, prompted by their topic being underlying principles and ontology (OED metaphysics *n.*). That the error was current in Shakespeare's time is clear from Faustus's love of 'These Metaphisicks of Magicians | And Negromantike bookes' (Marlowe 1604, A3r), but Gabriel Harvey, Thomas Heywood, and Francis Bacon all used the word correctly. In Lady Macbeth's mouth the slippage is, then, probably deliberate on Shakespeare's part: things that are in fact just nature she thinks have supernatural causes. This is a central misapprehension of the play.

And yet the play also insists upon the natural world responding to human actions, as in Lennox's description of the chaotic weather and animal behaviour on the night of Duncan's murder:

LENNOX
The night has been unruly. Where we lay
Our chimneys were blown down, and, as they say,
Lamentings heard i' th' air, strange screams of death,
And prophesying with accents terrible
Of dire combustion and confused events
New-hatched to th' woeful time. The obscure bird
Clamoured the livelong night. Some say the earth
Was feverous and did shake.
(*Macbeth* 2.3.53–60)

Lennox asseverates the merely natural (strong winds and owl sounds) but distances himself ('as they say' and 'Some say') from the potentially supernatural lamentings, screams, fires, and Earth tremors. The next scene continues the macrocosmic/microcosmic correspondence, including the Old Man's bizarre report (distanced by ''Tis said') of Duncan's horses eating one another, which Ross confirms. However, for Ross the macrocosmic happenings are not sympathetic but actively resistive: 'Thou seest the heavens, as troubled with man's act, | Threatens his bloody stage' (2.4.5–6). Correspondence between the planes in Tillyard's model need not mean mirroring and can include negative (opposing) reaction, a sense (shared by Macbeth) that nature can, like a mechanical 'governor', oppose human acts to restore equilibrium. As we can see, even expressions of this sense of macro/microcosmic correspondence are couched in distancing phrases, as though the speakers were reluctant to commit themselves to such a view.

The apparent impossibilities described by the witches' apparitions sound like rebellions in nature of the kind that Richard 2 hoped the affronted cosmos would generate in response to Bolingbroke's rebellion. The non-materialization of these impossibilities in the earlier play provided the key contrast between the fantasist king and the realist rebel, but in Macbeth the bizarre events reported by Lennox, Ross, and the Old Man raise audience expectation that the predicted miracles will come to pass and undo Macbeth. The most striking aspect of the ending of *Macbeth* is the frustration of this expectation, since the dramatic structure demands Macbeth's death yet the apparitions appear to have promised that only miracles can bring this about. Attentive first audiences might have heard in the Porter's references to equivocation a suggestion that the miracles have not in fact been promised, but even so the means by which the witches' words are literally fulfilled are so entirely banal that the effect must be disappointment. This deflation suits Macbeth's mood: the apparently supernatural backing for his reign turns out to have only ordinary, natural meaning.

However, the play appears to go too far in unnecessarily deflating audience expectations, since Macduff's delivery by what we call Caesarean section ('from his mother's womb | Untimely ripped' 5.10.15–16) surely counts as being 'born', which word was always related to the verb 'to bear' (OED bear $v.^1$ 42–4). Even with a shorter gestation – 'untimely' indicating, presumably, that he was cut out while his mother was dying – it is hardly reasonable to claim that she did not bear Macduff. We might say that at least the revelation of Macduff's birth is kept from the audience until the final moments of the play and offers something of a surprise. The apparent movement of Birnam Wood, on the other hand, is signalled to the audience before Macbeth knows about it, just as his promotion to the rank of Thane of Cawdor was pre-signalled. This drains the last hints of magic from the play, leaving only the pleasure of dramatic irony deriving from Macbeth's ignorance. As before, the audience could put Macbeth right and forestall his taking as supernatural a purely human event. Whereas quibbling on the meaning of the word 'born' could count as equivocation (as Macbeth calls it, fiends 'palter with us in a double sense' 5.10.20), the apparent movement of the forest cannot: the forest does not move. Malcolm's plan of having each soldier carry a bough replaces our uncertainty about the apparitions' meaning with mundane certainty, but as a military tactic its aim is exactly opposite: it is an effort at concealment.

It soon becomes an obviously pointless effort, for both sides are eager to do battle no matter what they discover about the other. In the end, the scales do not fall from Macbeth's eyes and he has not the audience's knowledge that humdrum reality meets the conditions that he took to be miraculous. His last words indicate that he believes that the supernatural prophecies have come true:

> [MACBETH]
> Though Birnam Wood be come to Dunsinane,
> And thou opposed being of no woman born,
> Yet I will try the last.
>
> (*Macbeth* 5.10.30–2)

The irony, of course, is that Macbeth believed that supernatural things (the wood moving, a man not being born of a woman) could not happen, even though he was told these things by what he took to be supernatural beings. The supernatural beings turned out to be saying only natural, everyday things, just as for Faustus the truths of the universe revealed to him by Mephistopheles turn out to be the ones his book-learning was bringing to him anyway.

*

In Shakespeare's usage, the word 'green' often means immature, and yet as we have seen the natural-world imagery of these three plays is concerned with things coming to ripeness or maturity. The obviously green-worldish *The Merry Wives of Windsor* has the most occurrences (11) of the word 'green' in all Shakespeare's plays, and *A Midsummer Night's Dream* comes an unsurprising second with 9 occurrences. *Richard 2* actually has a character called Green and another (equally appropriately) called Bushy, conveniently supplied by historical reality. These Shakespeare makes into 'caterpillars of the commonwealth' that Bolingbroke, mixing his metaphors, swears to 'weed and pluck away' (2.3.165–6), not least because contrary to their names they have abused his country estates, 'Disparked [his] parks and felled [his] forest woods' (3.1.23). Their decapitation is justified as a kind of horticultural tending in the play's Gardening Scene, which in likening humans to plants entangles itself in problems of reproduction and individuation:

> GARDENER [*to First Man*]
> Go, bind thou up young dangling apricots
> Which, like unruly children, make their sire
> Stoop with oppression of their prodigal weight.
> Give some supportance to the bending twigs.
> [*To Second Man*] Go thou, and, like an executioner,
> Cut off the heads of too fast-growing sprays
> That look too lofty in our commonwealth.
> All must be even in our government.
> (*Richard 2* 3.4.30–7)

Here the fruit of the tree are thought of as its children rather than its reproductive organs, as though the plant were a lineage not an individual. Likewise, if Green and Bushy are the 'sprays' that grew too fast, the Gardener's work is a kind of fascistic eugenics in which individuals may be sacrificed for the good of the collective.

Literary critics dismissing Tillyard's work have inferred from his claim that a general ideological consensus operated in Elizabethan England (for example, that they believed in natural order) an entirely unjustified opinion that Tillyard himself shared the Elizabethans' view and thought it essentially right. In the three plays we have looked at, there certainly is sufficient consensus about the analogies between plant and human life for the poetic images and tropes to be intelligible, but we find endless contestation about how these analogies are to be applied and we see awkward moments when the conventional and conservative meanings shear away and radical applications become possible. At worst, Tillyard's interpretation of the evidence could be characterized as 'green' in the common Shakespearian sense of naive: the radical possibilities of the same arguments were not drawn out. One of the reasons that Tillyard has been so misunderstood is that he ended his book with a cryptic allusion to the struggle against fascism occurring as he wrote:

> And, if we reflect on that [Elizabethan] habit [of mind], we may see that (in queerness though not in viciousness) it resembles certain trends of thought in central Europe, the ignoring of which by our scientifically minded intellectuals has helped not a little to bring the world into its present conflicts and distresses.
>
> (Tillyard 1943, 102)

A historiographer is entitled to model the Elizabethan habit of mind and to assert that it was effectively consensual without being accused of sharing those thoughts himself, and this is all the more true when he asserts that he can see how one strand of organic thinking feeds into fascism and Nazism. As Anna Bramwell shows, in one sense the Nazis were a Green party and too much emotional investment in an abstracted concept of the land tends towards irrationality and xenophobia. But to argue as Bramwell does that the late twentieth-century Green movement is 'based on the shift from mechanistic to vitalist thought in the late nineteenth century' (Bramwell 1989, xi) is to miss entirely the movement's indebtedness to the recent scientific dissolving of the Enlightenment's hard distinction of the mechanical from the organic. From the gene-centred perspective of modern zoology and the virtuous reductionism of the Gaia hypothesis we can see that life is essentially mechanical and that machines are increasingly modelled on organic processes.

3

# Food and biological nature
## *As You Like It, Antony and Cleopatra, Pericles, Cymbeline,* and *The Winter's Tale*

## *As You Like It*

For his encyclopaedic *Historie of Four-Footed Beasts* published in 1607, Edward Topsell borrowed heavily from Konrad Gesner's Latin *Historia Animalium* published in Zurich (1551–8), even to the extent of taking an explanatory epistle that justified the project of zoology, as his discipline was later to be known. Because animals are part of the same creation as ourselves, Gesner condemned those who think animals beneath their concern:

> But if any man be so Barbarous, as to thinke that the beasts and such other creatures, cannot affoord him any subiect woorthy of his contempaltion [*sic*], then let him thinke so of himselfe likewise; for what ignoble basenesse is there in bloode, flesh, bones, vaines, and such like? Doth not the body of man consist thereof? And then how abhominable art thou to thy selfe, that doest not rather looke into these which are so neere of kinde vnto thee?
>
> (Topsell 1607, ¶3v).

Topsell's spelling of 'abhominable' (for 'abominable') was the period's standard and reflects the mistaken belief that the word derived from the Latin phrase *ab homine*, meaning away from man and thus beastly (OED abominable, *a.* and *adv.*). Gesner's point, of course, is that humans and animals are not so far apart in physical nature, being made of the same stuff and also linked together in the Great Chain of Being that runs through

> the heauenly spirits and degrees of Angels and celestiall bodies ... the mindes of men ... and from men to other creatures that haue life or sence, as to plants and inanimate bodyes, so as the inferiors do alwaies so compose themselues to the imitation of their superiours, euen as their shaddowes and resemblaunces.
>
> (Topsell 1607, ¶4r)

It is easy to see what trouble this idea might lead to, and Gesner was quick to qualify his likening of the soul that suffused every part of the human body to the divine essence suffused through all creation. Whereas the soul suffered if any part of the human body was hurt, the divine essence 'is so communicated to creatures, as it neither is any part or matter, or forme of them; nor yet can be affected by any thing the creature suffereth, nor yet included in the creature'. To placate any reader baffled by this apparent contradiction regarding the suffering of animals and their closeness to human nature, Gesner sighed 'truely these thinges surpasse all the wit of man' (Topsell 1607, ¶4r).

Gesner's interest in animals here bears upon his Protestant religious orthodoxy (he was a typical product of the Swiss Reformation of 1522–3) and specifically the conviction that the divine presence in the sacrament of the Mass was attributable to omnipresence rather than a transformation of matter enacted by a priest. If Christ-the-man is everywhere, cruelty to animals is something like a repetition of the crucifixion. Gesner's rhetoric urgently backpedals when it seems to imply that the suffering of animals entails divine suffering, and he argues that consideration of the 'neather and backer partes of God', the meaner corners of his Creation, leads us by 'Prickes and Spurres' to the higher matters. These terms from the urging on of animals take Gesner into a standard biblical justification for human domination of the animal kingdom, from Genesis 1.25–6: 'dominion over the fish of the sea, and over the fowl of the air, and over the cattle ... and over every creeping thing'. This was a justification close to Topsell's heart too: the previous year he completed and saw into print Henry Holland's *The Historie of Adam* that used this dominion over the animals to illustrate the perfect state of prelapsarian humankind (Holland

1606, A3v–B1r). Although the standard justification was often repeated in the period, the ways in which humans were like animals were apparent to all and just which forms of domination were reasonable and humane was a matter of considerable difference of opinion. One notable exploration of the question is Shakespeare's *As You Like It*.

The play begins with a man who complains of being treated like an animal:

> [ORLANDO]          For my part, he keeps me rusticall
> at home – or, to speak more properly, stays me here at
> home unkept; for call you that keeping for a gentleman
> of my birth, that differs not from the stalling of an ox?
> His horses are bred better, for besides that they are fair
> with their feeding, they are taught their manège, and
> to that end riders dearly hired. But I, his brother, gain
> nothing under him but growth, for the which his
> animals on his dunghills are as much bound to him as
> I. Besides this nothing that he so plentifully gives me,
> the something that nature gave me his countenance
> seems to take from me. He lets me feed with his hinds,
> bars me the place of a brother, and as much as in him
> lies, mines my gentility with my education.
> *(As You Like It* 1.1.6–19)

Appropriately enough for a play about modern approximations of Eden, this opening complaint is addressed to an Adam. It is not clear from what Orlando says that he thinks himself essentially different from an animal (and hence mistreated to be kept like one): horses are 'bred better' while he only grows, and that from eating with 'hinds', which editors almost universally gloss as meaning farmhands or servants although in this context the sense of female deer is clearly also active.[13] Rather, it sounds as though Orlando fears actually becoming an animal because of his education, as though culture, not nature, will determine this. As Erica Fudge argues, in the Renaissance the humanist privileging of humankind had not fully taken hold, and a man might be thought capable of descending to the level of a dog by his behaviour (Fudge 2003). For us, of course, the work of Charles Darwin indissolubly links humankind to the animals (which is why it was so abhorrent to a certain strand of nineteenth-century humanist thinking), and we should always remember that for Shakespeare's contemporaries the 'beastilisation of humanity' as Fudge so aptly calls it (Fudge 2000) was always possible.

When the villain of the situation enters, Orlando acknowledges his superiority but only inasmuch as society (specifically, the custom of primogeniture) makes him so:

> OLIVER          Know you before whom [you stand], sir?
>
> ORLANDO Ay, better than him I am before knows me. I
> know you are my eldest brother, and in the gentle
> condition of blood you should so know me. The courtesy
> of nations allows you my better, in that you are the
> first-born; but the same tradition takes not away my
> blood, were there twenty brothers betwixt us. I have
> as much of my father in me as you, albeit I confess
> your coming before me is nearer to his reverence.
>
> (*As You Like It* 1.1.40–8)

It need not be like this. In one of his most optimistic happy endings, Shakespeare dramatized another pair of brothers deciding to let nature (their absolute physical equality) teach their humanity and to ignore this custom: '[DROMIO OF EPHESUS] let's go hand in hand, not one before another' (*The Comedy of Errors* 5.1.430). Once Orlando leaves, Oliver swears to do some of the brother-keeping that Orlando complains is neglected: 'Begin you to grow upon me? I will physic your rankness' (1.1.81–2). This is a horticultural image of Orlando as a plant choking Oliver, just as Prospero thinks of his brother Antonio as 'The ivy which had hid my princely trunk | And sucked my verdure out on 't' (*The Tempest* 1.2.86–7). But as Alan Brissenden observes (Shakespeare 1993, 1.1.82n), Oliver's use of the word 'physic' suggests not only horticulture but also surgery, which two domains Shakespeare allowed to overlap in a celebrated image of careful gardening: 'We at time of year | Do wound the bark, the skin of our fruit trees, | Lest, being over-proud in sap and blood, | With too much riches it confound itself' (*Richard 2* 3.4.59–61).

The central structural contrast of the play is, of course, between the sophistication and corruption of the court, where the entire first act is set, and the innocence and honesty of the country where almost all the remainder of the play is set. After the Fall there could be no hope of attaining a true natural paradise, but one might hope to recover something like it by returning to places that had not changed much over time. This sense of returning to a former, better state of things is clearly set up by the wrestler:

> CHARLES They say he is already in the forest of Ardenne, and a many merry men with him; and there they live like the old Robin Hood of England. They say many young gentlemen flock to him every day, and fleet the time carelessly, as they did in the golden world.
>
> (*As You Like It* 1.1.109–13)

Belief in a falling off since the golden age, a descent into corrupted sophistication, is apparent across early modern poetry and prose, and as Andrew Wear points out, 'The idea that fresh air, fresh food and freedom to move were good for pigs (and for men and women)' links the modern Green movement with these writers (Wear 1992, 146). The pigs enter the debate via Thomas Fuller's assertion that those running wild in Hampshire produce the best bacon because they eat the ready supply of fallen acorns, which were 'mens meats in the Golden, Hog's food in this Iron Age' (Wear 1992, 145). As Wear shows, the countryside was widely (and, statistics confirm, rightly) thought to be a healthier place to live than the city, and going there was a means to recover something of the physical vigour of prelapsarian humankind. Linking the physical and spiritual aspects, Holland's history of Adam completed by Topsell argued that religious correctness was also a means to the same end, as encapsulated in its subtitle: *The Four-Fold State of Man, Well Formed in his Creation, Deformed in his Corruption, Reformed in Grace, and Perfected in Glory* (Holland 1606).

That the countryside itself is the cause of the goodness of those who dwell in it is strongly suggested by the play's startling transformations of Oliver and Duke Ferdinand when they leave the court to enter the Forest of Ardenne. The only explanation offered for the latter's initially mean behaviour is Le Beau's 'The Duke is humorous' (1.2.256), which diction, Brissenden notes, appears at this point in the source but also alludes to the fashionable dramatic genre of humours comedy begun by George Chapman's *A Humorous Day's Mirth* at the Rose theatre in 1597 (Shakespeare 1993, 1.2.251n). In a brilliant analysis of this fashion, Martin Wiggins shows that Shakespeare absorbed the new style and made it his own (Wiggins 2000, 64–78), and indeed raw statistics confirm this picture. The words 'humour' and 'humourous' flood into Shakespeare's dramatic dialogue at the end of the sixteenth century. Taken in chronological order of composition, the word-counts are 8 in *1 Henry 4* (1596–7), 25 in *The Merry Wives of Windsor* (1597–8), 13 in *Henry 5* (1598–9), 9 in *Julius Caesar* (1599), and 8 in *As You Like It* (1599–1600), compared to a background average of 3 or 4 uses in each of his other plays.

The term 'humour' comes from classical medicine (primarily, the work of Galen of Pergamum, 129–*c*.216 CE) and refers to the effect upon personality of the predominance of one of the four fluids of the human body – bile (= choler), blood, melancholy (= black bile), and phlegm – which ought to be in a dynamic equilibrium. The comedy of humours differed from what went before in its concern with human agency, originating in bodily chemistry, above all else, and its relative neglect of plot. As Wiggins puts it, 'the events remain tightly under human control, created not by chance, still less by any supernatural force, but by the machinations, not always benevolent, of particular characters' (Wiggins 2000, 72). In having no supernatural agency at work, this kind of comedy lacks the macrocosmic/microcosmic correspondence that we saw in *Macbeth* where the natural world reacts to human behaviour. Instead, it has a concern for equilibrium centred on the human body, which reacts to external factors (including environment and diet) and which as a complex dynamic system can be brought back into order. This is essentially another kind of macrocosmic/microcosmic correspondence and one in which the body, not the cosmos, is responsive. Once the body is back in balance the social world is consequentially adjusted: the usurping brothers spontaneously restore what they took.

As Gail Kern Paster reminds us, the Galenic humoral model of human biology and psychology is utterly materialist. Not for its adherents the intangible mysteries of mental energy that Freud later tried to model, rather human thoughts and feelings are essentially a matter of hydraulics:

> For the early moderns, emotions flood the body not metaphorically but literally, as the humors course through the bloodstream carrying choler, melancholy, blood, and phlegm to the parts and as the animal spirits move like lightning from brain to muscle, from muscle to brain.
>
> (Paster 2004, 14)

A corollary of this view is an inherent link between the macro-cosm and the microcosm, although Paster avoids these unfashion-able terms, leaving them out of her highly detailed index. Nonetheless, they are central to her argument:

> to understand the early modern passions as embodying a histor-ically particular kind of self-experience requires seeing the passions and the body that houses them in ecological terms – that is, in terms of that body's reciprocal relations to the world. . . . The link between the inner and outer is often described in the language of the qualities, since the forces of cold, hot, moist, and dry not only determine an individual subject's character-istic humors and behaviors but also describe the characteristic behaviors of other living things – animate and inanimate.
>
> (Paster 2004, 19)

A ready way to influence one's fluid balance was diet, and belief that particular foods had particular humoral effects is evident throughout sixteenth-century printed dietaries (Fitzpatrick 2005). Thus to gloss Duke Senior's question to his men 'Come, shall we go and kill us venison?' (2.1.21), Brissenden is quite right to invoke contemporary beliefs about this meat promoting melancholy (Shakespeare 1993, 2.1.21n). As a fluid, melancholy itself is no bad thing, and one ought to promote its internal production when defi-cient. On the other hand, if one has too much melancholy then one ought to suppress its generation. Balance of the humoral levels is all, and one's dietary choices informed by knowledge of one's present state enable the body to exploit negative feedback to fine-tune the hydraulic system.

The pervasive classical mythology of the play, however, permits characters to ponder others' bodily systems and other principles of feedback and energy renewal. The collocation of the follow-ing remarks in the wrestling scene strongly suggests a particular classical mythological context:

> CHARLES Come, where is this young gallant that is so desirous to lie with his mother earth?
>
> [. . .]
>
> ROSALIND (*to Orlando*) Now Hercules be thy speed, young man!
>
> (*As You Like It* 1.2.188–98)

This talk of lying with the Earth, wrestling, and Hercules evokes the encounter with Antaeus: 'Being forced to wrestle with him, Hercules hugged him, lifted him aloft, broke and killed him; for when he touched the earth so it was that he waxed stronger, wherefore some said that he was a son of Earth' (Apollodorus 1921, 223, 2.5.11). In Greek wrestling the object was to repeatedly throw one's opponent to the ground (Hornblower and Spawforth 1996, 'wrestling'), but rather than defeating Antaeus such a fall only renews his energy. This positive-feedback loop – the snowball gathering momentum kind (see pp. 22–5 above) – must be broken by inverting the game's rules and holding him away from the source of his power. The point of this classical allusion is that mortals generally do not benefit from such positive feedback of strength, and that ordinary processes of adjustment and balance are the keys to human physical fitness.

Orlando's defeat of Charles has a hint of supernatural wonder about it, but is essentially mundane. A powerful animal can kill a man, and likewise a man can kill an animal. Orlando is strong, but Adam's warning 'This is no place, this house is but a butchery. | Abhor it, fear it, do not enter it' (2.3.28–9) reminds us of Orlando's opening complaint about being beastilized. Once in the forest, Orlando characterizes the relationship between men and beasts there as fairly evenly matched: 'If this uncouth forest yield anything savage I will either be food for it or bring it for food to thee' (2.6.6–7). This is the 'him or me' character of unmediated nature, and it runs counter to the understanding of the forest as a place where humans can recover their natural dominance over animals. Just as individual living creatures are out to kill and eat one another, so with humankind: in the forest the essential equality of animals and humans is reasserted. On the other hand, scene 2.6 is played on a stage that still contains the banquet laid out at the end of the previous scene, which will succour Orlando and Adam in the next. This suggests that human culture overcomes natural forces, as does culturedness in the sense of refined and gentle behaviour: 'ORLANDO Speak you so gently? Pardon me, I pray you. | I thought that all things had been savage here' (2.7.106–7). He assumed the countryside would be wild but in fact it is peaceful, but only because the good courtiers have brought with them their good manners. However, to agree to Orlando's interpretation would be premature: the play holds culture and nature in tension and refuses to confirm the triumph of either.

Orlando has no sooner carried off Adam than Duke Senior enters with his lords and makes explicit what is at stake: 'I think he [Jaques] be transformed into a beast, | For I can nowhere find him like a man' (2.7.1–2). The transformations at work here go both ways: venison makes a man melancholy and melancholy makes a man like a beast. Duke Senior's qualms about hunting venison were not so much about the violence itself as the proprieties of place:

> [DUKE SENIOR]
> And yet it irks me the poor dappled fools,
> Being native burghers of this desert city,
> Should in their own confines with forkèd heads
> Have their round haunches gored.
>
> (*As You Like It* 2.1.22–5)

According to the First Lord's description, Jaques's response to the spectacle of a wounded stag crying into a brook made the same distinction about where (rather than whether) animals should be killed, but first comes a description of utter pathos:

> [FIRST LORD] . . . a poor sequestered stag
> That from the hunter's aim had ta'en a hurt
> Did come to languish. And indeed, my lord,
> The wretched animal heaved forth such groans
> That their discharge did stretch his leathern coat
> Almost to bursting, and the big round tears
> Coursed one another down his innocent nose
> In piteous chase. And thus the hairy fool,
> Much markèd of the melancholy Jaques,
> Stood on th' extremest verge of the swift brook,
> Augmenting it with tears.
>
> (*As You Like It* 2.1.33–43)

In its diction of 'Coursed' and 'chase', the touching image of the animal's big tears rolling down its face carries a fractal (that is, self-similar) miniature representation of the chase that led to its predicament, and his leathern 'coat' painfully anticipates what will become of his skin if his body falls into human hands. Even this, however, is framed within language that suggests the town rather than the country. The animal is 'sequestered' in the sense of cut off from his fellows, but also perhaps (and anticipating Jaques's financial metaphors) in the legal sense of a debtor's wealth being seized to pay creditors (OED sequester *v.* 3).

Once Jaques begins to 'moralize this spectacle' (2.1.44), the language is almost entirely urban:

> [FIRST LORD]
> First, for his weeping into the needless stream;
> 'Poor deer,' quoth he, 'thou mak'st a testament
> As worldlings do, giving thy sum of more
> To that which had too much.' Then being there alone,
> Left and abandoned of his velvet friend,
> ''Tis right,' quoth he, 'thus misery doth part
> The flux of company.' Anon a careless herd
> Full of the pasture jumps along by him
> And never stays to greet him. 'Ay,' quoth Jaques,
> 'Sweep on, you fat and greasy citizens,
> 'Tis just the fashion. Wherefore should you look
> Upon that poor and broken bankrupt there?'
> Thus most invectively he pierceth through
> The body of the country, city, court,
> Yea, and of this our life, swearing that we
> Are mere usurpers, tyrants, and what's worse,
> To fright the animals and to kill them up
> In their assigned and native dwelling place.
>                     (*As You Like It* 2.1.46–63)

This propriety of place does not bear close scrutiny, for it sounds as though Duke Senior and Jaques agree that animals who confine themselves to the countryside should be safe, which would imply that the ones in the city's abattoirs merely wandered there by mistake and, being where they do not belong, came to deserve their fate. Yet even this fragile distinction between country and city is threatened by Jaques's urban diction that suggests he cannot apprehend the countryside other than through his courtly mind. The dying creature is, in adding water to water, making a point-less will ('testament') as humans do, and the herd that goes by without regarding their fellow are like prosperous citizens that disdain the company of one in financial difficulty ('broken bank-rupt'). This is a keen sort of irony: only by putting the event into urban terms can Jaques stir his emotions about it. Or, to be more generous and give credence to the First Lord's interpretation,

Jaques equally pierces the natural and the human worlds by show-ing that they are essentially alike: human society is not so different from animal society.

There is more going on with Jaques and the stag beyond this moralizing, however. Winifred Schleiner draws attention to the contemporary belief that the tear of a stag (the *lapis bezoar*) was itself medicinal to the melancholic (Schleiner 1980), so that as Carol Falvo Heffernan points out there is an irony in Jaques foregoing the relief from his condition that is right in front of him (Heffernan 1995, 107). Human melancholics such as Jaques, and animal ones such as stags, were supposed to be drawn to water because of their dryness, and hence the animal's 'augmenting' of the stream with its tears is also an ironic failure to correct the bodily hydraulics. A melancholic should conserve rather than give up its moisture where the addition is negligible, hence the 'needless[ness]' of the stream.

And yet there might also be a kind of self-regulation at work here, perceptible if we recall that humoral theory precedes the mind/body split of Cartesian dualism: Elizabethans observed no sharp distinction between emotional drives and the bodily hydraulics. Indeed, our notion of bodily causation of mental states is itself anachronistic here: 'Melancholia is black bile. That's what it means. . . . black bile doesn't just cause melancholy; melancholy somehow resides in it' (Taylor 1989, 188–9). If Jaques got melan-cholic from eating too much stag (or indeed hare or rabbit, according to contemporary wisdom) then what follows might be his body's self-correction of this imbalance. By generating his emotional state of sympathy for the stag, his bodily appetites are altered (he swears off meat) and so the proper balance can be restored. If, as seems likely, the 'ab[h]ominable' (4.1.6), man-avoiding Jaques seeks Duke Frederick at the close of the play in order to emulate his religious isolation, the monastic life (from the Greek *mono-* meaning alone) will include vegetarianism that will cure his melancholy.

We tend to think of the green-world plays such as *As You Like It* in terms of plant and landscape imagery but in fact our rela-tions with animals are its central subject. That it seems otherwise is probably because the country world is first evoked in terms of plants and landscape ('tongues in trees, books in the running brooks, | Sermons in stones' 2.1.16–17) and the country songs are predominantly about these things ('Under the greenwood tree'

2.5.1, 'unto the green holly' 2.7.181, 191, 'o'er the green cornfield
. . . acres of the rye . . . life was but a flower' 5.3.17–29). The final
song signals the closing return to the urban with its repetition of
'every town' (5.4.141, 144). Yet all this talk of plants and landscape is confined to the characters' verbal descriptions of where
they are; when they come to talk of their own affairs and what
matters to them, nature is animal rather than vegetable. The accel-
erated pairings up of lovers towards the close release fresh possibilities in this regard, and given more lovers to mock besides
herself and Orlando, Rosalind launches on a fresh stream of animal
denigration, likening Celia and Oliver's instantaneous reciproca-
tion to 'the fight of two rams' (5.2.29–30) and the general exclam-
ations of love of Phoebe, Silvius, and Orlando to 'the howling of
Irish wolves against the moon' (5.2.104–5).

The likening of humankind to animals runs throughout the play:
'ROSALIND [I am as native] As the coney that you see dwell where
she is kindled' (3.2.329–30) and '[ROSALIND] boys and women are
for the most part cattle of this colour' (3.2.398–9). The animal
metaphors run alongside a minor stream of man-as-plant imagery
such as Rosalind's 'I'll graft it [the tree] with you [Touchstone]'
(3.2.115) and Celia's 'I found him [Orlando] under a tree, like a
dropped acorn' (3.2.229–30). Even with the human-as-plant
metaphors, the point is our vulnerability to being consumed, like
a medlar fruit or an acorn taken up by one of Fuller's Hampshire
hogs. This vulnerability to predation had since classical mythology
provided a ready analogy for relations of love: '[CELIA] He was
furnished like a hunter – | ROSALIND O ominous – he comes to
kill my heart' (3.2.240–1). The common Elizabethan pun on
hart/heart provides the connection between the idealized and
romantic and the mundane and bodily, and Rosalind's supposed
cure for love is a shock to the bodily system:

> [ROSALIND] . . . grieve, be effeminate, changeable,
> longing and liking, proud, fantastical, apish, shallow,
> inconstant, full of tears, full of smiles; for every passion
> something, and for no passion truly anything, as boys
> and women are for the most part cattle of this colour –
> would now like him, now loathe him; then entertain
> him, then forswear him; now weep for him, then spit
> at him, that I drave my suitor from his mad humour
> of love to a living humour of madness, which was to

> forswear the full stream of the world and to live in a
> nook merely monastic. And thus I cured him, and this
> way will I take upon me to wash your liver as clean
> as a sound sheep's heart, that there shall not be one
> spot of love in 't.
>
> (*As You Like It* 3.2.395–408)

For all that it replaces one malady (love) with another (madness), this presumably imagined cure is of a piece with descriptions of humoral balance elsewhere in the play and it has the outcome – retirement into religious solitude – that the arch-villain Duke Frederick chooses for himself at the close.

Aside from Duke Frederick, who becomes 'abhominable' in the contemporary sense of 'apart from man', the visitors to the forest return at the end of the play to the courtly lives that they earlier claimed to have found inferior to country life. To the duke's eulogy about 'this life more sweet | Than that of painted pomp' (2.1.2–3), Amiens responds 'I would not change it' (2.1.18), meaning the new life for any other. And yet he does change it at the end of the play. Agnes Latham warns us not to read this as satire:

> Life in Arden is natural and happy and wholesome and all good men flourish there. One after another the refugees from the world's unkindness arrive drooping and the forest revives them. . . . At the end of the play the company return refreshed and invigorated to take up their ordinary duties, after what has been a life-enhancing and not a self-deluding interlude. The fact that they return so promptly and so cheerfully is what validates their experience.
>
> (Shakespeare 1975, llx)

This sense of a trip to the forest as an invigorating tonic – much like a walk in the countryside in Jonathan Bate's account of Romantic poetry (pp. 38–44 above) – can only be sustained by ignoring the play's considerable power to disrupt our sense of country and city as separate domains. More simply, this reading is made possible only by mistaking exile for vacation.

As Jane Kingsley-Smith observes, exile and pastoralism already had a long-standing literary association when Shakespeare came to write *As You Like It*, yet there are 'points of conflict' in the association, most notably because the classical versions tended to show men banished from their farms while Renaissance pastoralists often 'are exiles from court' banished *to* the countryside. The latter direction exemplified the continued resonance of the idea that human beings 'belong in a garden rather than in a city' and hence that, paradoxically, in banishment the exile comes home (Kingsley-Smith 2003, 108–9). (Taken at its widest, the Christian story of paradise lost and regained is, of course, precisely of this structure.) In Shakespeare's time the familiar dramatic expression of this city/country distinction was the so-called city comedy in which innocents from the countryside brought their naivety to the town. Shakespeare produced no city comedies, but in *As You Like It* he engages with the genre's conventions by reversal: courtiers bring their urban ideas to the countryside and find that aspects of city life have preceded them there. The financial depredation that we hear in Jaques's responses to the dying animal – and perhaps also in Duke Senior's confirmation of having 'seen better days' (2.7.120) – is already a feature of the countryside, hence Corin's inability to succour the exiles in 2.4. Rather than conforming to the pastoral stereotype of the self-sufficient and idling keeper of sheep, Corin is a daily labourer ('shepherd to another man' 2.4.77) and can resume his occupation only when the aristocrats buy his master's farm. Of this countryside reality the duke's party seem entirely unaware. No one appears to be growing crops in the world of *As You Like It*; the rustics are all descendants of murdered Abel rather than murderer Cain.

To follow the biblical correspondences for a moment, we can observe that the story of Noah makes a strong distinction between the plant world, which is not rescued in the ark, and the animal kingdom, which is. The plant world, it seems, survives on its own and indeed its capacity to self-regenerate is an index of the water's abating: when a dove returns with an olive leaf, Noah knows that it is safe to leave the ark (Genesis 8.1). The story of the flood is a kind of exile and return that the play mirrors in the flight and return of its groups of main characters, and the two-by-two marches of unclean animals admitted by Noah is, as Jaques observes ('another flood toward' 5.4.35), mirrored in the final scene's pairing of couples. Jaques's allusion to the biblical flood is relevant for the play's various investigations of the natural, because it confirmed human beings' dominion over the animals:

And the fear of you and the dread of you shall be upon every beast of the earth, and upon every fowl of the air, upon all that

> moveth upon the earth, and upon all the fishes of the sea; into
> your hand are they delivered. Every moving thing that liveth
> shall be meat for you; even as the green herb have I given you
> all things.
>
> (Genesis 9.2–3)

If the trip into the forest apparently awoke disquiet about human/
animal relations, the analogy of the flood should allow the courtiers
to return newly invigorated (as Latham would have us believe) with
a sense of the rightness of human dominance of animals.

However, before this renewal of dominion over animals, God
apparently also relented regarding Adam's cursed agrarian labour.
For the original sin God had said 'cursed is the ground for thy
sake; in sorrow shalt thou eat of it all the days of thy life; Thorns
also and thistles shall it bring forth to thee; and thou shalt eat the
herb of the field' (Genesis 3.17–18), but after the flood

> the LORD said in his heart, I will not again curse the ground
> any more for man's sake; for the imagination of man's heart is
> evil from his youth; neither will I again smite any more every
> thing living, as I have done. While the earth remaineth, seed-
> time and harvest, and cold and heat, and summer and winter,
> and day and night shall not cease.
>
> (Genesis 8.21–2)

Whereas the attitude to animals is simply confirmed, the position
regarding cultivation seems like a reversal. And indeed, Noah
becomes a husbandman and plants a vineyard (whence wine),
which epitomizes the re-entry of pleasure into the world (Genesis
9.20).

Any contrast of the agrarian and the pastoral lives in Western
literature necessarily draws upon the story of Cain and Abel, which
mythologizes the triumph of farming. Once human beings became
mostly crop-planters rather than hunters, hunting became a recreational activity, especially for the wealthy. The exile of the courtiers
in *As You Like It* bringing with it the necessity to hunt is, in that
sense, also a forced return to an earlier form of production and
what was formerly the height of aristocratic leisure must be done
to survive. *As You Like It* is concerned with the moral correctness
of hunting itself. What links our time with Shakespeare's is a sense
that our relationships with animals are a part of what we consider
to be a healthy lifestyle. We, like them, worry about how far it is

justifiable to make animals suffer for our ends, how far we may treat them as merely instruments. In pondering those relations, we must remember that difference of scale is not difference of kind, for Isabella makes the entirely plausible claim that 'the poor beetle that we tread upon | In corporal sufferance finds a pang as great | As when a giant dies' (*Measure for Measure* 3.1.77–9). For us the debate takes the form of agonizing over whether organic, free-range farming might of itself constitute sufficient respect of animals' right to happy lives that we may with good conscience eat their bodies after quickly and painlessly dispatching them. This question went largely unasked (let alone answered) by most people in the eighteenth and nineteenth centuries.

For Enlightenment humanism, the inherent superiority of humankind did not need to be argued for, it could merely be assumed. René Descartes's great rationalist breakthrough in *Meditationes de Prima Philosophia* (1641) avoided solipsism by splitting the unitary (in his terms, unextended) mind from the divisible (extended) body, and privileging the former as the location of distinct innate ideas placed there by God. This polarization of function reduced the body to a mere machine, and although this had a positive effect in promoting materialist medicine it clearly overstated the unembodiedness of the mind. Moreover, Cartesian dualism treats the human body as essentially like an animal inasmuch as it is a machine, albeit one inhabited by a soul. Descartes's supporters went further and claimed that animals could not feel pain (Thomas 1983, 33–6). As machines, they could not suffer but only react and hence the howls of an animal being dissected without anaesthesia were no different from the discordant blasts produced by randomly depressing a palmful of keys on a pipe organ. Descartes's view filled the growing need to feel comfortable with animal misery: it took from animals everything that might make their oppression disturbing. In the twenty-first century we are coming back to an idea that we have much in common with the animals, and in *As You Like It* we find a shared anxiety about the lives of animals. Descartes's rationalization ameliorated the anxiety that is evident in Gesner's rhetoric with which we started, and these share a concern to give their zoological practice a theological basis. In Shakespeare, on the other hand, we see a radically sceptical consideration of the human/animal relationship, explored in the courtiers' attempt to get back to nature in Ardenne.

## Antony and Cleopatra

In a number of ways, Shakespeare's *Antony and Cleopatra* simply does not add up. Cleopatra's last act before her suicide is to present Caesar with a false inventory of her wealth, which her treasurer (perhaps by prior arrangement) refuses to certify:

> CLEOPATRA What have I kept back?
>
> SELEUCUS
> Enough to purchase what you have made known.
>
> (*Antony and Cleopatra* 5.2.143–4)

Seleucus' answer is a roundabout way of saying 'at least half', and it signals a bookkeeper's concern for the zero-sum principle of a balance sheet. Nothing is lost, nothing gained in buying one half of one's wealth with the other. If this scene of apparent betrayal is indeed feigned to reassure Caesar that Cleopatra still imagines a future for herself (rather than intending to commit suicide), then its exploitation of an accountant's precision is a subtle device indeed, for that is just the kind of thinking she has actively resisted all her life. Cleopatra, like Timon of Athens and unlike Wilkins Micawber,[14] refuses to live her life as a zero-sum game.

In that regard, Cleopatra finds Antony a kindred spirit. Asked for an accurate account of the quantity of his love, he distinguishes between the merely finite (into which category fall the small and great) and its true opposite, the infinite: 'There's beggary in the love that can be reckoned' (1.1.15). Rather than quantities totalling up, losses balancing gains, the desire of Antony and Cleopatra is a paradoxical positive-feedback loop: whatever should check increase only accelerates it. Thus, in Enobarbus' description of Cleopatra's barge upon the Cydnus she personifies fire itself:

> [ENOBARBUS]                On each side her
> Stood pretty dimpled boys, like smiling Cupids,
> With divers-coloured fans whose wind did seem
> To glow the delicate cheeks which they did cool,
> And what they undid did.
>
> (*Antony and Cleopatra* 2.2.208–12)

We saw in *Coriolanus* (pp. 63–6 above) this paradox of blown air making a fire hotter or putting it out, and in *Antony and Cleopatra* it is but one of several such paradoxes conveying the strange nature of Cleopatra's sexual allure: 'Other women cloy | The appetites they feed, but she makes hungry | Where most she satisfies' (2.2.242–4). For Enobarbus this is a matter of wonder, and even Philo's disapproving language captures the extraordinary 'less-is-more' quality of it: '[Antony's heart] is become the bellows and the fan | To cool a gipsy's lust' (1.1.9–10).

We might expect all this talk of self-reinforcing arousal to lead to 'increase' of the biologically creative kind, but the play is remarkably coy about Cleopatra's fertility and her children have only a shadowy role. Caesar's complaint about the couple's dynasty-founding ritual glances at them in passing, and only because they compounded the offence:

CAESAR
Contemning Rome, he has done all this and more
In Alexandria. Here's the manner of 't:
I' th' market place on a tribunal silvered,
Cleopatra and himself in chairs of gold
Were publicly enthroned. At the feet sat
Caesarion, whom they call my father's son,
And all the unlawful issue that their lust
Since then hath made between them.
                                    (*Antony and Cleopatra* 3.6.1–8)

In the play's final manoeuvrings Caesar employs a thinly veiled threat to persuade Cleopatra against suicide 'you shall . . . put your children | To that destruction which I'll guard them from' (5.2.126–8). As Michael Neill notes, existing plays on the subject of Antony and Cleopatra made much of these children, while Shakespeare grants them only a 'nominal presence' (Shakespeare 1994a, 5.2.130–3n).

It is not that the play avoids the topic of fertility, only that the concern is with the peculiarly non-human and even non-biological: the strange fertility of the Nile itself. Even when Cleopatra's women ask a soothsayer to predict their sex-lives, they expect the answer to be connected to the river's fertility, as when teasing that a wet hand is like wet land: 'IRAS There's a palm presages chastity, if nothing else. CHARMIAN E'en as the o'erflowing Nilus presageth famine' (1.2.42–4). The likening of human female fertility with the fertility of the Earth is, of course, a major poetic trope present in every culture and underlying the common metaphor of Mother Earth.[15] Here, however, the Nile is treated as a special case within the wider trope and it is related back to the special case of Cleopatra.

The play begins and ends with the Earth Mother trope, but only to acknowledge it before a perfunctory dismissal. In the first minutes of a performance, Antony disdains his summons from Rome by contrasting coupling with Cleopatra against the merely reproductive biology of the Earth:

ANTONY
Let Rome in Tiber melt, and the wide arch
Of the ranged empire fall. Here is my space.
Kingdoms are clay. Our dungy earth alike
Feeds beast as man. The nobleness of life
Is to do thus; when such a mutual pair
And such a twain can do 't.

*(Antony and Cleopatra* 1.1.35–40)

Most editors put a stage direction for his embracing her at 'to do thus', and even performed most chastely this gesture necessarily implies that whereas the Earth's reproductive principle generates food, their coupling is something better because non-reproductive. Heroic disdain of food while on military campaign is the subject of Caesar's apparently sincere eulogy in his first monologue: Antony drank 'The stale of horses, and the gilded puddle', ate the 'roughest berry', the 'barks of trees', and even 'strange flesh' that killed others (1.4.62–7). Although the sensual indulgence of the Egyptian court is amply described later, in Antony's embrace of Cleopatra he seems to retain a disdain for the generative principle of earthly biology, for the way that the 'dungy earth . . . feeds' people. The actor playing Cleopatra was a boy no older than 19 so we might here also catch a hint of the classical disdain for merely procreative heterosexuality evident in such stories as Aristophanes' account of the origin of love in Plato's *Symposium* (Plato 1871, 506–9).

In the closing minutes of a performance, Cleopatra uses the same language of disdain when describing death's quietus that: 'ends all other deeds . . . shackles accidents . . . bolts up change . . . sleeps and never palates more the dung, | The beggar's nurse, and Caesar's' (5.2.5–8). Just as ordinary love unites great and small in common finitude, so ordinary appetite for food unites beggar and monarch in sucking sustenance from the dungy Earth. On the other side stand the extraordinary, the infinite, death. We might also hear in this idea of palating the dungy Earth the reverse meaning: not to taste but to 'make palatable' (OED palate *v.* 2). Such a reversal gives Hamlet his grim joke about Polonius being at supper with the worms, 'Not where he eats, but where a is eaten' (*Hamlet* 4.3.20), and here it suggests Cleopatra's anxiety about feeding the Earth with her dead body. Indeed, it is possible to see the final scene's repetition of the word 'worm' (nine times, against a background average of one or two instances per play) as a mantra of death, just as it is in *Hamlet*.

Between these opening and closing glances at humanity's reciprocal relations with the reproductive Earth the images of reproduction are intensely focused on the principle of spontaneous generation by which ordinary matter becomes alive. Thus, thinking of the death of Fulvia, the rise of Pompey, and his need to return to Rome, Antony remarks: 'Much is breeding | Which, like the courser's hair, hath yet but life, | And not a serpent's poison' (1.2.184–6). Lewis Theobald (Shakespeare 1733b, 220n8) was the first to gloss this with belief in spontaneous generation evident in Holinshed's description of England:

> I might finallie tell you, how that in fennie riuers sides if you cut a turffe, and laie it with the grasse downewards, vpon the earth, in such sort as the water may touch it as it passeth by, you shall haue a brood of eeles, it would seeme a wonder; and yet it is beleeued with no lesse assurance of some, than that an horse haire laid in a pale full of the like water will in short time stirre and become a liuing creature.
>
> (Holinshed 1587, U3v, p. 224)

A few minutes later, in the next scene, Antony affirms his belief in such things by swearing 'By the fire | That quickens Nilus' slime' (1.3.68–9), which goes directly to the point about what was supposed to be special about the Nile.

In his favourite classical text, Ovid's *Metamorphoses*, Shakespeare found the following account:

> So when the seven-mouthed Nile has receded from the drenched fields and has returned again to its former bed, and the fresh slime has been heated by the sun's rays, farmers as they turn over the lumps of earth find many animate things; and among these some, but now begun, are upon the very verge of life, some are unfinished and lacking in their proper parts, and

oft-times in the same body one part is alive and the other still
nothing but raw earth.

(Ovid 1916a, Book 1 lines 422–9)

The play is clearly informed by this imagery of the Nile spontaneously generating life, and indeed we might well suppose that the
sex-without-generation of the protagonists is somehow related to
this generation-without-sex of creatures in the Nile. Thus in an
exchange mocking Lepidus' equal love for his fellow triumvirs,
Agrippa calls Antony 'thou Arabian bird' (3.2.12), meaning the
phoenix (OED Arabian *a.*, bird *n.* 4a). This implies Antony's singularity (there was only ever one phoenix alive at a time) and hints
at his immortality, but most famous of all is the phoenix's asexual
reproduction by self-immolation. Enobarbus tops Agrippa's jest
with 'They [Caesar and Antony] are his shards, and he [Lepidus]
their beetle' (3.2.20), which Neill suspects is a glance at Plutarch's
account of the asexual reproduction of the scarab or dung beetle
(Shakespeare 1994a, 3.2.20n).

Antony's pet name for Cleopatra is 'my serpent of old Nile'
(1.5.25), and indeed her endless transformations – what she calls
her 'becomings' (1.3.97) that cause Antony to liken her to the
shape-shifting Thetis (3.7.60) – could be imaged as the shedding
of so many snake-skins. Edward Topsell's follow-up to his history
of four-footed beasts was a history of serpents, in which he recounted the various stories of their spontaneous generation before
giving what we would consider the true account of their copula-
tion (Topsell 1608, B3v–B5r). The latter includes a detail that
explains how the former came about: the young are hatched from
eggs hidden in the ground, which would give the appearance of
their arising directly out of the material in which they were buried.
Contemporary classifications such as Topsell's treated the crocodile as a kind of serpent, and we might wonder whether Lepidus'
drunken enquiry about the nature of the Egyptian crocodile is
really an enquiry about Cleopatra herself.

The enquiry occurs in the banquet scene that begins in earnest
upon the entry of the triumvirate with Pompey and their respec-
tive attendant captains. The triumvirs are mid-conversation:

ANTONY (*to Caesar*)
Thus do they, sir: they take the flow o' th' Nile
By certain scales i' th' pyramid. They know
By th' height, the lowness, or the mean, if dearth

Or foison follow. The higher Nilus swells
The more it promises; as it ebbs, the seedsman
Upon the slime and ooze scatters his grain,
And shortly comes to harvest.

LEPIDUS You've strange serpents there?

ANTONY Ay, Lepidus.

LEPIDUS Your serpent of Egypt is bred now of your mud
by the operation of your sun; so is your crocodile.

ANTONY They are so.
(*Antony and Cleopatra* 2.7.17–28)

The account moves smoothly from plants to animals, from human tending of crops to the spontaneous generation of animals, because the Nile's extraordinary fertility elides the difference between the two. Flooded Egypt itself virtually comes alive. Lepidus wants to know more about these Egyptian serpents:

LEPIDUS What manner o' thing is your crocodile?

ANTONY It is shaped, sir, like itself, and it is as broad as
it hath breadth. It is just so high as it is, and moves
with it own organs. It lives by that which nourisheth
it, and the elements once out of it, it transmigrates.

LEPIDUS What colour is it of?

ANTONY Of its own colour, too.

LEPIDUS 'Tis a strange serpent.

ANTONY 'Tis so, and the tears of it are wet.
(*Antony and Cleopatra* 2.7.40–8)

Antony's tautologous answers give Lepidus nothing, although they have the linguistic form of learned knowledge.

And yet, the point of this exchange might be its very tautological pointlessness. Any attempt to pin down language's meaning necessarily sets off a process of chasing differences, since definition is just a succession of qualifying statements, as the ancient philosophers had noticed. A well-known joke about philosophers extending their definitions to cover new and unexpected cases was told by Diogenes Laertius in an account of his (unrelated) namesake Diogenes the Cynic:

Plato defined man thus: 'Man is a two-footed, featherless animal', and was much praised for the definition; so Diogenes plucked a cock and brought it into his school, and said 'This is Plato's man'. On which account this addition was made to the definition, 'With broad flat nails'.

(Laertius 1891, 231)

The process of refinement is potentially endless, and in general we stop when a sufficient confidence of non-ambiguity has been reached. Coming from Antony and within a play so concerned to contrast the finite and the infinite, tautology is a consummate evasion. To say 'it is what it is' short-circuits the deferral of linguistic gratification, and recalling Julia Kristeva's likening of sexual and linguistic gratification (Kristeva 1984) we might suppose there is also a hint of short-circuiting physical gratification too. As we have seen, Cleopatra is characterized by paradoxical inversions – fans that cool lust and inflame it, food that stimulates appetite as it satisfies it – that gesture at an insatiable desire. The point of this Bacchanalian scene is to show the differing responses of the triumvirs to bodily temptation. Lepidus succumbs to drunkenness while Caesar, painfully aware of his physical susceptibility, exercises an iron self-control. Antony, whose reputation for excessive indulgence in Egypt raises an expectation of riot, is forearmed with tautology and seemingly inviolable.

Caesar, picking up the sense of gratification, does not think Antony's speech will do: 'Will this description satisfy him?' and Antony replies that it will, 'With the health that Pompey gives him; else he is a very epicure' (2.7.49–51). Universally ignored and unglossed by editors until the twentieth century, this reference to the philosophy of Epicureanism is cryptic, but John Wilders captures the two main possibilities that it either means Lepidus is 'devoted to sensual pleasure' and hence hard to satisfy – the only sense offered by Neill (Shakespeare 1994a, 2.7.52n) – or that he really is a follower of Epicurus (371–270 BCE) and hence does not believe in the transmigration of souls (Shakespeare 1995, 2.7.53n). Earlier in the play Pompey had hoped of Antony that 'Epicurean cooks | [would] Sharpen with cloyless sauce his appetite' (2.1.24–5) so that with corporeal satiety he would be distracted from matters of war. The gluttony invoked is not a matter of quantity but of quality, which is significant because Cleopatra's paradoxical inversions serve to undermine precisely this distinction: the quality of sexual pleasure she gives defers gratification indefinitely, so no amount is enough. In this regard Cleopatra feminizes Antony, making his bounded masculine desire into the boundless feminine desire that contemporary misogynists warned about.

From such a reference to bodily satisfaction we might infer that the play's engagement with Epicureanism is superficial, for the philosophy was considerably subtler than the simple ideas about bodily pleasure that it has come to stand for in common usage. However, the play's engagement with Epicureanism might also be subtler than at first appears. Epicureans were proto-Utilitarians in their concern with pleasure above all else, but for them the pleasures of the mind were more important than those of the body and the starting point for mental satisfaction was the elimination (not the exaltation) of bodily wants. Moreover, Epicureanism is a markedly materialist philosophy upon which was based a distinct doctrine of ethics, and it shares Utilitarianism's sense that ethics cannot be grounded in nebulous transcendental categories of good and evil but rather must be based on quantifiable phenomena such as pleasure and pain. It was this that attracted the young Karl Marx to the philosophy, and he wrote his Ph.D. thesis on the differences between the physics of Democritus and Epicurus and their implications for ethics (Marx 1967). Democritus' model of physical interactions was deterministic and allowed no place for chance in the workings of nature, whereas (much preferably, Marx thought) Epicurus insisted that at the smallest scale interactions had random elements, unpredictable swerves in the movements of atoms, and hence that the universe was not determined. For Marx, Epicurus' view allowed for human freedom: spontaneity and hence human liberty arose from the very nature of matter.

Marx was wrong about this: indeterminism is not logically essential to free will, as the philosopher Daniel Dennett has brilliantly demonstrated (Dennett 2003, 97–139). The play's treatment of how human beings relate to physical nature – explored in relation to the unquantifiable, the insatiable, and the limitlessness of earthly biology – suggests that Shakespeare, like Marx, took materialism and determinism seriously. As Diogenes Laertius recorded, Epicurus taught a materialist zoology and warned:

> Let us also beware of thinking that animals are derived from the infinite; for there is no one who can prove that the germs from which animals are born, and plants, and all the other objects

which we contemplate, have been brought from the exterior in such a world, and that this same world would not have been able to produce them of itself. This remark applies particularly to the earth.

(Laertius 1891, 451)

Read in this light, Antony's description of the crocodile might be entirely un-ironic in its denial of external causes. The Earth brings forth peculiar things that arise out of the nature of matter, things that need (indeed, admit) no external explanation but are of their own shape and colour, and are their own cause. For us in the twenty-first century, evolution is the all-embracing theory that – in the teeth of our instinctive demand for reasons – insists that the bare facts of biology admit no reasons. Among the seventeenth-century materialists, Isaac Newton stands as the greatest because his laws of motion simply bypassed the traditional Aristotelian questions about why things move as they do and confined themselves to describing, almost perfectly, how they move. Fittingly, Newton wished to express his indebtedness to Epicurus in this regard, and there will be more to say about that connection with *The Tempest* (pp. 148–9 below).

I claimed that Antony's answers to Lepidus are perfectly tautologous, which is not quite true. They contain one positive assertion: that the Egyptian crocodile's soul transmigrates. Wherever else he might have come across this idea of Pythagoras', Shakespeare undoubtedly found it in Ovid's *Metamorphoses*. Like spontaneous generation, transmigration of souls denies the special condition of humanity; in poststructuralist terminology it decentres humankind, demoting us to mere containers:

> Our souls are deathless, and ever, when they have left their former seat, do they live in new abodes and dwell in the bodies that have received them. . . . All things are changing; nothing dies. The spirit wanders, comes now here, now there, and occupies whatever frame it pleases. From beasts it passes into human bodies, and from our bodies into beasts, but never perishes. And, as the pliant wax is stamped with new designs, does not remain as it was before nor keep the same form long, but is still the selfsame wax, so do I teach that the soul is ever the same, though it passes into ever-changing bodies. Therefore, lest your piety be overcome by appetite, I warn you as a seer, do not drive out

by impious slaughter what may be kindred souls, and let not
life be fed by life.

(Ovid 1916b, Book 15 lines 158–75)

To see how twenty-first century science returns us to ancient philosophical questions one only has to substitute 'genes' for 'souls' in
the above passage and observe that it is essentially correct. The
new gene-centred perspective raises the unsettling Pythagorean
insight that we are merely the vehicles for entities within us that
we can scarcely comprehend.

While Antony is aboard Pompey's barge describing Egypt's
animals, Cleopatra remains in Egypt receiving information about
him. To evoke her African location, Shakespeare has Cleopatra
repeatedly refer to the creatures for which it was famous, but
this is more than mere dramatic colouring. Railing on the
messenger who brings the news of Antony's marriage to Octavia,
Cleopatra images the collapse of human society in terms of the
transformations of animals:

CLEOPATRA
Some innocents 'scape not the thunderbolt.
Melt Egypt into Nile, and kindly creatures
Turn all to serpents! Call the slave again.
Though I am mad I will not bite him.

[. . .]

MESSENGER
Should I lie, madam?

CLEOPATRA                    O, I would thou didst,
So half my Egypt were submerged and made
A cistern for scaled snakes.

(*Antony and Cleopatra* 2.5.77–96)

Once things start to go seriously wrong, Cleopatra's rhetoric turns
these liquid transformations – 'Melt', 'submerged', 'Dissolve',
'discandying' – upon herself and her family:

[CLEOPATRA]
From my cold heart let heaven engender hail,
And poison it in the source, and the first stone
Drop in my neck: as it determines, so
Dissolve my life! The next Caesarion smite,

> Till by degrees the memory of my womb,
> Together with my brave Egyptians all,
> By the discandying of this pelleted storm
> Lie graveless till the flies and gnats of Nile
> Have buried them for prey!
>
> *(Antony and Cleopatra* 3.13.162–70)

The long final scene of the play, lasting around 20 minutes, is intensely focused upon the transformation of Cleopatra's body after death. Rather than be shamefully exhibited to the Roman 'varletry' by Caesar in triumph, Cleopatra imagines giving herself up to the transformatory creatures of her own country:

> [CLEOPATRA]    Rather a ditch in Egypt
> Be gentle grave unto me; rather on Nilus' mud
> Lay me stark naked, and let the waterflies
> Blow me into abhorring;
>
> *(Antony and Cleopatra* 5.2.56–9)

Neill detects in '*gentle* grave' a pun on the name of the fly maggots that will enter and transform her body (Shakespeare 1994a, 5.2.58n), and if accepted this pun also alludes to fishing, as the OED definition makes clear: 'A maggot . . . employed as bait by anglers' (OED gentle *n.* 3). Five to ten minutes earlier, Cleopatra herself was angling, for the raising of Antony to the top of her monument in 4.16 put into action an imagined scene of fishing from the middle of the play: '[CLEOPATRA] My bended hook shall pierce | Their slimy jaws, and as I draw them up | I'll think them every one an Antony, | And say "Ah ha, you're caught!"'' (2.5.12–15). For Shakespeare, fishing provided a sharp illustration of death's ironical transformations: as Hamlet put it, 'A man may fish with the worm that hath eat of a king, and eat of the fish that hath fed of that worm' (*Hamlet* 4.3.27–8).

Organic recycling in death is the point of the worm that comes in a basket of food, but to eat rather than be eaten. As Neill notes, Cleopatra's 'Will it eat me?' associates this worm with the ones of her grave (Shakespeare 1994a, 5.2.270n) and perhaps her final words repeat the pun on the anglers' name for a maggot: 'as soft as air, as gentle' (5.2.306). An additional irony, of course, is that this wormy death is itself central to her legend, which endures. The repeated tellings of it (including this one) give a kind of immortality. In that sense, she is indeed as she calls herself 'marble-constant' (5.2.236), not merely in sticking to her plan but in becoming legendary: 'Not marble nor the gilded monuments | ... shall outlive this powerful rhyme' (Sonnet 55). Her last great speech about Antony memorializes him too ('His legs bestrid the ocean ... His voice ... as rattling thunder' 5.2.81–5), but the description is undermined by our last glimpse of Antony falling far short of the hyperbole.

Perhaps sensing that something less exalted might be better, Cleopatra switches to more ordinary comparisons:

> [CLEOPATRA]        For his bounty,
> There was no winter in 't; an autumn 'twas,
> That grew the more by reaping. His delights
> Were dolphin-like; they showed his back above
> The element they lived in.
>
> (*Antony and Cleopatra* 5.2.85–9)

The first, agricultural image is even stronger in the Folio text: 'For his Bounty, | There was no winter in't. An *Anthony* it was, | That grew the more by reaping' (Shakespeare 1623, zz1r). Emrys Jones defended the Folio reading, noting that, although the logical sense slips in this passage, an audience would have no difficulty understanding the idea of 'Antony as a perpetually plenteous harvest' (Shakespeare 1977, 5.2.87n). In fact, that is not quite the idea at stake. Cleopatra makes Antony a paradox of positive feedback like herself: he grows all the more by reaping. Whereas the lesson learnt by Timon of Athens is that things do, eventually, have to add up, here is claimed a contradictory exceeding of all bounds. This insistence upon breaking limits is followed even more aptly with the image of the dolphin, which as Tillyard explained is king of the fishes precisely because it will not remain in its proper element (water) but insists upon raising itself beyond it (Tillyard 1943, 32). As Tillyard rightly commented, the image makes no sense without a model of orderliness and proper place, but equally it achieves its full power by exception from the very rules that give it meaning.

## Pericles, Cymbeline, and The Winter's Tale

We can pursue these ideas regarding food, genetics, and the origins of life through the last of Shakespeare's plays, which are overtly concerned with the dangers of incest. The historical Cleopatra was incestuously married to her younger brother, which fact Shakespeare glances at in having Caesar call her 'the queen of Ptolemy' (1.4.6). The context is a discussion of Antony's faults, which Lepidus dismisses as 'hereditary | Rather than purchased' (1.4.13–14), meaning excusable because not chosen. Although Shakespeare makes nothing of the incest, the verbal collocation with hereditary faults is significant because, of course, these things go together. Improperly applied in literary studies, social constructivist ideas about the relationship between nature and culture can easily mislead on this point, as can be seen in the introduction (freshly rewritten specifically for university students) to John Ford's *'Tis Pity She's A Whore*, which claims that:

> Incest is a social construction attached to a relatively unimportant biological fact. To many the very idea is repugnant, yet human beings have no inborn aversion to it. . . . Horror of incest is a product of culture and of particular family structures
>
> (Ford 1997, 6)

The 'evidence' adduced in support of this extraordinary claim is that unrelated children brought up together find one another sexually unattractive, and conversely that related children brought up apart and unaware of their genetic connection can easily be attracted to one another. Because the cultural conditions of upbringing seem the stronger force here, the editor concludes that the taboo is cultural not genetic. The truth, of course, is that there is a powerful genetic pressure not to have sex with those with whom one is raised, since they are most likely close relatives. The incest taboo is an evolutionarily selected behavioural habit generated by the relative unhealthiness of individuals whose parents are genetically alike.

In *Antony and Cleopatra* we saw the classical philosophy of Epicureanism treated in its familiar vulgar sense of mere sensuous gluttony – 'Eight wild boars roasted whole at a breakfast' (2.2.186) – and in its more sophisticated mode as a theory regarding material nature and spontaneous generation. These two senses become intertwined in Shakespeare's recurrent connection of incest with eating. To early moderns, it was clear that something transformative occurred in eating as life of one kind or another (plants or animals) cultivated by humans (farmers) died to make food that somehow gave life again to humans. Whatever their particular models of how this happened – perhaps via the Galenic humoral model recently advanced as essential context for the plays by Gail Kern Paster (Paster 2004) – the baffling fact was that life and not-life seemed convertible by processes of nourishment, and this formed a necessary analogy with procreation.

Written a year after *Antony and Cleopatra*, Shakespeare and George Wilkins's *Pericles* engages directly with the seemingly miraculous transformations of sex and nourishment, principally via its arboreal imagery. When a genealogy is drawn as a family tree, the incest taboo promotes the fanning out of lines of descent and prevents the formation of genetically closed loops of relative-sex, which are generally less fecund because the resulting children die out. The family tree of an incestuous relationship would tend towards a denuded bough, its branches withering from disease. Pericles' sexual desire for the daughter of Antioch is articulated in arboreal terms: 'To taste the fruit of yon celestial tree' (1.64). It is not clear if the daughter is the fruit and her father the celestial tree, or perhaps she is the tree and the fruit is the sexual enjoyment of her. Her father, however, calls her 'this fair Hesperides, | With golden fruit' (1.70–1), which metaphor casts his daughter as a living contradiction, since she is the object of men's desire and simultaneously the guardian of that object.

The riddle Pericles is to solve is written from the mute daughter's point of view and, as riddles often are, is based on apparent self-contradiction:

[PERICLES]
[*He takes up and*] *reads aloud the riddle*
I am no viper, yet I feed
On mother's flesh which did me breed.
I sought a husband, in which labour
I found that kindness in a father.
He's father, son, and husband mild;
I mother, wife, and yet his child.
How this may be and yet in two,
As you will live resolve it you.
Sharp physic is the last.

                                     (*Pericles* 1.106–15)

Even once this is understood to be about incest, the problem of the riddle is not entirely eliminated, since one can see how her father would, in an incestuous relation, be her father and husband, but not her 'son', and equally mysterious is why she thinks herself not only his wife and child but also his 'mother'.

Parallel phrasing occurs in Pericles' soliloquy after Antiochus leaves:

> [PERICLES]
> Where now you're both a father and a son
> By your uncomely claspings with your child –
> Which pleasures fits a husband, not a father –
> And she, an eater of her mother's flesh,
> By the defiling of her parents' bed,
> And both like serpents are, who though they feed
> On sweetest flowers, yet they poison breed.
> (*Pericles* 1.170–6)

This presents the same type of puzzle as the riddle: why should he call Antiochus 'both a father and a son' rather than father and husband, and why is the daughter 'an eater of her mother's flesh'?

The answer might lie in the drawing of family trees. In the making of pedigrees, horizontal lines are used to link mates and vertical lines are used to link parents and their offspring, and there is no simple way to represent parent-child incest without duplicating one of the parties to be both parent (or sibling) and mate. The representation of incest makes a family tree, which should fan out, fold back on itself, or else it requires paradoxical duplication, as in the daughter of Antiochus being both the fruit and the guardian of that fruit. Sterility is a common consequence of inbreeding, and the device that Pericles presents to Thaisa before the tournament, 'A withered branch that's only green at top' (6.47), might stand for his avoidance of this evil. Antiochus calls Pericles a tree (1.157), but Pericles thinks of himself as 'the tops of trees' (2.30) that protect the lower-class roots. The image of the tree unites social hierarchy with the abiding theme of these late plays, incest. As Katherine Duncan-Jones has shown, Shakespeare's own family tree had to be established for him to purchase a 'gentle' status, and the resultant family crest was indebted to the tradition of chivalric devices, known as *imprese*, carried in tournaments (Duncan-Jones 2001, 92). That Shakespeare had something of a personal involvement with *imprese* is clear: he wrote the text for one painted by Richard Burbage for Francis Manners, sixth Earl of Rutland, to use at the tilt on 24 March 1613, the king's accession day (Rutland 1905, 494).

Humans avoid incest by being able to recognize their offspring and distinguish them from others. *Pericles* (like *The Winter's Tale* and *Cymbeline*) is much concerned with the ability to recognize one's offspring, and Thaisa does not even know if she has a daughter, the shipboard delivery being somehow forgotten:

> THAISA That I was shipped at sea
> I well remember, ev'n on my eaning time,
> But whether there delivered, by th' holy gods
> I cannot rightly say.
>
> (*Pericles* 14.4–7)

She does not know it, but the child was a girl so there is no danger of their later meeting and incestuously mating. But Pericles does indeed meet Marina without knowing who she is, and his language on recognizing her invokes precisely the contradictory self-parenting language of Antiochus and his daughter: 'Thou that begett'st him that did thee beget' (21.183).

The genetic pressure not to commit incest unknowingly is at least part of the motivation unconsciously driving Pericles' and Marina's tense consideration of the means by which identity might be determined, as with her 'Is it no more | To be your daughter than to say my mother's name?' (21.196–7), which might carry the additional sense of 'is mentioning your wife enough to stop you thinking of me sexually?' In time of dearth, the failure of fertility, the people of Tarsus are ready 'To eat those little darlings whom they loved' (4.44), becoming literally feeders on their own flesh, whereas incest only metaphorically involves such self-consumption. From a genetic point of view, feeding one's children (rather than feeding on them) and not having sex with them have precisely the same point, the perpetuation of these tiny slivers of replicating DNA.

Incest also lies just beneath the surface of *Cymbeline* in the strong affection of Guiderius and Arviragus for their sister Innogen, which only her disguise suppresses: 'Were you a woman, youth, | I should woo hard' (3.6.66–7). In the surrogate family made of three men, achievement at hunting determines gender and domestic roles:

> BELARIUS
> You, Polydore, have proved best woodman and
> Are master of the feast. Cadwal and I
> Will play the cook and servant; 'tis our match.
>
> (*Cymbeline* 3.6.28–30)

When a real woman arrives, her proper place in this arrangement (male disguise notwithstanding) is not hard to guess:

GUIDERIUS But his neat cookery!

[BELARIUS]
He cut our roots in characters,
And sauced our broths as Juno had been sick
And he her dieter.

(*Cymbeline* 4.2.50–3)

Hunting, one kind of domination of nature, brings the raw material, but culture (via a woman) brings delight in feeding. With all the disguises removed at the close, these relations can come the right way out. In the wilderness scenes, however, no one is who they say or think they are, hence the danger of incest is high, and yet the gender-swapping disguise forestalls incest; even amidst all this culture in the depths of nature, 'normal' family relations can emerge so long as incest is averted.

Incest also structures *The Winter's Tale* although much less overtly than it structures *Pericles* and *Cymbeline*. Shakespeare toned down the incest in his source, Robert Greene's prose tale *Pandosto*, the title-page of which surprisingly promoted the book's capacity to bridge the generation gap: '*Pleasant for age to auoyde drowsie thoughtes, profitable for youth to eschue other wanton pastimes, and bringing both to a desired content*' (Greene 1588, A1r). Despite this warranty, in the story the father Pandosto unwittingly and extensively woos his lost daughter Fawnia and even threatens to rape her if she will not yield to him (Greene 1588, F4r–G3vr). Shakespeare attenuated this part of the plot but did not excise it altogether:

[FLORIZEL]                    At your request
My father will grant precious things as trifles.

LEONTES
Would he do so, I'd beg your precious mistress,
Which he counts but a trifle.

(*The Winter's Tale* 5.1.220–3)

Although the conditions for a resolution are in place – that which was lost has been found – there remains a kind of sterility in Sicilia. Normal family relations have not been restored, and the danger of incest remains. Throughout the play, the relations and the danger that ensues when they are disrupted are allegorized by relations and disruptions of earthly fertility and weather.

Two courtiers sent by Leontes to the oracle on the isle of Delphos find the location charming: '[CLEOMENES] The climate's delicate, the air most sweet; | Fertile the isle' (3.1.1–2). That the Sicilians find Delphos pleasant for its weather and verdancy is significant, for Sicilia and Bohemia come to be contrasted as places of dearth and foison, of sterility and fertility. The word 'climate' appears three times in the play: the above example, and when Leontes orders his child to be left exposed 'to it own protection | And favour of the climate' (2.3.178–9), and when Leontes welcomes Florizel to Sicilia with the imprecation 'The blessed gods | Purge all infection from our air whilst you | Do climate here!' (5.1.167–9). No other Shakespeare play uses 'climate' more than once, and most commonly it is a disyllabic synonym for 'clime' and means little more than a realm or region. Here, however, Shakespeare is clearly concerned with how the weather affects biological nature: Delphos' climate makes it fertile and the exposed child will have to take its chances for life or death according to the climate of the place 'out of our dominions' to which Antigonus chooses to take it (2.3.177).

The Earth's weather is so complex that it currently cannot (and might never) be predicted more than five days in advance, but the average weather for a region – its climate – is remarkably consistent, and has long been quantified. Antigonus might seem merely unfortunate, then, in choosing to deposit the babe where he does just as a storm is beginning. In an explanatory soliloquy, Antigonus relates that in a dream the ghost of Hermione instructed him to leave the babe in Bohemia; this serves to exculpate his behaviour and simultaneously to reinforce the audience's misapprehension that Hermione is dead. At this central hinge of the play, the recovery of the exposed babe marks the cyclical return to order and fertility. As the Old Shepherd characterizes the almost-simultaneous destruction of Antigonus and his companions and the discovery of the babe, 'Thou metst with things dying, I with things new-born' (3.3.110–11). Classical myths of cyclical regeneration – patterns of death and renewal – are clearly lying closely under the surface of this Mediterranean drama, breaking through to the explicit in such moments as Perdita's exclamation 'O Proserpina, | For the flowers now that, frighted, thou letst fall | From Dis's wagon!' (4.4.116–18). Proserpina was the daughter of

Ceres (goddess of corn) and her being forced to spend part of the year in Hell and part on Earth was an allegory of the seasonal renewal of agriculture (Hornblower and Spawforth 1996, 'Persephone'). In her Greek form as Demeter, the goddess of cereal most clearly links human and agricultural fertility: δη or δα was thought by the Romans to be the Greek for Earth (although Gaia was), and *-meter* has the same origin as *mater* meaning mother (Hornblower and Spawforth 1996, 'Demeter').

The likening of human female fertility with the fertility of the Earth is, of course, a ubiquitous poetic trope. The play repeatedly associates a man with the country he rules, considered in abstraction, and associates the actual land under his domination with femaleness. The association of man with the mastery of land underlies Camillo's 'Sicilia cannot show herself over-kind to Bohemia' (1.1.21–2) as well as Leontes' conception of his wife's imagined infidelity in terms of land-use rights ('[he] little thinks . . . his pond fished by his next neighbour') and of vaginas as 'gates' enclosing land (1.2.196–8). Polixenes too employs the language of land-use when referring to sexual intimacy between Florizel and Perdita: 'if ever henceforth thou | These rural latches to his entrance open' (4.4.437–8). The act of sexual infidelity is imagined by Leontes in terms of invasion by a foreign power, because 'a belly . . . will let in and out the enemy | With bag and baggage' (1.2.205–7). Finally, there is the almost ceremonial laying of Perdita upon the Bohemian soil:

> [ANTIGONUS] . . . it should here be laid,
> Either for life or death, upon the earth
> Of its right father.
>
> (*The Winter's Tale* 3.3.43–5)

Here the idea of the Earth as a kind of universal mother is activated in the custom – much discussed by classical authors (Hornblower and Spawforth 1996, 'children') – of abandoning babies upon a mountainside like seed thrown onto the ground. Perdita, the product of a transgressive procreation (so Antigonus wrongly believes) is being reconceived upon the correct female: the soil of Bohemia, possessed by its father.

Between Perdita's loss and her restoration the play is concerned almost entirely with events in rural Bohemia. Clearly, the shepherds are enjoying foison – a feast is being organized with Perdita at its centre – and since almost nothing else of Bohemia is shown the implicit contrast is between fertile Bohemia as a whole and sterile Sicilia. The sterility is conveyed by the death of Mamillius, the apparent death of Hermione, and by Paulina's description of Leontes' desperate state, which is virtually a curse:

> [PAULINA]                    A thousand knees,
> Ten thousand years together, naked, fasting,
> Upon a barren mountain, and still winter
> In storm perpetual, could not move the gods
> To look that way thou wert.
>                              (*The Winter's Tale* 3.2.210–13)

It is implied that the whole nation is in a kind of spiritual winter because of what has happened. At the sight of Florizel, Leontes exclaims 'Welcome hither, | As is the spring to th' earth' (5.1. 150–1). The way is almost clear for the comic resolution, although Shakespeare imposes one more obstacle by having Camillo, 'Whose honour and whose honesty till now | Endured all weathers' (5.1.193), betray the young couple to Polixenes.

It is unsurprising that with six occurrences, this play about seemingly random change has the most uses of the word 'weather' among Shakespeare's plays, nor that *The Tempest* has, for the obvious titular reason, the next highest with five. However, *The Winter's Tale* is markedly slippery about randomness and climate. Camillo's betrayal, explained only as a touch of homesickness (4.4.665–7), is as under-motivated as Leontes' sexual jealousy but whereas the latter is 'a feather for each wind that blows' (2.3.154) the former has seemingly been firm against 'all weathers' until now. Strangely, part of Leontes' welcome to Florizel invokes a unique sense of the word 'climate' that may help us to understand how Shakespeare is allegorizing the weather here: 'The blessed gods | Purge all infection from our air whilst you | Do climate here!' (5.1.167–9). This is the only recorded instance of 'climate' meaning 'To sojourn in a particular region or climate' (OED climate *v.*), which runs counter to the prevailing sense of climates being attached to particular geographical locations. While the first half of Leontes' imprecation seems to call for Sicilia's weather to be purified to suit the visitor from somewhere else, the second suggests that the visitor has brought his own local weather with him. This seeming contradiction is smoothed when we realize that in inadvertently bringing Perdita back to Sicilia, Florizel has allegorically brought the weather of spring with him. Understood in just the way that Geoffrey Bullough rejected – he insisted it was 'not . . . a fertility myth' (Bullough 1975, 135) – *The Winter's Tale* is archetypally Green in its insistence that human productive capacities and the Earth's are interdependent.

At over 840 lines, the sheep-shearing feast of 4.4 is fully a quarter of the play and this alone makes clear the play's concern with agricultural production.[16] Representing the weather as not merely accident that befalls us, and the environment as not merely an inanimate place where we happen to be, the play reworks myth to make a strikingly modern point about the artificiality of our distinction between nature and culture. To be sure the point is made, Shakespeare has Polixenes and Perdita discuss hybridity in a way that ties incest into a wider survey of the nature/culture distinction. In the light of his subsequent 'divorce' (4.4.417) of the young couple, we might suspect that behind Polixenes' vehemence is his feeling that, as B. J. Sokol argues (Sokol 1995, 124–30), although Perdita is not suitable to be Florizel's wife, she is suitable to be his concubine and bear him children. Reading backwards, that is what we might hear in their discussion of horticultural grafting.

The exchange starts with Polixenes praising Perdita's choice of suitable flowers for himself and Camillo. As in Chaucer's *The Miller's Tale* about January and May, an aged man can be allegorized as an aged year: 'POLIXENES Shepherdess, | A fair one are you. Well you fit our ages | With flowers of winter' (4.4.77–9). Perdita's cryptic response invokes the cyclical processes of nature, thereby effectively denying the allegory since old men are not renewed, and relocates the principle of appropriateness in suiting the season, not suiting the receiver:

> PERDITA    Sir, the year growing ancient,
> Not yet on summer's death, nor on the birth
> Of trembling winter, the fairest flowers o' th' season
> Are our carnations and streaked gillyvors,
> Which some call nature's bastards.
>
> (*The Winter's Tale* 4.4.79–83)

At this transitional moment of cyclical change, nature itself cannot easily generate these flowers, and Perdita will have nothing to do with genetic engineering: 'Of that kind | Our rustic garden's barren, and I care not | To get slips of them' (4.4.83–5). That is, the only way Perdita might cultivate these flowers is by getting a cutting from an existing plant (OED slip *n.*[2] 1), and this she is loath to do.

Pressed to explain why, she responds:

> PERDITA          For I have heard it said
> There is an art which in their piedness shares
> With great creating nature.
> > (*The Winter's Tale* 4.4.86–8)

Editors generally gloss this as Perdita's objection to grafting, but that is not at all what Perdita means. She objects to 'carnations and streaked gillyvors' not because they are artificially created, but because even though naturally created (by cross-pollination from proximity) they *look* like hybrids that result from human interference in nature. Even though she knows them to be entirely natural, they are to her impure by likeness. Like many editors, Polixenes misses her point and responds as though she were objecting to human interventions in natural processes:

> POLIXENES          Say there be,
> Yet nature is made better by no mean
> But nature makes that mean. So over that art
> Which you say adds to nature is an art
> That nature makes. You see, sweet maid, we marry
> A gentler scion to the wildest stock,
> And make conceive a bark of baser kind
> By bud of nobler race. This is an art
> Which does mend nature – change it rather; but
> The art itself is nature.
> > (*The Winter's Tale* 4.4.88–97)

It is not capitulation but resignation in the face of his miscomprehension that makes Perdita reply blankly 'So it is' (4.4.97). From Polixenes' point of view, his explanation that nature's over-arching (or all-embracing) universality naturalizes art has trumped her distinction of nature and culture. This can be summed up as a statement of the facile thesis that nature embraces everything. Human beings are products of nature, so anything they do must perforce be a natural act. This claim is rather like the one, popular in recent literary criticism, that everything is political and/or ideological. Such attempts to deny that there are areas of human existence outside the realm in which one is interested necessarily drain all force from the distinctions that make the terms intelligible in the first place. If everything is nature (or politics, or ideology), then nothing is, for the word has nothing from which to distinguish itself.

In fact, Perdita pre-empted the dissolving of the nature/culture binary herself. Nature too produces hybrids, she pointed out, and this offends her as much as cultural hybridity. Although the play leaves the connection implicit, we can see here too a concern with incest as natural hybridity. Looking back through historical time, the family trees of everyone alive today necessarily converge upon the vanishing point of a single ancestral pair; going sufficiently far back, we are all related. In the Christian tradition, the story of origins avoids early incest by inventing a wife for Adam and Eve's son Cain without explaining her parentage (Genesis 4.16–19). The same problem would recur seven generations later with the Flood, which certainly condemns the unclean animals to incest since only two of each are preserved in the Ark (Genesis 7.2). Humankind is spared this fate because more are saved: 'And Noah went in, and his sons, and his wife, and his sons' wives with him' (Genesis 7.7).

In the Greek version of the Flood, however, incest is inevitable because only Deucalion and his wife Pyrrha survive (Hornblower and Spawforth 1996, 'Deucalion'). At the end of the sheep-shearing scene, Polixenes threatens Florizel by invoking the Greek Flood to image the extent to which father could repudiate son: 'Not hold thee of our blood, no, not our kin, | Farre than Deucalion off' (4.4.430–1). Ironically, of course, the point of Deucalion's story is that we are all related, that human kinship cannot be denied since we share a common ancestor. In the version that Shakespeare would have known from Ovid's *Metamorphoses* (Ovid 1916a, Book 1 lines 313–415) the world is repopulated when Deucalion correctly interprets the goddess Themis' instruction that he and Pyrrha should throw behind them their grandam's bones. This, he realizes, means stones (the bones of mother Earth) and those thrown by Deucalion become men and those thrown by Pyrrha become women. As François Laroque has pointed out, this story of stone turned into human flesh must be at least part of what was in Shakespeare's mind when he wrote the scene in which what everyone (including the audience) thinks is a stone statue turns out to be the living person of Hermione (Laroque 1984).

*

The Deucalion story in Ovid's *Metamorphoses* would have brought
Shakespeare back to Epicurean concerns, for what Laroque did
not observe is that the very next thing Ovid recounted was how,
once the humans were back, nature brought back the animal
kingdom too. This is the passage about the spontaneous generation ('So when the seven-mouthed Nile . . . ') that we encountered
earlier in relation to Egyptian fertility (pp. 111–12 above). These
plays are overtly concerned with kinship relations: from the familiar
sister-cousins of *As You Like It* (somewhat reprised from Hermia
and Helena in *A Midsummer Night's Dream*) through the incestuous
Cleopatra and the intermingling of politics and family in Antony's
marriage to Octavia to the more deeply troubling inability of
Pericles and Leontes to recognize their daughters, and an adopted
family's willingness to throw off the adoptee when she brings
trouble (*The Winter's Tale* 4.4.687–702). Put in this sequence, we
can see that Shakespeare increasingly tackled these matters of
family relations in a wider context of the relatedness of all living
things, the plants and animals included and incorporating a notion
of the Earth itself being alive. Tracing kin relations back to
Deucalion or Noah emphasized that there must be an origin point
before which life was not human and after which it was.
Somewhere, the inanimate became animate and although in
Christian ideology this is a matter of divine inspiration ('God . . .
breathed into his nostrils the breath of life' Genesis 2.7), Shakespeare had access to equally powerful alternatives. With the final
scene of *The Winter's Tale* he daringly dramatized one of them.

# 4

# Supernature and the weather
## *King Lear* and *The Tempest*

Any sufficiently advanced technology is indistinguishable
from magic.

(Clarke 1972, 147)

## *King Lear*

Dividing in three his kingdom to give it away in the first scene,
Lear describes it not in terms of cities nor inhabitants, but as natural
countryside: 'shady forests and wide skirted meads' (1.59) comprised of 'space, validity, and pleasure' (1.76). In the final moments
of the play the three-way division of authority is repeated, but now
the kingdom is conceived as a sensible body: '[ALBANY] (*To Kent
and Edgar*) Friends of my soul, you twain | Rule in this kingdom,
and the gored state sustain' (24.314–15). Whereas land can be
divided with tools such a maps, a living body cannot, and the play
closes with a real change in attitude regarding monarchial authority. Shakespeare had previously dramatized in *As You Like It* such
movement from an objective and contemplative relation to the
land to a sensible one in which it is apprehended 'feelingly'. Duke
Senior's speech about the sweet uses of adversity – 'counsellors |
That feelingly persuade me what I am' (2.1.10–11) – reflected upon
bodily experience of the weather: 'The seasons' difference, as the
icy fang | And churlish chiding of the winter's wind, | Which
when it bites and blows upon my body' (2.1.6–8). For aristocratic
characters who normally are protected from the environment, these
bodily experiences produce a conviction that the inanimate
world itself is alive, that humanity can be found in nature: 'tongues
in trees, books in the running brooks, | Sermons in stones'

(2.1.16–17). A typical modern reaction is to dismiss this as a senti-mental attitude towards the natural world, one that might have persisted in Shakespeare's time but was even then open to mockery. *King Lear* presents us with versions of this modern reaction and invites us to mock those for whom human affairs and the wider cosmos are inextricably bound together. However, it is also seems intent on making us reconsider this mockery and to see merit in the mocked view.

The play's prime rationalist mocker is clearly Edmund, who wit-tily diagnoses the psychological imperative behind superstition:

> EDMUND This is the excellent foppery of the world: that
> when we are sick in fortune – often the surfeit of our
> own behaviour – we make guilty of our disasters the
> sun, the moon, and the stars, as if we were villains by
> necessity, fools by heavenly compulsion, knaves,
> thieves, and treacherers by spherical predominance,
> drunkards, liars, and adulterers by an enforced
> obedience of planetary influence, and all that we are
> evil in by a divine thrusting on. An admirable evasion
> of whoremaster man, to lay his goatish disposition to
> the charge of stars! My father compounded with my
> mother under the Dragon's tail and my nativity was
> under Ursa Major, so that it follows I am rough and
> lecherous. Fut! I should have been that I am had the
> maidenliest star of the firmament twinkled on my
> bastardy.
>
> (*King Lear Quarto* 2.113–28)

Edmund here targets his father, who believes that 'These late eclipses in the sun and moon portend no good to us' (2.103). According to Edward Capell, Shakespeare made Gloucester believe in astrology in order to convey his weak-mindedness, and hence to make his incredulity plausible (Capell and Collins 1779–80a, 147). William Warburton identified such belief as an impiety imported from Italy (whence 'most other unnatural crimes and follies of these latter ages'), which impiety was most clearly dis-played in the idea that planetary configurations at the moment of birth would shape human character (Shakespeare 1747b, 20n9). Warburton's comment goes rather beyond what Gloucester claims, which is simply that earthly miseries are caused by heavenly dis-turbance, although he was right to make the Italian connection:

we still call the malady supposedly brought by flux from the stars by its Italian name of influenza. Indeed, in Shakespeare, the word 'influence' only ever means the process whereby superlunary bodies affect sublunary ones. Ben Jonson's commendatory verse prefixed to the 1623 Folio imagines the deceased Shakespeare made into a star that will 'with rage, | Or influence, chide, or cheere the drooping Stage' (Shakespeare 1623, πA4v). To articulate such ideas, then, was not a clear sign of stupidity or naivety.

About a year before writing *King Lear*, Shakespeare had written another speech about stellar influence:

> HELEN
> Our remedies oft in ourselves do lie
> Which we ascribe to heaven. The fated sky
> Gives us free scope, only doth backward pull
> Our slow designs when we ourselves are dull.
> *(All's Well that Ends Well* 1.1.212–15)

This accords with Edmund's view that people use stellar influence as an excuse for their own weakness, but admits the possibility of influence in one direction at least: the stars reinforce any reluctance we might have. Otherwise, according to Helen, we and not the stars are masters of our destinies. Characters that Shakespeare apparently wants us to take sympathetically seem to hold roughly Helen's line: there is stellar influence, but it does not entirely constrain human behaviour. Science now knows that there really *is* stellar influence: a flux emanates from the Sun and during periods of high sunspot activity it brings strong magnetic fields that block high-energy galactic cosmic rays and lower the amount of carbon-14 created in the atmosphere and absorbed by living things. The Little Ice Age of Shakespeare's time was probably caused by diminution in this flux. In the now familiar pattern traced by this book, we find yet again that the latest materialist explanations return us to ways of thinking that have long been dismissed as mere superstition, and demand that we take the old ideas seriously.

Edmund has his own rationalist explanation for why he is the way he is:

> EDMUND
> Why brand they us with 'base, base bastardy',
> Who in the lusty stealth of nature take

More composition and fierce quality
Than doth within a stale, dull-eyed bed go
To the creating a whole tribe of fops
Got 'tween a sleep and wake?
                    (*King Lear Quarto* 2.10–15)

The belief that what happens to the couple during the act of conception shapes the individual conceived has a long history, from the story of Jacob setting parti-coloured wands before Laban's sheep to make them conceive parti-coloured lambs (Genesis 30.31–40) told in *The Merchant of Venice* (1.3.70–89) to the question from his wife ('have you not forgot to wind up the clock?') that distracts Walter Shandy in the making of their son Tristram (Sterne 1760, 3). For Edmund, this kind of influence is natural (since 'lusty stealth' itself is natural) and makes for differences between people that culture unfairly ignores. For us this belief about what happens to the couple during conception is, like the belief in planetary influence, easily dismissed as superstition, but it is worth noting that these ideas differ only in the scale of the forces that are considered dominant. For Edmund the local events matter most, and he mocks those who think that heavenly configuration is the dominant force.[17] The difference, then, is not really between rationalism and superstition but between competing rationalisms, for what else is astrology but a form of hyper-rationalism that insists upon explanations for everything?

The play periodically returns to this opening debate between differing explanations for human personality. Kent is perhaps the play's most highly sympathetic character and although he is not consistently likeable – tripping Oswald to gain Lear's admiration is a notable low (4.83–6) – the following is clearly meant as a sincere attempt to make sense of human differences: 'It is the stars, | The stars above us govern our conditions, | Else one self mate and make could not beget | Such different issues' (17.33–6). Although Edmund has the attractive elements of an Elizabethan stage anti-hero (sex appeal, daring, and a hard-luck story), we cannot say that his rationalism is validated by the events of the play and that the superstitions of Gloucester and Kent are shown to be delusory. Indeed, in general the play avoids explaining human personality, which avoidance is a dramatic device apparent in the character of Hamlet and honed in *Othello* (Iago's malice is as under-motivated as his master's credulity) and used again in *The Winter's Tale* (where

Leontes' jealousy seems groundless). The most we can say is that the play goes along with its characters' explanations of the world only for poetic justice, as when Edgar credits Edmund's conception with some explanatory power: 'The dark and vicious place where thee he got | Cost him [Gloucester] his eyes' (24.168–9). To this Edmund accedes.

We must, of course, put these ideas about personality in their dramatic context: Lear's is supposed to be a pre-Christian England in which pagan gods and heavenly bodies are worshipped. Shakespeare strenuously evokes this context from the beginning, with Lear swearing his rejection of Cordelia 'by the sacred radiance of the sun, | The mysteries of Hecate and the night, | By all the operation of the orbs | From whom we do exist and cease to be' (1.102–5). Lear's intended impositions upon his daughters' hospitality are timed by the moon ('monthly course' 1.124), which necessarily implies inconstancy: '[GONORIL] I think our father will hence tonight. REGAN That's most certain, and with you. Next month with us. GONORIL You see how full of changes his age is' (1.275–9). Edmund too privileges the lunar over the solar calendar: in soliloquy (and hence in honesty) he calls himself 'some twelve or fourteen moonshines' the younger brother (2.5). Edmund knows the rhetorical power of lunar association, as when he claims that Edgar stood before him 'conjuring the moon | To stand 's auspicious mistress' (6.38–9). Refusing to join the plot against Gloucester, Edmund claims to have 'told him [Edgar] the revengive gods | 'Gainst parricides did all their thunders bend' (6.44–5), evoking the pagan gods and their control of the weather. Shakespeare also sprinkled astrological terms across the play, such as 'cadent' (4.278), 'aspect' (7.102) 'influence' (7.103), and 'starblasting' (11.52) in places where the context scarcely calls for them. The effect is to evoke a world of deep astrological belief.

Having carefully set up this pre-Christian context, it is no accident that for his great apostrophe to nature Shakespeare makes Lear leap forward to a recognizably modern religious world in calling for the rain to continue until it has 'drenched the steeples' (9.3). This proleptic aspect of the play was amplified in the revisions for a revival around 1610 (Shakespeare 2000a, 3–9; Taylor and Warren 1983) inasmuch as the Folio text also has the marvellously contorted chronology of the Fool's prophecy – frequently mangled by editors (Egan 2004, 115–18) – which he leaves Merlin

to make, 'for I live before his time' (*King Lear Folio* 3.2.95–6). Even
in the quarto version, Lear's confrontation with the elements is
proleptically described before it is shown:

> [KENT]                Where's the King?
>
> FIRST GENTLEMAN
> Contending with the fretful element;
> Bids the wind blow the earth into the sea
> Or swell the curlèd waters 'bove the main,
> That things might change or cease; tears his white hair,
> Which the impetuous blasts, with eyeless rage,
> Catch in their fury and make nothing of;
> Strives in his little world of man to outstorm
> The to-and-fro-conflicting wind and rain.
>                                    (*King Lear Quarto* 8.2–10)

In this account, Lear is competing with the weather and trying to
'outstorm' it, and the macrocosm/microcosm correspondence is
clear: the 'little world of man' mirrors the greater. Amplifying the
point, Shakespeare has the First Gentleman describe himself as
'minded like the weather' (8.1). In this gentleman's account, Lear
anticipates great social alteration from this unexpected weather –
it is an 'out-of-season threat'ning dark-eyed night' (6.119) – so that
things might 'change or cease'. However, whether the tempest is
the cure or the symptom of human disorder is never clear. The
out-of-season aspect necessarily recalls the bad weather described
in *A Midsummer Night's Dream* (2.1.88–117) that is caused by conflict between the fairy monarchs, so to that extent it seems like a
consequence of the Lear family affairs.

The storm starts at the end of an exchange in which Lear
complains of his mistreatment and invokes the pagan gods as
potential agents of justice, upon whom he has not called:

> [LEAR]
> I do not bid the thunder-bearer shoot,
> Nor tell tales of thee to high-judging Jove.
>
> [. . .]
>
> I will have such revenges on you both
> That all the world shall – I will do such things –
> What they are, yet I know not; but they shall be

> The terrors of the earth. You think I'll weep.
> No, I'll not weep. [*Storm within*]
> 
>                            (*King Lear Quarto* 7.385–442)

Here there is more than an echo of the divine assistance that we saw Richard 2 expecting to follow from his subjects' rebellion, and amid the endless astrological imagery and pagan theology an audience could hardly be blamed for anticipating something supernatural. Indeed, the conventions of the Jacobean stage demanded such an expectation. Having surveyed hundreds of stage directions as preparation for the making of a dictionary of them, Leslie Thomson became aware that, as a rule, the theatrical sound-and-light effect of thunder and lightning did indeed signal that something supernatural was about to happen (Thomson 1999). The association was traditional and firmly held as causal in the period: witches and gods really were thought to be the causes of these phenomena. Giving examples from more than a dozen plays, Thomson argues that when stage directions call for thunder and lightning, it is almost always as 'a conventional code for staging the supernatural' (Thomson 1999, 16). However, Thomson insists that the linking 'was not theatrical in origin' but rather that the theatre emulated what was 'generally believed' to be a real connection (Thomson 1999, 11). It is hard to be sure what (if anything) was generally believed, of course, and a weak association in some spectators' minds might in time have been reinforced by the theatre itself, just as the horror film genre in the twentieth century strengthened the association between lightning and moments of heightened fear.

The technology of theatre (*pace* Thomson) undoubtedly strengthened an association between thunder and lightning and theophany (the dramatic appearance of a god). The winch used to lower a 'flying' god-actor literally creaked, as we know from Jonson's promise in the prologue to the Folio edition of *Every Man in his Humour* that his play would have no such cheap crowd-pleasing stage effects in it (Jonson 1616, A3r). Covering the unwanted noise from the winch with thunder would have suited the conventional association of gods with loud noises while serving a theatrical necessity, and that there was indeed this practical motivation seems corroborated by the alterations to practice that were made when possible. The Blackfriars building had a heavy ceiling that was not altered when it was turned into a playhouse in 1596 (Hosley 1975,

205), and that this ceiling masked the sound of the descent machine installed in the room above is suggested by George Chapman's *The Widow's Tears* having a descent of Hymen in 3.2 (the only relevant example) that is accompanied by music rather than noise (Chapman 1612, G2v). Similarly, the late revisions to Marlowe's *Doctor Faustus* include the visual juxtaposition of hell's torments represented by something from the stage trap with heavenly bliss cued by the stage direction 'Musicke while the Throne descends' (Marlowe 1616, H2r). A descent car containing a blissful vision rather than a person was presumably light enough to keep the winch from creaking.

Lear's speeches to the gods of weather suggest that he shares the audience's expectation that thunder and lightning presage a theophany, but the play – so much concerned with what is natural in individuals and in society – seems deliberately to withhold the usual collocation. As Thomson points out, 'it *is* only a storm', as the stage directions indicate, for all that the sound effects hint otherwise (Thomson 1999, 16). The temptation to personalize nature, to see an agency where there is only a meteorological phenomenon, is a trap that the character and the playhouse audience are led into. Shakespeare rarely misled his audience in this way and usually we enjoy a privileged position from which the misunderstandings of the characters can be measured against a notional narrative truth. Two obvious exceptions are *The Comedy of Errors*, in which the audience learn the identity of the Abbess only when it is revealed to the onstage characters at 5.1.346, and, at the other end of Shakespeare's career, Paulina's revelation that Hermione is alive at the end of *The Winter's Tale* is a similar surprise for the audience.

In *King Lear*, however, Shakespeare sprung three such deceptions on his audience. Philip C. McGuire argues that the supposed ascent of the Dover Cliff by Gloucester and Edgar in *King Lear* is such a deception (McGuire 1994, 87–90). On the flat non-scenic Shakespearian stage, characters' descriptions of their surroundings are the audience's only clues to what they are supposed to imagine, as with Northumberland's 'These high wild hills and rough uneven ways | Draws out our miles and makes them wearisome' (*Richard 2* 2.3.4–5). An audience trained to accept such descriptions at face value are likely to wonder whom to believe when faced with this exchange:

GLOUCESTER
When shall we come to th' top of that same hill?

EDGAR
You do climb up it now. Look how we labour.

GLOUCESTER
Methinks the ground is even.

EDGAR                                    Horrible steep.
                                    (*King Lear Quarto* 20.1–3)

McGuire describes the likely reaction of the first audience to this
as 'a combination of uncertainty and suspense' (McGuire 1994,
89) for not only is Edgar's intention unclear – will he help his
father to die? – but also the audience cannot tell where the action
is set. Strong encouragement to believe that father and son are to
be imagined standing at the top of a cliff comes in Edgar's speech
describing the perspective foreshortening of the birds, people, and
boats he claims to see below (20.11–24). Edgar's ambiguous aside
'Why I do trifle thus with his despair | Is done to cure it' (20.33–4)
would presumably reinforce the scepticism of an audience member
who thought she knew what kind of deception was coming, but
on its own would not be enough to change the mind of someone
who was taking literally the dialogue of the scene.

The third deception of the audience is the unexpected death of
Cordelia. The story of King Lear had circulated in a number of
forms (play, prose, and poetry), all of which had the king's youngest
daughter leading a French army into England, defeating her
father's enemies, and restoring him to the throne. The existing
play ended at that point and was printed in 1605, probably giving
Shakespeare the idea for his play (Knowles 2002). Other tellings
continue the narrative to the king's natural death, his daughter's
succession, and a rebellion that leads to her death in prison,
although this might simply form a coda to the story, as in William
Warner's *Albion's England* where the account ends with a couplet
summarizing what will not be described: 'Not how her nephews
war on her . . . / Shall follow' (Bullough 1973, 338). The genre
expectations thrown up by the simplest distinction between comedy
(in which no one good should die) and tragedy (in which the good
must die) were already clouded by the emergence around the turn
of the century of what Martin Wiggins calls the hermaphrodite
genre of tragicomedy (Wiggins 2000, 102–22). Thus the horrible

violence in the middle of Shakespeare's *King Lear* would not have given the audience warning that, unlike the story they knew, this afternoon's entertainment was going to end unhappily. If anything, those 'in the know' about this story would have been convinced that the body Lear carries on in the final moments of the play will recover.

So, to return to the first of these three deceptions, Lear's great speech to the tempest treats it as divine retribution for human sin:

> LEAR
> Blow, wind, and crack your cheeks! Rage, blow,
> You cataracts and hurricanoes, spout
> Till you have drenched the steeples, drowned the cocks!
> You sulphurous and thought-executing fires,
> Vaunt-couriers to oak-cleaving thunderbolts,
> Singe my white head; and thou all-shaking thunder,
> Smite flat the thick rotundity of the world,
> Crack nature's mould, all germens spill at once
> That make ingrateful man.
>
> (*King Lear Quarto* 9.1–9)

The elemental conflict here is like the biblical flood not only in the sense of washing away human sin, but also in the idea of the Earth at war with itself: the air displacing the water to destroy natural fertility. Coining the word 'germens', as Wells points out,

> Lear seems oddly close to the modern biological use of 'germ' for 'the female reproductive element, in opposition to *sperm-*' (*OED, germ, sb.* I) as if he were thinking of the world as a vast woman from whom all the means of conception could be squeezed out.
>
> (Shakespeare 2000a, 9.8n)

This image connects the speech to a genetic theme that runs through the play and is especially concerned with self-cancelling vice.

Just as we saw Polixenes disown his son with an image of un-relatedness, so Lear disowns Cordelia by saying that she will be no closer to him than the absurdly self-defeating barbarian who 'makes his generation | Messes to gorge his appetite' (1.110–11). Such images of perverted human biology are close to the surface throughout the play, as when Lear wishes Gonoril were sterile: 'Hark, nature, hear: | Dear goddess, suspend thy purpose if | Thou didst intend to make this creature fruitful' (4.268–70). If fertility itself cannot be thwarted, it can nonetheless be the vector by which the absurdity of human selfishness is made apparent, since one gets children like oneself. In a sense, genetics provides a material basis for the Christian Golden Rule of 'whatsoever ye would that men should do to you, do ye even so to them' (Matthew 7:12). Shakespeare does not treat virtue and vice as equally consistent behaviours, since whereas the former sustains itself down the generations, the latter runs counter to the replicating principle because the child inheriting it will punish the parent: '[LEAR] If she must teem, | Create her child of spleen, that it may live | And be a thwart disnatured torment to her' (4.274–6). In other words, what makes sense for an individual might become self-negating when considered socially. Goodness, we might say, evolves.[18]

What is at stake here is the degree to which the human body, the family, society, the Earth, and the wider cosmos necessarily follow analogous principles. As we saw in *Coriolanus* and *Henry 5* especially, analogies from nature are rhetorically powerful but multi-edged in their effects. Filial ingratitude is like a kind of rebellion in the body: '[LEAR] Is it not as this mouth should tear this hand | For lifting food to 't?' (11.15–16). Even the expression 'my flesh, my blood', spoken of a child, is only an analogy (children have just half the genes of a parent), and hence after Lear calls Gonoril 'my flesh' to make her ashamed of herself he immediately revises the image from bodily self-rebellion to infection: 'Or rather a disease that lies within my flesh' (7.380). As we saw in Chapter 2 (pp. 51–66 above), two or three years later in *Coriolanus*, Shakespeare used similar imagery for the antisocial behaviour of Caius Martius: 'SICINIUS He's a disease that must be cut away. MENENIUS O, he's a limb that has but a disease' (*Coriolanus* 3.1.296–7). Lear's speech to the tempest addresses the largest possible such body, the Earth, and speaks of it as diseased and in need of cure, using clearly biological terminology: not only 'germens', but also 'rotundity' suggests pregnancy, and 'mould' means 'pattern for replication' and also the dome of an infant's head (OED mould *n.*²) growing inside the womb and forming a fractally miniaturized version of its rotundity. Lear's speech is about *Mother* Earth, rising up to chastise her children.

It is not clear whether Lear considers himself one of those to be chastised, for he invites punishment ('Singe my white head' 9.6) and yet calls himself 'a man more sinned against than sinning'

(9.60). This latter phrase occurs when Lear considers what effect the tempest should have on the guilty:

> LEAR                       Let the great gods,
> That keep this dreadful pother o'er our heads,
> Find out their enemies now. Tremble, thou wretch
> That hast within thee undivulgèd crimes
> Unwhipped of justice; hide thee, thou bloody hand,
> Thou perjured and thou simular man of virtue
> That art incestuous; caitiff, in pieces shake,
> That under covert and convenient seeming
> Hast practised on man's life;
> Close pent-up guilts, rive your concealèd centres
> And cry these dreadful summoners grace.
> I am a man more sinned against than sinning.
> (King Lear Quarto 9.49–60)

The point here is that there are no great gods, only theatrical sound effects. As with the 'Mousetrap' in *Hamlet*, the concern is with the power of dramatic representation (a falsehood) to elicit from the guilty their unwilling but terrified confession (a truth). If we attribute to Lear a pantheistic conflation of Mother Earth and the great gods, this sounds like a devious account of how the guilty can be manipulated into confession by the power of shows. That is to say, it sounds ideological. However, although 'I am a man more sinned against than sinning' is usually taken as Lear's statement of his own case – that such terrors can wrest no confession from him for his withers are unwrung – it might in fact complete the 'cry' of the previous line. In the quarto of 1608 there is a comma, not a period, after 'grace', so that Lear might be advising the guilty to cry out 'Grace! I am a man more sinned against than sinning' (Shakespeare 1608, F4v). Read this way, Lear would appear to be saying that all are perpetrators and yet also victims of sin, which is of course the way things are in a society: even without genetic ties we are bound together by the reciprocity of our actions. Society *is* like a body, like a family, and like the Earth.

From a performative point of view, the problem of the tempest is how to prevent its representation taking over (aurally drowning) the scenes in which it must be portrayed. Understood as the manifestation of divine displeasure (as the audience are encouraged to expect), the tempest would be one kind of macrocosmic/microcosmic correspondence: the petty events on Earth being but

a version of the greater strife. Deliberately thwarting this interpretation by not providing a theophany, Shakespeare emphasized
instead the other macrocosmic/microcosmic correspondence: the
weather is a version of the storm in Lear's mind. Tillyard's terminology of correspondence between the planes is just right for this
relation (reflection is too mechanistic a notion), for the weather
and Lear's agitation are artistic versions of one phenomenon. This
was Harley Granville-Barker's view as he addressed the practical
problem of preventing the storm's effects dominating the scenes in
which they occur:

> And he [Shakespeare] solves his problem by making the actor
> impersonate Lear and the storm together, by identifying Lear's
> passion with the storm's. Mere association will not serve; there
> must be no chance left of a rivalry of interest. . . . this is the
> basis of his stagecraft, to make Lear and the storm as one.
> (Granville-Barker 1927, 142)

The brilliance of this solution lies in the fact that it disables at a
stroke two interpretations that, as Jonathan Dollimore shows, tend
to promote human suffering as the purpose of existence (Dollimore
1984, 189–203).

A Christian reading of the play would interpret suffering as a
necessary experience on the path to redemption, and a humanist/
existential reading could use the same terminology to argue that
human beings redeem themselves in their responses to suffering.
(For the latter, the key articulation is Gloucester's 'As flies to
wanton boys are we to th' gods; | They kill us for their sport'
15.35–6.) Dollimore's materialist reading, however, does not avail
itself of Barker's escape route and instead argues rather implaus-
ibly that experiencing suffering for himself reveals to Lear a reality
that empty forms and rituals have kept from him, and that the
play in general tends to disclose the ideological apparatuses of an
oppressive social order. The play does indeed offer an ideological
critique, but not by having a veil of ignorance fall from Lear's
eyes, nor from those of Gloucester who utters the almost Marxist
sentiment that 'distribution should undo excess' (15.68). Rather,
by bringing the means of presentation into the critique (that is, by
frustrating the audience's expectations with theatrical tricks), the
play presents something rather more experientially disquieting
that forces attention upon an urgent question about the weather.

It is the question that mad Lear' asks of mad Tom O'Bedlam: 'What is the cause of thunder?' (11.142). In the Globe playhouse in 1605, as across the globe today, the cause of unseasonal weather is not divine and not mysterious, it is human action.

It might be objected that suffering is nonetheless the key to knowledge, as Wells (the most recent of many) argues when explaining that in the following passage Lear 'recognizes that suffering has brought insight, seeing more clearly in his madness than when sane, as Gloucester does in his blindness' (Shakespeare 2000a, 20.98–103n):

> [LEAR]
> When the rain came to wet me once, and the wind to
> make me chatter, when the thunder would not peace
> at my bidding, there I found them, there I smelt them
> out. Go to, they are not men of their words. They told
> me I was everything; 'tis a lie, I am not ague-proof.
> (*King Lear* 20.99–102)

To read this speech as Wells does is to overlook the fact that Lear's account of his own actions is false: he did not bid the thunder stop; he urged it to do its worst. George Steevens's long-forgotten gloss is germane here: 'This seems to be an allusion to king Canute's behaviour when his courtiers flattered him as lord of the sea' (Shakespeare 1778b, 523n7). Canute 1 (994/5–1035 CE) is most commonly remembered for foolishly commanding the tide to halt before his throne, although of course his real intention was to prove to his flatterers that a monarch's power is subordinate to raw nature (Speed 1612, Ttt2v). Lear's apostrophe to the tempest ('Blow, wind, and crack your cheeks! . . .') was spoken as though a soliloquy, although the Fool was also present, and it takes on another colour again once Lear misreports it. Rather than the acquisition of real knowledge through suffering, Lear's exposing himself in the storm appears rather more of a melodramatic gesture that exploits his body's capacity to bear a meaning to his enemies. Look at what your lies misled me to do, he seems to say, and see by how much nature is stronger than man. Cordelia appears to have heard the most sympathetic version of that night, for she asks 'And wast thou fain, poor father, | To hovel thee with swine and rogues forlorn | In short and musty straw?' (21.36–8). Well, no, he was not fain. Kent and Gloucester invited Lear into the hovel seven times

(11.1, 4, 5, 21, 135, 143, and 158) before he acceded, and performers can make this reluctance to go in appear as maddeningly wilful self-abuse.

   To read Lear's intention this way is not to deny that he becomes mad, nor to minimize the play's concern with suffering. Exposure to nature makes Lear mentally ill, and (with a pleasing poetic balance) nature provides the cure too. At least, this is what the doctor appears to say:

> DOCTOR     There is means [to recover him], madam.
> Our foster-nurse of nature is repose,
> The which he lacks. That to provoke in him
> Are many simples operative, whose power
> Will close the eye of anguish.
>
> CORDELIA                    All blest secrets,
> All you unpublished virtues of the earth,
> Spring with my tears, be aidant and remediate
> In the good man's distress!
>
> (*King Lear Quarto* 18.12–19)

Like the herb-collecting Friar Laurence, this doctor believes that dialectic nature can cure as easily as kill: 'Two such opposed kings encamp them still | In man as well as herbs' (*Romeo and Juliet* 2.2.27–8). Of course, anyone with access to herbs can, in our terminology, self-medicate, which is what Frank McCombie thinks Lear has been doing in 'searching the ditches for remedies for his pains and sickness' (McCombie 1981, 133). Thus Cordelia's description of the garland Lear makes for himself includes weeds known to have specific medicinal properties:

> [CORDELIA]     Why, he was met even now,
> As mad as the racked sea, singing aloud,
> Crowned with rank fumitor and furrow-weeds,
> With burdocks, hemlock, nettles, cuckoo-flowers,
> Darnel, and all the idle weeds that grow
> In our sustaining corn.
>
> (*King Lear Quarto* 18.1–6)

Fumitor, McCombie reports, was known to be good for curing scabs, furrow-weeds for fresh wounds, burdocks for animal bites, hemlock provides anaesthesia, nettles are an anti-venom, cuckoo-flowers clear blemishes from the skin, and darnel combats sores and ulcers.

It is conceivable that Shakespeare's audience spotted these medicinal associations, although fashioning plants into a garland is a peculiar way to receive their benefits. A much stronger context for the named weeds lies within Shakespeare's own body of work, for as we saw in an earlier play also about war between France and England (pp. 66–82 above), these are (as Cordelia calls them) the idle weeds that flourish when people neglect agriculture to make war:

> [BURGUNDY] [Peace] hath from France too long been chased,
>                     ... her fallow leas
> The *darnel, hemlock,* and *rank fumitory*
> Doth root upon, while that the coulter rusts
> That should deracinate such savagery.
> The even mead ...
> Wanting the scythe, all uncorrected, rank,
> Conceives by idleness, and nothing teems
> But hateful *docks,* rough *thistles,* kecksies, *burs*
>                     (*Henry 5* 5.2.38–52 [emphasis added])

Rather than looking back to what has happened to him, Lear's garland might be an anticipation of the evil of war between France and England. The plants flourish by idleness because in war the tools of farming fall idle: swords and ploughshares cannot be handled at once. In his magnificent chronological account of Shakespeare's growing disgust at militarism dramatized in the sequence of plays from *Henry 5* to *The Tempest,* Robin Headlam Wells skipped over *King Lear* as providing no evidence for his argument (Wells 2000). In fact, its plant imagery reinforces the relation between the green world and peace, between plants that grow in the agricultural idleness that war enforces and Lear's restorative repose. By the dialectic that makes a darnel a poison or a cure, a bill is a weapon of war and also a kind of scythe (OED bill *n.*[1] 1–2, 4). We might recall, then, that the man who coined the name Green Peace because it combined ecology with anti-militarism had the entirely apposite name Bill Darnell.

## The Tempest

In his poem 'Lamia', John Keats complained of the 'cold philosophy' of scientific discovery threatening to 'clip an angel's wings' and, no doubt thinking specifically of Isaac Newton's optics, to 'unweave a rainbow' (Keats 1820, 2.230–7). Fear that knowing too much about the universe might tarnish its beauty is a characteristic Romantic reaction to scientific and technological progress, and it marks the emergence of an intellectual division that in the mid-twentieth century C. P. Snow characterized as the two isolated cultures of art and science (Snow 1959). It is a division that would have made little sense in the seventeenth century. Working on the second edition of his *Philosophiae Naturalis Principia Mathematica* – the title itself straddles Snow's boundaries – Newton decided to include 90 verses from the poem *De rerum natura* (*On the nature of things*) by Titus Lucretius Carus (*c*.95–63 BCE). Lucretius' poem is an extended Epicurean argument for atomism, showing how it accounts for the soul, sensory perception, the evolution of people and society, and the natural phenomena of the earth and the sky. Newton claimed to have found in Lucretius' poem the idea for his principle of inertia, although historians of science have long rejected this claim and instead stressed its dependence on the medieval scientific tradition (derived from Aristotle) and the work of René Descartes. William L. Hine has shown that we should take Newton's claim seriously, and hence that one of the cornerstones of Enlightenment thinking was indeed recovered from the ancients (Hine 1995). To argue, as this book has done, for a reconsideration of long-abandoned ideas to make sense of new discoveries is not to deny the forward progression of human knowledge nor claim that our endeavours are circular. Rather, it is to acknowledge (as Newton did) that progress depends not on being cleverer than our ancestors but on building upon their achievements: 'standing on ye shoulders of Giants', as Newton wrote to Robert Hooke (Merton 1965, 31). For this, long-dead giants are no worse than living or recent ones.

Although none of it was published before the twentieth century, Newton's most extensive writing was on the subject of alchemy, the transmutation of ordinary metal into gold. This might easily seem to us to be intellectual folly – a great mind led astray by mysticism – but in fact the atomic model is entirely compatible with the transmutation of elements. When Dmitri Mendeleev ordered the known elements by their atomic weight in 1869 he left gaps for elements predicted by his model but which had not been discovered, and when in due course they were found (and with just the characteristics he predicted) Mendeleev's Periodic Table gained wide acceptance. However, the great error of Mendeleev's career was his unshakeable conviction that the elements were, as their name implies, immutable so that a material occupying one position in his table could never be altered to occupy another. Work on the natural radioactive decay of elements by Mendeleev's French contemporaries Henri Becquerel, and Marie and Pierre Curie led Ernest Rutherford to demonstrate the first artificial disintegration in 1919: collision with an alpha particle turned an atom of nitrogen into an atom of oxygen and an atom of hydrogen. The Italian Enrico Fermi continued this work using slow-moving neutrons striking a target of uranium and on 16 January 1939 atomic fission was announced in a letter to the journal *Nature*. As we saw in Chapter 1 (pp. 17–18), the energy released by atomic fission made Fermi's the first generation of humans capable of destroying the world. To this the Green movement of the 1960s is a direct reaction.

Shakespeare's *The Tempest* is clearly concerned with the possibilities of transmutation, especially regarding human flesh, and this is most commonly understood as the influence of Ovid. Jonathan Bate puts the case baldly – '*The Tempest* is Shakespeare's last revision of the *Metamorphoses*' (Bate 1993, 245) – and supports the claim in 20 pages of close textual argument. To make sense of the relation of Ovid and Shakespeare, Bate had previously tried to use the notion of 'anxiety of influence' where even its inventor, Harold Bloom, thought it did not apply (Bate 1990), only to abandon it as too ahistorical when revising the argument (Bate 1993, xi). Raphael Lyne tried the same tack, making a virtue of ahistoricity and calling 'influence' by its more racy *nom de plume* of 'intertextuality'. Without abandoning this educational context (that is, what Shakespeare learnt at school), we can read *The Tempest* in a couple of historical contexts that have recently become available, and within which it seems even more grimly pessimistic than recent (especially postcolonial) criticism has allowed. The new contexts are concerned with the knowledge of science, and with the costuming of the play.

In a brilliant reading of Ariel's line 'Those are pearls that were his eyes', B. J. Sokol shows that Shakespeare was aware that Pliny's account of how pearls are formed had been supplanted by recent scientific discovery (Sokol 2003, 30–47). Just as a pearl is made by an oyster to smooth over an irritating foreign body, so, long before the action of the play, Alonso's guilt ('my trespass' 3.3.99) had been an irritant that his conscience worked upon:

> implicit in Ariel's eyes-become-pearls image lies the possibility that a living human eye can become either filmed over or hardened, made nacreous or mineral-callous, by habitual mental evasions and hypocrisies. . . . As in shellfish physically, so in a human spirit morally, irritants (or painful truths) may be coated over by anodyne smooth secretions which harden around them.
>
> (Sokol 2003, 46)

For Sokol, the late Shakespeare plays are almost obsessively concerned with biological recovery: Pericles is awakened from catatonia, his wife brought back from the dead, and a stone Hermione appears to transmute into human flesh. However, these are not quite the sea changes that Sokol presents them as, for the key fact about these apparent transmutations is that they are only apparent, not real. Like *King Lear*, *The Tempest* is concerned with transformatory power, but it is always in the form of theatrical power. The Dover Cliff trick played upon Gloucester by his son may strike us as tawdry, but it was entirely successful in curing the old man's sinful despair. Likewise the theatrical trick of withholding the expected theophany: the association of bad weather with divine retribution might well, as Lear says, be powerful to make the guilty divulge their secrets. What governs these plays is the power to give the appearance of a transformation, belief in which then performs a real transformation. We have seen hints of this concern in the plays already considered – in the Welsh Captain's self-fulfilling prophecy in *Richard 2* and in the witches' apparent promises in *Macbeth* – and it provides the climax of *The Winter's Tale*: Leontes is truly transformed by witnessing what he thinks is the transformation of his wife's statue. In *The Tempest*, Shakespeare explored to its logical conclusion the ideological power of theatre to transform its spectators, placing special emphasis on illusions that seem the irruption of the supernatural in the natural world.

It has now been established to most people's satisfaction that around 1610 Shakespeare returned to *King Lear* and partially rewrote it (Taylor 1983). The theatrical trick of the deceptive

tempest in the old play must have given Shakespeare the idea for
an even more audaciously deceptive tempest to start a new play.
Some of the key words he simply copied out again, others he
adapted:

> [LEAR]
> You *sulphurous* and *thought-executing* fires,
> *Vaunt-couriers* to oak-cleaving *thunderbolts*,
> > (*King Lear Quarto* 9.4–5, emphasis added)

> [ARIEL]                    Jove's lightning, the *precursors*
> O' th' dreadful *thunderclaps*, more momentary
> And *sight-outrunning* were not. The fire and cracks
> Of *sulphurous* roaring the most mighty Neptune
> Seem to besiege
> > (*The Tempest* 1.2.202–6, emphasis added)

The compound adjectives 'thought-executing' and 'sight-out-
running' are not just grammatically alike (abstract noun yoked
to a gerund) but also both convey in different ways the sense of a
human faculty (thinking, seeing) surpassed by the instantaneous
brightness of lightning flashes that are advance warnings ('vaunt-
couriers', 'precursors') of the boom of thunder that will follow.[19]
The tempest in *King Lear* was a demonstration of the ideological
power of theatrical convention – specifically, a means to terrify the
guilty into submission – and this idea Shakespeare expanded upon
in *The Tempest*, which is almost entirely concerned with Prospero's
exploitation of theatrical power, dressed up as a magic, to control
his enemies.

The play's opening stage direction ('tempestuous noise of
thunder and lightning heard') was, according to Andrew Gurr, a
deliberate shock tactic: the noisy sound effect from an open-air
amphitheatre was thrown at a genteel indoor Blackfriars audience
who were used to being lulled by the venue's famous musicians
(Gurr 1989, 95). Even more clearly than the Dover Cliff scene in
*King Lear*, this is not only a shock but also a deception of the audience, who have no reason to suppose that the tumult of the first
scene is an illusion created by Ariel. As Peter Holland points out,
theatre and film directors who show Prospero and/or Ariel in a
manipulative capacity in the first scene spoil this crucial point about
agency (Holland 1995, 224; Holland 1997, 172). On the other
hand, we do not know that the play was written with performance

at the Blackfriars in mind, and there would have been much to recommend performance at the open-air Globe too. As Brian Gibbons observes, 'there are, as in a ship, trapdoors in the floor/deck, doors in the facade and a gallery above; stage posts correspond to masts', and perhaps the opening scene 'exploits the fact that the Elizabethan stage is made of the same materials as Captain Drake's ship that went around the world' (Gibbons 1996, 42).

The location of performance might not even be the most important context, and Gurr elsewhere suggests that *The Tempest* could be Shakespeare's answer to Jonson's *The Alchemist* (in which Lovewit represents mercurial Shakespeare), and an answer that mocks Jonson's devotion to the classical unities in a virtuoso adherence to them (Gurr 1999, 17–18). There is certainly a vein of alchemical imagery running through *The Tempest*, not only in Alonso's bones and eyes becoming coral and pearls, but also in Prospero's 'project' that must 'gather to a head' with charms that do not 'crack' (5.1.1–2), which as Stephen Orgel notes is alchemical terminology that would be familiar to those who had attended the same company's performances of Jonson's play on the topic (Shakespeare 1987, 5.1.1n, 2n). Orgel even wonders if Caliban's initial conclusion that Stefano and Trinculo are 'spirits' bearing 'celestial liquor' (2.2.114–15) might have struck audiences as allusions to the process of distillation (Shakespeare 1987, 2.2.112n). However, the alchemical imagery in the play is sporadic, and only by an absurd literalism regarding the events – the splitting of a ship (*separatio*), the falling into the sea (marination), the being driven to despair (*distractio* and condensation), the wetted costumes (calcination), and so on – is Peggy Muñoz Simonds able to read the entire play as chemistry (Simonds 1998).

Two additional contexts for *The Tempest* have recently emerged. The first is that a pair of sea-creature costumes came into the King's Men's possession while Shakespeare was composing the play and their availability seems to have shaped the depictions of Caliban ('[TRINCULO] a man or a fish?' 2.2.25) and of Ariel-as-sea-nymph (Saenger 1995; Egan 1997). These were made for a sea-pageant on the Thames celebrating the investiture of Prince Henry as Prince of Wales, described in a pamphlet by Anthony Munday. On 5 June 1610 Richard Burbage and John Rice (John Heminges's apprentice) were rewarded by the London Corporation for their performance in this sea-pageant by being allowed to keep the expensive costumes that they wore. The second context concerns the play's main textual source, the account of the wreck of the *Sea Venture* at Bermuda, en route to the English colony in Virginia (Bullough 1975, 275–94). The discovery of part of a thermoscope during an archaeological dig at the site of the Jamestown colony shows that in the earliest days of the settlement (before 1610) somebody there was experimenting with devices that were used to measure and predict the weather, and which certain showmen claimed could be used to control the weather (Sokol 2003, 97–124). Shakespeare apparently knew those involved in the Virginia project – he certainly had access to an unpublished account of the shipwreck – and if he knew that it included a proto-scientist doing climatic experiments then this doubtless shaped the character of Prospero. The play is utterly ambiguous about the kind of control over the physical world that Prospero's knowledge gives him, and by probing this question (what *is* his 'art'?) we can begin to see the ecological significance of *The Tempest*.

The opening scene establishes the location as a ship at sea, and ends with Gonzalo's wish to be anywhere else: 'Now would I give a thousand furlongs of sea for an acre of barren ground: long heath, broom, furze, anything' (1.1.61–3). The Folio text has 'Browne firrs' where editors generally modernize to the low shrub 'furze', although Orgel acknowledges that the fir tree might instead be intended and retains the word 'brown' (Shakespeare 1987, 1.1.66n). However, Gonzalo clearly means something that he can stand upon, and pursuing Gibbons's likening of the Globe stage to ship we might hear in the Folio's 'firrs' the word meaning shaped boards 'call'd Furrs' nailed to warped floor timbers to make them level (OED fur *n.*[1] 7). The timbers of the Globe playhouse were at least 34 years old when *The Tempest* was first performed (having been recycled from the Shoreditch Theatre erected in 1576), and when Philip Henslowe contracted the builder Gilbert Katherens to erect the Hope theatre a couple of years later he insisted that 'no furr tymber' was to be used (Greg 1907, 20). As Herbert Berry showed (Berry 1987, 189–92), this must refer to timbers that had been 'furred' – made straight by nailing on boards – and a witness required to state the scrap value of the materials from the second Globe playhouse in 1634 explained that it was for the most part only 'ffurr Tymber' and hence not worth as much as one might think. If Gonzalo is referring to the playhouse fabric just as the scene closes then his wish acquires the ironic overtone of wanting to be anywhere but the dramatic location (aboard ship), including being where he actually is, standing on the stage. This would give the opening scene of *The Tempest* the same quality as the analogous Dover Cliff scene in *King Lear* that likewise deceives its audience: theatre convention constructs Gloucester and Edgar's steep climb in our minds while they (actors and characters) remain dramatically and figuratively 'on the level'. Gonzalo *is* standing on brown furs, but special ones that have the quality of evoking a ship at sea during a storm.

The next scene begins with Miranda saying that she has seen what we in the audience think we have seen ('A brave vessel . . . Dashed all to pieces' 1.2.6–8) and her father reassuring her that she saw only a show, a 'direful spectacle' (1.2.26). Once Miranda is asleep, Ariel confirms that he created not a storm but only the likeness of one:

> [ARIEL]
> I boarded the King's ship. Now on the beak,
> Now in the waste, the deck, in every cabin,
> I flamed amazement. Sometime I'd divide,
> And burn in many places; on the top-mast,
> The yards, and bowsprit, would I flame distinctly;
> Then meet and join. Jove's lightning, the precursors
> O' th' dreadful thunderclaps, more momentary
> And sight-outrunning were not. The fire and cracks
> Of sulphurous roaring the most mighty Neptune
> Seem to besiege, and make his bold waves tremble,
> Yea, his dread trident shake.
> (*The Tempest* 1.2.197–207)

Ariel compares each aspect of his simulated storm with the real thing: his fake lightning was as brief as real lightning, his sounds and sights appeared to besiege the sea-god himself, and by these tricks he 'flamed amazement' in the boat's occupants. The point of the storm was to induce 'a fever of the mad' (1.2.210) in Prospero's enemies, although understandably such an 'art' might frighten the innocent too, as it does Miranda. 'Art' is the word Miranda uses for her father's power and although it could mean magic the dominant senses of this word were skill and science. Prospero's usage of 'pluck my magic garment from me . . . Lie there, my art' (1.2.24–5) yokes together these heterogeneous senses, but we are not bound to accept his elision of the semantic difference. Indeed, the play repeatedly asks us to reject the elision, as we shall see.

Shakespeare weaves in a separate and familiar horticultural/arboreal strand when Prospero informs Miranda of their past. Antonio, he says, became habituated to command: 'how to grant suits, | How to deny them, who t' advance and who | To trash for over-topping' (1.2.79–81). We have seen (pp. 70–9 above) how the scything of overgrown plants collocates with mention of suits (via the unspoken term 'weeds'), and here Prospero evokes the familiar image of a monarch as a tree: 'my princely trunk' (1.2.86) that Antonio sought to 'extirpate' (1.2.125), which literally means to displant, roots and all. In Shakespeare's time the verb 'to supplant' also had this sense of uprooting, and it is used that way by Sebastian and Ariel-as-harpy regarding Prospero's usurpation ('You did supplant your brother' 2.1.276, 'you . . . did supplant good Prospero' 3.3.69–70) and by Stefano as a threat: 'I will supplant some of your teeth' (3.2.50). The dynastic connotations of the monarch-as-tree that we saw in *Richard 2* (pp. 89–91 above) are present here too when Prospero warns that Miranda's 'virgin-knot' – an image obscurely connected to the 'knotty entrails' (1.2.296) into which Ariel might be pegged – must not be prematurely broken, else the heaven will 'bestrew | The union of your bed with weeds' (4.2.20–1). This marriage bed is also a seed-bed of the new royal stock and must be kept free of weeds that would choke it.

This recurrent arboreal imagery has a very real point in the play, for Prospero's main activity since his arrival on the island has been its deforestation. The play is insistent about this activity and its rapidity: 'Fetch in our wood' (1.2.314); 'There's wood enough within' (1.2.316); 'Fetch us in fuel. And be quick' (1.2.368); '*Enter Caliban . . . with a burden of wood*' (2.2.0); 'torment me | For bringing wood in slowly' (2.2.15–16); 'I'll bring my wood home faster' (2.2.71–2); 'I'll . . . get thee wood enough' (2.2.160); 'I'll bear him no more sticks' (2.2.162); 'Nor fetch in firing | At requiring' (2.2.180–1); '*Enter Ferdinand, bearing a log*' (3.1.0); 'no more endure | This wooden slavery' (3.1.61–2); 'Am I this patient log-man' (3.1.67). Suffering this relentless arboreal labour, it is hardly surprising that Caliban's fantasy of revenge includes the poetic justice of killing Prospero with a stake through the stomach (3.2.91). So repetitively does the play refer to the axeing of trees that it might not be inquiring too curiously to wonder whether Prospero accidentally 'made gape | The pine' (1.2.293–4) and let Ariel out of his confinement, and only after thought to lay the credit to his magical 'art'.

Anyone who came to the first performances of *The Tempest* knowing that it was at least partly based on the true story of the wreck of the *Sea Venture* might well have thought they knew what all these trees were being cut down for. In William Strachey's account, the remedy of their situation soon occurred to the survivors:

> In the meane space did one Frubbusher (a painefull and well experienced Shipwright, and skilfull workman) labour the building of a little Pinnace: for the furtherance of which, the Governour dispensed with no travaile of his body, nor forbare any care of study of minde, perswading . . . by how owne performance, then by authority, thereby to hold them at their worke, name to fell, carry, and sawe Cedar, fit for the Carpenters purpose
>
> (Bullough 1975, 286)

What Prospero has told Caliban about his plans is unclear, and the latter's 'He has brave utensils, for so he calls them, | Which when he has a house he'll deck withal' (3.2.97–8) might mean that Prospero anticipates leaving the island or only that he wants to make improvements to his 'poor cell' (1.2.20). (Such improvements might just account for all the wood.) Antonio and Sebastian certainly anticipate leaving the island, else their assassination plot in 2.1 makes no sense, and Sebastian is explicit about his aim: 'I'll come by Naples' (2.1.297). Since they think their ship wrecked, it is not clear how they imagine encompassing their removal. Taken in this light, the plot of Trinculo and Stefano to dominate the island upon which they consider themselves trapped is much the more sensible plan. In Strachey's account there were indeed rebels who refused to chop trees and were all for remaining in Bermuda rather than attempting to cross to Virginia (Bullough 1975, 287–91). Ferdinand's delighted response to the masque, 'Let me live here forever! . . . this place [is] paradise' (4.1.122–4) is of course retrograde to Prospero's desire and is peremptorily hushed.

Howsoever the expected action of a shipwrecked man in possession of wood is to make a boat, nothing in the play suggests that Prospero is doing this. What, then, would an early audience have understood from all this deforestation? The answer appears to be colonization. Postcolonial readings of the play have emphasized that the closest and best-known colonial endeavour undertaken by the English in Shakespeare's time was the planting of Ireland, and critics have stressed just how like Ireland is the play's supposedly uninhabited island (Brown 1985) and that Caliban resembles contemporary stereotypes of the Irish (Callaghan 2000, 97–138). A major part of the effort to subdue Ireland in the sixteenth and seventeenth centuries was to clear its forest:

> Woodland covered about one-eighth of the country at the beginning of the seventeenth century, but was gradually being cleared for fuel, for timber used in building and for making barrel staves and implements, for charcoal (used in iron-making), and for strategic purposes. . . . a common complaint of English soldiers was that the 'woods and bogs are a great hindrance to us and help to the rebels', the latter being able, with only a handful of men, to engage in 'ambushcados' and, when necessary, escape with ease.
>
> (Butlin 1976, 143–5)

Eileen McCracken has traced the rapidly accelerating deforestation from this gradual start to the end of the seventeenth century when most of the woods were gone, marked for destruction because 'they had been a serious obstacle to the Tudor conquest and colonization of Ireland' (McCracken 1959, 287). If the play's insistent references to deforestation struck the early audiences as a sign that Prospero's intention was to colonize the island, we have yet another confusing signal. Prospero wants to leave, but he is not making a boat. Prospero captures a passing boat as a means of escape – giving specific instruction that it is not to be damaged, confirmed by Ariel's 'Safely in harbour' (1.2.227) – but continues clearing wood as though he meant to stay and colonize the island. To treat the matter with such literalism might seem pedantic, but in fact this second scene's insistence on Prospero's magical power necessarily forces the audience to consider just what keeps Prospero on the island. Possession of the kind of power boasted of by Prospero in his famous act of abjuration would seem to mock his own captivity. What is the nature of that power?

The most striking thing about Prospero's power is that it is almost entirely mediated through Ariel, via whom he controls the lesser native spirits that he calls 'meaner ministers' (3.3.87) or worse 'the rabble' (4.1.37), which terminology is reason enough to credit Caliban's claim that 'they all do hate him | As rootedly as I' (3.2.95–6). As many critics have noted, this relationship is reminiscent of Oberon and Robin Goodfellow in *A Midsummer Night's Dream* and there are a number of connections suggesting that this early work was in Shakespeare's mind as he wrote *The Tempest*. Caliban's 'What a pied ninny's this!' (3.2.64) revives a word meaning simpleton that Shakespeare had not used since Flute-as-Thisbe and Bottom-as-Pyramus, reworking the laugh Elizabethan schoolboys got from Ovid's *'ad busta Nini'* (Rudd 2000, 116), had mispronounced 'Ninus's tomb' (*A Midsummer Night's Dream* 3.1.91–2, 5.1.201, 258). The instantaneous love of Ferdinand and Miranda has overtones of the drug-induced passions of the Athenian youth in the forest, and Ariel's instigation of a quarrel by ventriloquism in *The Tempest* 3.2 repeats the trick performed by Robin Goodfellow in *A Midsummer Night's Dream* 3.2. Most significantly, the same kind of misrecognition of the everyday occurs in both plays: there is real magic, but also the imputing of supernatural causes to what are really only ordinary effects.

Despite the fish-like costume that the actor playing Caliban is wearing, Trinculo revises his first opinion: 'This is no fish, but an islander that hath lately suffered by a thunderbolt' (2.2.35–6). This might remind us that upon seeing Hermia and Lysander sleeping apart (as she had most properly insisted upon), Robin Goodfellow read their physical separation not as modesty but disdain, and so decided that here was the unrequiting youth his master sent him to drug (*A Midsummer Night's Dream* 2.2.76–83). Similarly, Alonso's astonished reaction 'But how should Prospero | Be living and be here?' (5.1.121–2) treats as though supernatural a perfectly ordinary piece of good luck: their boat, like his, brought Prospero and Miranda safely to the island. This subtle irony matches Oberon's response to seeing Demetrius pursue Hermia: 'What hast thou done? Thou hast mistaken quite, | And laid the love juice on some true love's sight' (*A Midsummer Night's Dream* 3.2.88–9). Robin had indeed made this mistake, but that is not why Demetrius is pursuing Hermia: he has been doing that, unaided by drugs, since the start of the play. Finally, there are the mariners left dozing from the second to the penultimate scene of *The Tempest*, for whom the play's little life is indeed rounded with sleep, which is a version of what Robin says in his epilogue.

What Shakespeare chose to handle differently this time was metamorphosis: there is nothing in *The Tempest* to match the translation of Bottom in *A Midsummer Night's Dream*. However, Prospero's theatricality is clearly indebted to the earlier play's self-referentiality in which the theatre tiring-house stood for a hawthorn brake that Quince remarked would make a good tiring-house, just as the rushes-strewn stage stood for a 'green plot' that conveniently makes a stage (*A Midsummer Night's Dream* 3.1.3–4). When Bottom exited to fetch the ass-head he entered a real theatre tiring-house and returned with one of its properties; this closed the self-referential circuit, shutting down access to a vantage point from which we might assert what is 'real' in the play. Likewise in *The Tempest* there are aspects of the island that its representation refuses to address: is it 'lush and lusty' and 'green', as Gonzalo says or 'tawny' as Antonio claims (2.1.57–9)? The unadorned stage is silent on the matter, but that is not to say that according to the characters' subjective responses the same landscape will be described as beautiful or ugly. Rather, the open-ended potentiality of the unlocalized stage accurately conveys the island's condition of being neither one thing nor another: the island – land, water, plants, and animals – mediates the power of whoever controls it.

This principle of mediation is first evident in Prospero's account of Ariel's confinement (derived ultimately from Ariel's memory, of course), which emphasizes not so much the spirit's pain, nor even his crying out, but rather the pain caused to others by hearing his cries:

> [PROSPERO]          Thy groans
> Did make wolves howl, and penetrate the breasts
> Of ever-angry bears; it was a torment
> To lay upon the damned
> > (*The Tempest* 1.2.288–91)

Hurting Ariel was a way to make animals frightened, so that even while being punished the rebellious servant was conveying Sycorax's power. Prospero knows the trick and uses it too:

> [PROSPERO]
> If thou neglect'st or dost unwillingly
> What I command, I'll rack thee with old cramps,

Fill all thy bones with aches, make thee roar,
That *beasts shall tremble* at thy din.

CALIBAN No, pray thee.

(*The Tempest* 1.2.370–3 [emphasis added])

Torturers know the power of vicarious punishment, and just as
Prospero and Sycorax can summon up sounds that terrify, so too
can Sebastian and Antonio: 'a din to fright a monster's ear' is how
Antonio describes the noise that made him draw his sword while
Alonso and Gonzalo slept (2.1.319). Shakespeare subtly indicates
the effect upon Caliban of being repeatedly punished by spirits that
are merely conduits for Prospero's power (he hurts them, they
hurt Caliban). When Trinculo starts to shake from fear as they hide
together under a gaberdine, Caliban interprets this as the beginning
of another punishment:

CALIBAN (*to Trinculo*) Thou dost me yet but little hurt.
Thou wilt anon, I know it by thy trembling. Now
Prosper works upon thee.

(*The Tempest* 2.2.79–81)

Far from being immutable in his nature, as Prospero claims,
Caliban has developed the recognizable symptom of the mentally
traumatized: everything (including another's reaction to fear) seems
to threaten new pain. This is why he responds to perfectly ordinary
thunder as though it were the reaction of Prospero's agents to his
cursing:

CALIBAN [*throwing down his burden*]
All the infections that the sun sucks up
From bogs, fens, flats, on Prosper fall, and make him
By inch-meal a disease! [*A noise of thunder heard*] His spirits
      hear me

(*The Tempest* 2.2.1–3)

And it is why he mistakes Trinculo for an agent of retribution:
'Here comes a spirit of his, and to torment me | For bringing
wood in slowly' (2.2.15–16).

It is in this light that we should consider the transformatory
power of Prospero's terrifying theatrical illusions. The first illusion
is the tempest itself that made the 'bold waves tremble' (1.2.206)
– yet more terrified mediators of fear – and was intended to 'infect
[the] reason' to cause 'a fever of the mad' in Prospero's enemies
(1.2.209–10). The reactions of the low characters who experienced

this terror are no different to the reactions of the high characters: they thereafter take the natural for the supernatural. Ferdinand takes Miranda for a goddess (1.2.424) and Stefano mistakes Caliban and Trinculo for a pair of devils (2.2.57). Working especially on the Italian aristocrats, Prospero redoubles the fear with lies mediated through Ariel-as-harpy:

> [ARIEL]                    Thee of thy son, Alonso,
> They [the seas, shores, and animals] have bereft, and do
>     pronounce by me
> Ling'ring perdition – worse than any death
> Can be at once
> (*The Tempest* 3.3.75–8)

The lies are plausible: Ferdinand seems drowned and it seems an island 'Where man doth not inhabit' (3.3.57).[20] These terrified aristocrats do not return to the stage until their entrance with 'frantic gesture[s]' expressing their 'boiled' brains (5.1.57, 60) in the last scene. In modern performance these descriptions are not usually taken literally, although some notable exceptions that made clear the 'ordeal and distress' are recorded by Christine Dymkowski (Shakespeare 2000b, 5.1.57n).

The last illusion is the hunting of Stefano, Trinculo, and Caliban by *'divers spirits in shape of dogs and hounds'* (4.1.254), which symbolically reduces them to the level of beasts. As with the highly contentious 'reconciliation' of the final scene – 'Antonio does not repent . . . he is, indeed, not *allowed* to repent' (Shakespeare 1987, 53) – it is far from clear that the hunted are truly changed by the experience. They are forgiven but not necessarily repentant. Moreover, Caliban has long been hunted by Prospero's ministers without being reduced to the status of an animal. Prospero's admission that Caliban is necessary to Prospero and Miranda's lifestyle includes the fact that 'He does make our fire' (1.2.313), which has long been understood as an ability that marks humankind off from the animals. Indeed, as far as Miranda is concerned Caliban is a man. Were he not, Ferdinand would (after her father) count as only the second man she has seen, but she counts three: 'This | Is the third man that e'er I saw' (1.2.447–8). At least, she counts three when talking to herself in an aside. When talking openly to Ferdinand, she drops Caliban from the count of men: 'nor have I seen | More that I may call men than you, good friend, | And my dear father' (3.1.50–2).[21] Man enough to threaten Miranda's chastity, Caliban is not (despite his own claim at 1.2.343) man enough to count as a subject when Prospero is explaining himself to Alonso: 'subjects none abroad' (5.1.169). Others' perspectives and perhaps his fishy stage costume cast Caliban as a liminal figure between humankind and animal, and his own view on the matter seems markedly Althusserian. That is, Caliban seems to think that the subject is interpellated by the role that others create for him, that the man is made by the nature and behaviour of the master: "Ban, 'ban, Cacaliban | Has a new master. – Get a new man!' (2.2.183–4).[22]

To say that the hunting of Stefano, Trinculo, and Caliban is Prospero's last illusion would seem to leave out the most important one: the masque to celebrate the betrothal of Ferdinand and Miranda, future monarchs of Naples. For Orgel this masque is the 'prime example' of Prospero's art and he treats it as 'Shakespeare's most significant essay in this courtly genre', although warning that it is of course not itself a masque but a dramatic allusion to the form (Shakespeare 1987, 43–4). If for no other reason than that it is designed to please rather than terrify, the masque in *The Tempest* needs to be treated separately from the rest of Prospero's illusions. Of course, pleasing royalty is itself a political act, and it is worth recalling Munday's sea-pageant to flatter Prince Henry where the most knowing of *The Tempest*'s original audiences would first have seen the Caliban and Ariel-as-sea-nymph costumes:

> Wherefore let vs thinke of *Neptune*, that out of his spacious watrie wildernes, he then suddenly sent a huge Whale and a Dolphin, and by the power of his commanding Trident, had seated two of his choycest Trytons on them, altring their de-formed Sea-shapes, bestowing on them the borrowed bodies of two absolute Actors, euen the verie best our instāt time can yeeld; & personating in them, the seuerall *Genii* of *Corinea*, the beauti-full Queene of *Cornewall*, and *Amphion* the Father of hermonie or Musick.
>
> (Henry 1610, B4r)

Munday's description inverts the impersonation and describes the tritons as being made man-like, which presumably means becoming bipedal in order to sit astride their mounts. But the impersonation does not end there. One of the tritons has to play the part of Corinea and the other Amphion. When these costumes were first used, then, the conceit was not that actors played tritons but that tritons were translated into (given the 'borrowed bodies' of) human actors in order to impersonate Corinea and Amphion. As with the property ass-head fixed on the actor playing Bottom in *A Midsummer Night's Dream*, the self-referentiality circuit is thereby closed.

In an extended literary 'stage direction' that recreates the scene for the reader, Munday describes Corinea's approach to Prince Henry:

> CORINEA, a very fayre and beautifull Nimphe, representing the Genius of olde Corineus Queene, and the Prouince of Cornewall, suited in her watrie habit yet riche and costly, with a Coronet of Pearles and Cockle shelles on her head, saluteth the PRINCE.
>
> (Henry 1610, C1v)

Munday's 'stage direction' for Burbage's 'entrance' in the sea-pageant includes similar head-gear:

> AMPION [*sic*], a graue and iudicious Prophet-like personage, attyred in his apte habits, euery way answerable to his state and profession, with his wreathe of Sea-shelles on his head, and his harpe hanging in fayre twine before him: personating the Genius of Wales, giueth the Prince this Farewell.
>
> (Henry 1610, C4r).

That these expensive costumes so well suit fishy Caliban and Ariel-as-sea-nymph, and that we know Burbage and Rice were permitted to keep them by the London Corporation just as *The Tempest* was being written, makes their use in the play almost undeniable (Saenger 1995). Ariel is a singing role suited to a boy actor, so the obvious assignment is that the adult-size Amphion costume became Caliban and the boy-sized Corinea costume became Ariel-as-sea-nymph.[23]

Removing all doubt on the point, Shakespeare put into *The Tempest* an unmistakable allusion to this sea-pageant:

> ADRIAN (*to Gonzalo*) 'Widow Dido' said you? You make me study of that: she was of Carthage, not of Tunis.
>
> GONZALO This Tunis, sir, was Carthage.
>
> ADRIAN Carthage?
>
> GONZALO I assure you, Carthage.
>
> ANTONIO (*to Sebastian*) His word is more than the miraculous harp.

SEBASTIAN He hath raised the wall, and houses too.

ANTONIO What impossible matter will he make easy next?

SEBASTIAN I think he will carry this island home in his pocket, and give it his son for an apple.

(The Tempest 2.1.86–96)

As Capell was the first to record (Capell and Collins 1779–80b, 62), the 'miraculous harp' alludes to Amphion, founder of Thebes who built its seven-gated wall by charming the stones into place with the music from his lyre (Hornblower and Spawforth 1996, 'Amphion and Zethus').[24] Burbage played Amphion in the sea-pageant for Prince Henry, and as the leading actor of the King's Men presumably played Prospero in *The Tempest.* Surveying the various accounts of Amphion and his muscle-bound brother Zethus, James George Frazer observes that the comparisons 'suggest the feebleness of brute strength by comparison with the power of genius' (Apollodorus 1921, 338n1–339n2, 3.5.5), which is of course also the point of Prospero's charming of Ferdinand's sword (1.2.469) and Ariel-as-harpy's charming of Alonso, Sebastian, and Antonio's swords (3.3.60–8). As Prospero, Burbage retains more than something of the creative power he had as Amphion, and the actor playing Caliban, now wearing the same costume, has more than something of the bodily indeterminacy of the bipedal triton impersonating Amphion: '[TRINCULO] Legged like a man, and his fins like arms!' (2.2.33–4). Caliban is Prospero's descendant ('I acknowledge mine' 5.1.278–9) not by paternity, as Dympna Callaghan suggests (Callaghan 2000, 134–8), but by theatricality: he is a cast-off.

Sebastian mocks the power of Gonzalo's word to raise up Carthage by conflating it with Tunis, and urged on by Antonio he imagines the whole island pocketed up and given to his son for a gift. The point of the sea-pageant was to mark that the investiture of King James's son as Prince of Wales formalized his inheritance of an island of seafarers that Neptune himself gave to his fourth son Albion, and in Munday's account the winds and waves 'were whist and still' in honour of the occasion (Henry 1610, B3r–v, C3r). Shakespeare's only use of the adjective 'whist', meaning silent, is in Ariel's song: 'kissed | The wild waves whist' (1.2.379–80), and Ferdinand confirms this power to silence and still the waves: 'This music crept by me upon the waters, | Allaying both their fury and my passion' (1.2.394–5). Shakespeare's creative imagination seems indebted to the sea-pageant not only for the costumes that shaped the characters of Ariel and Caliban, but also for the idea that having raised the waves Prospero can allay them with his 'art'. Recalling that Prospero did not raise the waves in the first place – there was no storm, only the likeness of one – we should understand that this apparent reversibility is illusory. Ferdinand stops experiencing the tempest when Ariel stops imitating it.

Reversibility is the key to the pageant that Prospero puts on for his heirs, the masque of Ceres, Iris, Juno, and the nymphs and reapers. In an obvious way this is made clear at the end of the masque by Prospero's dissolving of his own construction (a vision 'melted into air' 4.1.150), plucked down by recollection of the conspirators just as Antonio and Sebastian pluck down what they see as Gonzalo's baseless fabric. But the matter of reversibility enters into the masque, unseen, right at the beginning in the words of Iris. Clearly, the classical character of Ceres symbolizes the hoped-for fertility of the marriage union, but so too does Iris. She is the rainbow goddess, and in the biblical account of the worst tempest ever, God set a rainbow in the sky to signify that there would be no more such floods and that every plant and animal on Earth would thereafter be subordinate to human needs (Genesis 9.1–17). Reflecting on that moment, it is easy to see why Lynn White Junior describes Christianity as 'the most anthropocentric religion the world has seen' (White Junior 1967, 1205), although Keith Thomas is doubtless right that White overstates the power of religion *vis-à-vis* economics (Thomas 1983, 23). Of course, the theological context of Ceres, Iris, and Juno is pagan not Christian Rome, but it is worth observing that much of the masque (4.1.86–101) is concerned with establishing that, like the Christian God, these gods will now leave the happy couple alone. Iris confirms that Venus and Cupid were on their way to ruin the occasion by stimulating pre-marital lust ('Some wanton charm upon this man and maid' 4.1.95) but the danger is averted: Cupid has, as Prospero will, broken the source of his power. This seems to leave the way clear for an entirely joyous celebration, but as critics now constantly emphasize it is a pleasure cut short by Prospero's recollection of a loose end.[25]

However, what is generally overlooked by critics searching for something sour in the masque is that it begins with a description of the countryside that seems idyllic but contains a hint of environmental degradation:

IRIS
Ceres, most bounteous lady, thy rich leas
Of wheat, rye, barley, vetches, oats, and peas;
Thy turfy mountains where live nibbling sheep,
And flat meads thatched with stover, them to keep;
Thy banks with peonied and twillèd brims
                              (*The Tempest* 4.1.60–4)

The meaning of 'peonied and twilled brims' (in the Folio it is
'pioned, and twilled brims') has long been debated, and Furness's
Variorum could not compress the debate (up to 1892) into fewer
than six full pages (Shakespeare 1892, 195–201, 4.1.43). In 1910
Thomas P. Harrison hit upon 'pioned' being the past participle of
the verb 'to pion', meaning to excavate a trench (as pioneers do)
and so produce an embankment of earth. Since 'to twill' is to weave
so as to produce diagonal ridges, the idea is of the banks of a
stream 'artificially heaped up for protection . . . and criss-crossed
with branches of trees' so that the tops (brims) are attractively
hatched (Harrison 1910, 9). The important word here is 'artificially', for whereas George Lyman Kittredge took the meaning to
be natural patterning – cut 'by the current and by the weather of
winter and early spring' (Shakespeare 1946, 4.1.64n) – Harrison's
point had been that human effort to diminish erosion by weath-
ering was the line's essence. Indeed, Harrison was so annoyed by
Kittredge's adoption of the thrust of his explanation while turning
it to the opposite sense that he published another note directing
the reader to descriptions and illustrations of similar earthworks in
the US Department of Agriculture Forest Service *Handbook of
Erosion-Control Engineering on the National Forests* (Harrison 1943,
425). As Kermode and Orgel record, Harrison's explanation – that
Iris is referring to human efforts to prevent soil erosion – has
prevailed (Shakespeare 1954, 4.1.64n; Shakespeare 1987, 4.1.64n).
In this context, Prospero's deforestation of the island could be
understood as a reaction to erosion (he is making earthworks to
protect the natural) or alternatively as its cause (his chopping down
of trees is making it worse). There is little to help us choose between
these alternatives, although Ariel's report that he has gathered the
king and his followers in a small wood that 'weather-fends' (5.1.10)
Prospero's home does rather suggest that chopping down this
wood is folly.

Still, a man such as Prospero who can command the weather
has no need of the natural protection of trees. On the other hand,
as we have seen, the extent of Prospero's magic is recurrently ques-
tioned in the play and, although critics have tended to treat him
as a sorcerer, there is little shown to the audience that has to be
understood as magic. Moreover, as in *A Midsummer Night's Dream*,
the play shows an unmistakable concern with natural phenomena
being taken for magic. The greatest claims for Prospero's magic
are made just as he abjures it:

> PROSPERO
> Ye elves of hills, brooks, standing lakes and groves,
> And ye that on the sands with printless foot
> Do chase the ebbing Neptune, and do fly him
> When he comes back; you demi-puppets that
> By moonshine do the green sour ringlets make
> Whereof the ewe not bites; and you whose pastime
> Is to make midnight mushrooms, that rejoice
> To hear the solemn curfew; by whose aid,
> Weak masters though ye be, I have bedimmed
> The noontide sun, called forth the mutinous winds,
> And 'twixt the green sea and the azured vault
> Set roaring war – to the dread rattling thunder
> Have I given fire, and rifted Jove's stout oak
> With his own bolt; the strong-based promontory
> Have I made shake, and by the spurs plucked up
> The pine and cedar; graves at my command
> Have waked their sleepers, oped, and let 'em forth
> By my so potent art. But this rough magic
> I here abjure.
>
> (*The Tempest* 5.1.33–51)

Impressive as this catalogue of tricks is, there seems little possibility
that an audience will take it seriously. Whose graves might Prospero
be referring to, here on this island? Prospero we know is defor-
esting the island, but the recurrent references are to logs cut with
an axe (3.1.0, 10, 17, 24, 67; 3.2.90) not whole trees 'by the spurs
plucked up'. The rifting of a stout oak sounds like the release of
Ariel from the pine in which Sycorax imprisoned him, and we
might wonder if this speech was written before 1.2 where we heard
of Ariel's confinement.

In fact, it was written long before in the sense that it was lifted largely from Medea's speech in Ovid's *Metamorphoses*:

> Ye Ayres and windes: ye Elves of Hilles, of Brookes, of
>     Woods alone,
> Of standing Lakes, and of the Night approche ye
>     everychone.
> Through helpe of whom (the crooked bankes much
>     wondring at the thing)
> I have compelled streames to run cleane backward to their
>     spring.
> By charmes I make the calme Seas rough, and make the
>     rough Seas plaine
> And cover all the Skie with Cloudes, and chase them
>     thence againe.
> By charmes I rayse and lay the windes, and burst the
>     Vipers jaw,
> And from the bowels of the Earth both stones and trees
>     doe drawe.
> Whole woods and Forestes I remove: I make the
>     Mountaines shake,
> And even the Earth it selfe to grone and fearfully to quake.
> I call up dead men from their graves: and thee O lightsome
>     Moone
> I darken oft, though beaten brasse abate thy perill soone.
> Our Sorcerie dimmes the Morning faire, and darkes the
>     Sun at Noone.
>
>                                   (Ovid 1567, M3v)

As Geoffrey Bullough notes, Shakespeare's version is indebted to Ovid's Latin and to Arthur Golding's English translation (Bullough 1975, 315), and Lyne understands Prospero's act of resurrection to be this very use of Ovid itself, a 'rough' kind of magic because mediated through Golding's English (Lyne 2000, 159–61). Bate, on the other hand, thinks that here Prospero realizes that his magic is seductive and open to abuse – raising the dead being a divine prerogative – and hence abjures it to distinguish himself from the dark practices of Sycorax and Medea (Bate 1993, 252).

Lyne and Bate are right to focus on resurrection, and it should be noted that other Shakespeare plays from this period share the concern: Thaisa is apparently resurrected by Cerimon in *Pericles*, Hermione is apparently resurrected by Paulina in *The Winter's Tale*,

Cornelius's switching of potions makes possible Imogen's recovery from apparent death in *Cymbeline*, and in *The Tempest* Ferdinand is apparently brought back from the dead. Most importantly, these are only apparent resurrections and they have material explanations. Despite their intense interest in the minutiae of how Shakespeare used his source, Lyne and Bate overlook a crucial difference between Medea's speech and Prospero's regarding the larger matter of reversibility in general, of which resurrection is but the most impressive particular. Prospero claims to have dimmed the sun, and summoned winds and rough seas, but not to have undone these acts. Medea, by contrast, can reverse what she does: 'I make the calme Seas rough, and make the rough Seas plaine | And cover all the Skie with Cloudes, and chase them thence againe. | By charmes I rayse and lay the windes'. Even more than Prospero's, Medea's interventions in the natural landscape sound like acts of human civilization that the original audiences and readers would have recognized: clearing woods and forests and making mountains shake.

Caliban is described in the Folio list of parts as a 'saluage' man (from *silva*, Latin for wood), and his carrying of logs is not only a menial duty but also a mark that the world from which he comes is being destroyed by his settler-master. Although we must not mistake subsequent resonances for original ones, later audiences and readers familiar with the effects of nineteenth-century industrialization would also get the sense that this is about the advance of human civilization from the reference to dimmed skies. In fact, London suffered coal-fire smog as early as the thirteenth century (White Junior 1967, 1204). Prospero's tricks, the real and sordid domination of nature, are irreversible. Like Sycorax, who imprisoned Ariel but could not release him, Prospero has the power to change the world in ways that he cannot undo. The ship is whole at the end of the play not because Prospero put it back together but because it was not smashed in the first place. Alonso can receive Ferdinand as if back from the dead only because he was never in danger. Prospero's apparent magic represents human ingenuity at its peak, not supernature at all. Most importantly, the one-way transformatory power of Prospero's 'art' (in which we may read the new technologies of commercial exploitation) illustrates that the only way to hold on to what one most wants to preserve is not to discover how to bring it back once it is gone, but to learn not to destroy it in the first place. For all that the showmen who used the kind of thermoscope recently discovered in Jamestown pretended to be able to control the weather, their experiments were limited to measuring it and, at the very best, predicting how it might change. Such knowledge can give us the power to predict the future effects upon Gaia of our actions, and to plan accordingly. As the ecocritics must be aware, there is an alternative: Gaia's responses can easily eliminate the cause of global harm by eliminating us.

*

The second book of Lucretius' *De rerum natura* (*On the nature of things*) begins:

> Pleasant it is, when over a great sea the winds trouble the waters, to gaze from shore upon another's tribulation: not because any man's troubles are a delectable joy, but because to perceive what ills you are free from yourself is pleasant.
>
> (Lucretius Carus 1924, 85, Book 2 lines 1–4)

Hans Blumenberg points out that this is not smugness:

> It has nothing to do with a relationship among men, between those who suffer and those who do not; it has rather to do with the relationship between philosophers and reality; it has to do with the advantage gained through Epicurus' philosophy, the possession of an inviolable, solid ground for one's view of the world.
>
> (Blumenberg 1997, 26)

Paradoxically, a philosophy based on the randomness of atomic movements gives solid ground from which to observe the randomness of a ship tossed on the raging sea, and it was for this sense of solidity, of having a material atomistic basis for one's principles, that Newton valued Epicurus and sought to include his verses in the second edition of *Principia Mathematica*. Shakespeare constructed *The Tempest* so that Miranda's position on shore watching the ship in distress at sea is coterminous with the audience's, but whereas she suffers with those she thinks she has seen (1.2.5–6) we, like Lucretius, see that their ills are illusory. The power of Newton's contribution to science was predictability: for almost all that human beings want to do – including Stefano's claimed trip from the moon to the Earth (2.2.136–8) – Newton's three laws of motion are suffi-cient. Newton could not have foreseen this use of his laws, but because they are essentially true (the Einsteinian differences being irrelevant for most purposes) they are endlessly applicable in new contexts. So too with art. Shakespeare's play proleptically links colonization, deforestation, and extreme weather in ways that can now be seen as prescient.

# Conclusion
# EcoShakespeare

The Shakespearian scholar Edmond Malone was the first to apply serious effort to the recovery of the original performance context of Shakespeare's plays, and he concluded that the Globe playhouse was hexagonal in shape on the outside and circular on the inside (Shakespeare 1780, 5). Malone thought he had eyewitness evidence for this, because his friend Hester Thrale (subsequently Hester Piozzi), whom he knew through Samuel Johnson, owned the site of the Globe and told him what she had seen. While working on her property, builders had uncovered the 'really curious remains of the old Globe Playhouse, which though hexagonal in form, was round within' (Piozzi 1910, 28; Chambers 1923, 428). Malone's era, the early eighteenth century, was the age of coal, which displaced timber as the prime source of industrial energy and remained so until the more cleanly burning hydrocarbon, oil, became widely and cheaply available 100 years later (McNeill 2000, 55–63). Malone pioneered the academic methodology of reaching into the past to make sense of Shakespeare in the present, recovering authentic fossils of evidence (original records, verifiable accounts, unedited texts) and discarding their later descendants (De Grazia 1991). This new method emerged, by chance, just as industrial technology abandoned the fuel of felled trees in preference for the hydrocarbons of their more densely compacted fossilized ancestors.

That burning coal and oil releases more energy than timber was empirically obvious long before the chemical structures of these hydrocarbons were known. In the mid-nineteenth century Friedrich A. Kekulé was working on the atomic bonding of carbon atoms, and puzzling what kind of structure could account for the known valencies. In a dream, Kekulé saw the troublesome atoms dancing in a line before transmuting into a serpent that turned back on itself to eat its own tail, and upon waking he realized that this solved the puzzle. By connecting the last atom to the first, he produced the now familiar arrangement of the benzene ring symbolized by a circle inside a hexagon (Figure 5).

Rounded in Kekulé's sleep, the carbon atom chain formed the shape that Hester Thrale saw emerging from the grounds of her South London brewery as the Globe foundations were uncovered. It happens that Thrale was wrong: all authoritative representations show that the Globe had many more than six sides – but the coincidence of shapes is instructive, for although the detail was wrong Malone's method remains with us.[26] Likewise Kekulé was wrong. Or rather, just as Newton's rules are qualified by relativity, so Kekulé's account of the carbon bonds was qualified by quantum mechanics in the work of Linus Pauling. At the heart of quantum mechanics' counter-intuitive account of the physical world is the inherent indeterminacy (specifically, the immeasurability) of forces and masses at the subatomic level. Embedded in the new mechanics that swept away Newtonian determinism was a modern form of the Epicurean indeterminacy, the unpredictable

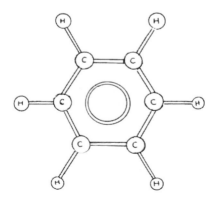

*Figure 5* The benzene ring. C is a carbon atom, H a hydrogen atom.

atomic swerve that gives us free will (Lucretius Carus 1924, 101–9, Book 2 lines 216–332) and that Newton found so valuable.

These homologous accounts usefully illustrate the uneven progression of knowledge, and how elements derived from ancient ways of thinking may be the spurs to new ideas. As this book has tried to show, ecocriticism treats with scepticism the Enlightenment certainties about organic and inorganic processes, and disdains its classificatory systems that arbitrarily separate parts from the wholes they comprise. Once those certainties are abandoned, some ancient ideas about humankind and all other life (including the Earth itself) are revealed as startling prefigurations of recent work in genetics and Systems Thinking. The more we discover about animals the harder it is to maintain the hard distinctions between them and us that have become so firmly entrenched since Shakespeare's time, and the more we learn about the exchange of chemicals and energy between the oceans and the atmosphere the less quaint seems the system of correspondences that E. M. W. Tillyard claimed were the commonplaces of Elizabethan cosmology. From this viewpoint, Shakespeare's plays start to seem not only keenly observed accounts of how philosophical commonplaces are put to rhetorical (and especially political) use, but also investigations of the commonplaces themselves. Contrary to the thrust of recent radical criticism (especially British Cultural Materialism), Shakespeare found much to admire in the cosmological commonplaces of his age. We should admire them too, for they anticipated some key ideas that will dominate twenty-first century science and culture.

During the sixteenth and seventeenth centuries a new view of nature began to take shape in distinction from the inherited Greek tradition: instead of an organism, the universe could better be thought of as a machine (Collingwood 1945, 4–9, 93–112). We have seen the two views in competition in Shakespeare's plays, and in particular we have seen how things that appear magical or organic are really mundane or inorganic. The plays do not, however, simply validate the new thinking since (as for example with Prospero's devices) it takes a kind of trickery to pass off nature as supernature. Since the Enlightenment the idea that the Earth is alive has seemed superstitious and archaic thinking, and the idea that it is a machine has seemed obviously right, but with the newest science (Gaia and neo-Darwinism) we can see that things that appear mechanical can be alive and things that seem magically alive can be essentially mechanical. Artificial Intelligence, which cannot be far off, will doubtless show that the difference is not qualitative. Likewise the nature/culture distinction is essentially false, as indeed its etymology tells us: culture, in Raymond Williams's long-derived definition, means at its simplest the tending of natural growth (Williams 1958, 335). The new science invokes ideas not current since Shakespeare's time, although reached by completely different routes. We can revisit the philosophical implications of those old ideas, which is what the plays reflect upon, to see the implications of the new science on our sense of who we are.

With the work of critics such as Gail Kern Paster we are returning to some old concerns with a new realization that they are not necessarily conservative or reductive. The distinctive contribution of Green thinking broadens our view of why these ideas are worth returning to. It is not simply that the critical pendulum has swung back again in favour of stressing orderliness over disruption. Indeed, quite the opposite is true. The latest science undermines key aspects of the Enlightenment and this, rather than postmodernism, is the truly politically and culturally disruptive thinking of our time. It is a matter of urgency that new ways of thinking about humankind's relations with the Earth are put to use, for disrupting the still-persisting habits of thought under which industrial capitalism emerged and flourished is the most important intellectual project for the twenty-first century. If it fails humankind is unlikely to witness the twenty-second century. Science takes us back to a kind of transformation of not-life into life that for Enlightenment thinkers was the height of absurdity and which, since Darwin, has had a material basis that makes all religious, and many philosophical, explanations superfluous. Just as politicized radical criticism based on gender, race, and sexual orientation takes in the full range of cultural articulations, so Green criticism has an application beyond the obviously green-world plays such as *A Midsummer Night's Dream*, hence the choice of plays considered in this book. It is hoped that the readings offered here show the potential for a new kind of criticism that uses as a cultural lens the most pressing concerns of our time.

# Notes

1 A calenture is 'A disease incident to sailors within the tropics, characterized by delirium in which the patient, it is said, fancies the sea to be green fields, and desires to leap into it' (OED calenture *n.* 1), which sounds rather suspiciously precise. The OED's examples of the uses of 'calenture' all refer to generic fevers until Jonathan Swift, in a poem full of Shakespeare allusions, used the term like this:

> So, by a Calenture misled,
> The Mariner with Rapture sees,
>   On the smooth Ocean's azure Bed,
> Enamel'd Fields and verdant Trees.
> (Swift 1721, lines 25–8)

It is impossible not to suspect that Theobald's use of word was prompted by this poetic sharpening of the term.

2 In 1948 the Hungarian scientist Dennis Gabor invented a means of improving the resolving power of the electron microscope by photographing not the image produced by the beam of electrons bouncing off an object but instead the interference pattern between this beam and a beam reflected by the object's background. Viewed in a coherent light (that is, one with its waves in phase), this photograph reveals depth-information about the object, making a three-dimensional picture rather than a two-dimensional picture. With the development of lasers as sources of bright, coherent light in the 1960s it became possible to make three-dimensional pictures stored on two-dimensional planes of glass: holograms.

3   In the snowflake, the Star of David pattern of two overlapping triangles governs the overall shape and is fully repeated, at a small scale, in each of the corners. Each of these six corners is itself made of a further six Star of David patterns, and so on down through the scale. Expressed as a mathematical function, this principle of self-repetition goes on indefinitely. In the example of the fern too, the overall shape of the leaf is repeated in each petal of the leaf, and each petal is made of still smaller versions of the same shape. The example of the fern leaf is particularly instructive because it indicates the informational economy of reusing at different scales a single set of genetic instructions for growth, which brevity is doubtless advantageous to an organism. Similarly, as Richard Dawkins showed, the simple instruction for a growing limb to branch can be reused throughout an organism to produce the great variety of physical structures that we see in living things (Dawkins 1986, 43–74).

In another way too, the Tillyardian holographic principle applies to biology. Every cell in the human body contains a full set of instructions, genes, necessary for making the whole body. Indeed, each contains not only the instructions for making the individual but also the instructions (inherited from the parent of the opposite sex) for making body parts the individual does not possess but which will be needed by his or her child of the opposite sex. Men carry unexpressed genes for making breasts, ovaries, and a womb, and women carry unexpressed genes for making a penis and an Adam's apple. Each of us contains information that is redundant to ourself as an individual and that expresses our place in a lineage of genes, for the correct way to think about it is not that we carry genes in order to propagate ourselves but that the genes made us (in two kinds) to carry and propagate them.

4   It could be argued that calling Empson a New Critic understates the degree to which he was his own man. However, as a recent biography of Empson up to the age of 33 makes clear, his dependence upon the ideas of his tutor I. A. Richards (for example in claiming that literary meaning is inherently overdetermined) was extensive (Haffenden 2005). While the differences between Richards, Empson, and F. R. Leavis were as important as their collective differences from the American branch of New Criticism, what this generation of critics had in common and differentiated them from previous generations is coherent enough to form a family resemblance and hence a single label.

5   Wiener's comments on modern country life occur in the midst of an argument that in a sense we all live on borrowed time because we rely on technological solutions not yet invented to ensure that our children have a future (Wiener 1950, 20–58). This was also the insight of Jay Wright Forrester's modelling that underlay the alarming Club of Rome report *Limits to Growth*, which commented that 'Applying

technology to the natural pressures that the environment exerts against any growth process has been so successful in the past that a whole culture has evolved around the principle of fighting against limits rather than learning to live with them' (Meadows *et al.* 1972, 150).

The danger of what the report's authors call 'technological optimism' (Meadows *et al.* 1972, 154) is easily illustrated from the nuclear power industry, which, having no means to render harmless its waste products, buries them in the ground in the hope that either these burial sites will remained undisturbed for the thousands of years necessary for the radiation to decay to natural levels, or that new technologies will be invented to hasten the process. It is salutary to recall that although we can (just about) read papyri from 3,000 years ago, data written to computer storage media such as magnetic disks as recently as the 1970s are quite unrecoverable now, even using machines preserved in science museums. Writing the locations of nuclear dumps on paper might, for all this technological optimism, be the safest way to preserve such valuable knowledge.

6  This point is humorously made by the visiting alien in the television comedy *Mork and Mindy*, who cannot comprehend his human girl-friend's objection to the construction of a nearby nuclear power station, since any accidental spills can easily be removed with the everyday cleaning product 'Nuke-Away'. Horrified to learn that humankind has no 'Nuke-Away', Mork protests that without it nuclear power is the height of recklessness.

7  Or it might be Antium; compare 'Your native town' (5.6.49) said to Aufidius with 'in Corioles' (4.6.92).

8  As Jonathan Culler points out, from a structuralist point of view such movement from singularities to collectivities and back again (that is, the movement called synecdoche) is the essence of metaphor (Culler 1975, 180–1). Typically, a metaphor (say, iron horse) is made of two class synecdoches – from member (horse) to class (rideable and loco-motive) to member (train) – but it works equally with movement between parts and wholes, whence our comic sense of the absurd oneness of sex from Iago's phrase. Shakespeare was as capable of staging this movement dramatically as he was of encapsulating it poet-ically, and hence the comedy of the composite beast with four legs and two voices (comprised Trinculo and Caliban under a gaberdine) in *The Tempest*. Significantly for our understanding of Caliban's bodily nature, the composite beast strikes Stefano as a marketable oddity (2.2.68–70) just as Caliban's (also composite?) physiognomy strikes Trinculo (2.2.27–30).

9  In *King John* Prince Arthur imagines that the fire Hubert uses to heat irons to put out his eyes 'is dead with grief' (4.1.105) and Hubert imagines rekindling it with breath; the child's pathetically innocent talk is, of course, the wind that has cooled Hubert. In *Richard 2* the deposed king imagines that his story told at a fireside would make the

brands 'in compassion weep the fire out' (5.1.48), and likewise Miranda imagines that the wood Ferdinand carries will, when burned, 'weep for having wearied you' (*The Tempest* 3.1.19).

10  *2 Henry 4* has directions for a character named Silence and *3 Henry 6* calls for characters to enter silently (Shakespeare 1623, p6v). The Oxford Complete Works text of *The Merchant of Venice* twice invents directions for characters to 'speak silently' to one another (1.3.38, 5.2.126) without explaining what this means (Wells *et al.* 1987, 324, 327).

11  In fact the sobriquet 'black prince' is unrecorded prior to its appearance in the index to Richard Grafton's prose *Chronicles* (Grafton 1569, c2r).

12  Lisa Hopkins thinks that the image of 'high upreared and abutting fronts' suits not so much the 'restricting "girdle"' of the playhouse as 'the typical design of a London street, in which houses built with projecting jetties jutted across at each other over the cluttered space below' (Hopkins 1997, 9). In my reading, the same structural opposition was visible in the incomplete building and then softened by its final O-ness.

13  The only exception I have found is John F. Andrews's Everyman Shakespeare edition, which offers both senses (Shakespeare 1997, 6n20).

14  In Charles Dickens's *David Copperfield*, Micawber offers the precept 'Annual income twenty pounds, annual expenditure nineteen nineteen six, result happiness. Annual income twenty pounds, annual expenditure twenty pounds ought and six, result misery' (Dickens 1850, 125–6).

15  Critiquing this association is a central concern of ecofeminist theory and criticism, as exemplified in Branch *et al.* 1998, Bowerbank 2004, and Phillips 2004. Of the wider concerns of ecofeminism, Mellor 1996, Soper 1996, Kirk 1997, and Nanda 1997 are typical, although it should be understood in relation to the last that the 'green revolution' means the application of science to majority world agriculture in the 1960s.

16  That shepherds live from the sale of wool, not lamb, was apparently unknown to those responsible for the production of *The Winter's Tale* at the London Globe replica in 1997. Covering the stage with nearly 100 sheepskin rugs for this scene gave the distinct impression that the entire flock had been slaughtered for the occasion.

17  There are two moments that we might fix upon in this regard, conception and birth, and Edmund mocks both: 'My father compounded with my mother under the Dragon's tail and my nativity was under Ursa Major, so that it follows I am rough and lecherous. Fut!' (2.123–6). Normally, of course, the date of conception determines the date of birth (which follows 266 days later), and the play has a loose end in that Shakespeare began by making Edmund abnormal in this

regard too: '[GLOUCESTER] this knave came something saucily into the world before he was sent for' (1.21–2). Possibly this characterological furrow about premature birth was abandoned early in composition because Shakespeare recalled that he had ploughed it exhaustively in *Richard 3*.

18 Paulina puts her finger on another aspect of the paradoxical inheritance of vice when trying to convince Leontes that the baby Perdita is his:

> [PAULINA]
> [She is] So like to him that got it, if thou hast
> The ordering of the mind too, 'mongst all colours
> No yellow in 't, lest she suspect, as he does,
> Her children not her husband's.
> (*The Winter's Tale* 2.3.105–8)

That is, the baby is so much the inheritor of its father's characteristics that it might even, as an adult, suspect (as Leontes does) that its children are not really its own, and this even though it is female and hence biologically enabled to be certain who its children are. Leontes' fears are absurd because they cannot be inherited.

19 An additional small piece of linguistic evidence that Shakespeare re-read *King Lear* before writing *The Tempest* is that only these two plays use the word 'kibe' (chilblain) in connection with the mind: *King Lear Quarto* 5.8–9 and *The Tempest* 2.1.280–1.

20 The play audience knows both claims to be untrue, but readers are treated to an additional irony about the latter. The Folio's *dramatis personae* names the scene as 'an vn-inhabited Island', only to follow this by identifying at least 22 of its inhabitants (Shakespeare 1623, B4r).

21 In what we should presumably read as Freudian repression, Prospero does not count himself as one of the men Miranda has seen, but includes Caliban: 'Thou think'st there is no more such shapes as he, | Having seen but him and Caliban' (1.2.481–2).

22 Editors since Edward Capell (Capell and Collins 1779–80b, 65), including the recent Oxford Shakespeare and Arden Shakespeare, have taken 'Get a new man!' to be contemptuously addressed to Prospero. Since Prospero is not present and there are no other candidates to fill Caliban's post, this is implausible. The point of Caliban's freedom song is how his life, not Prospero's, will be transformed by his new post, and for the Variorum Horace Howard Furness supplied the much better suggestion that 'get' means 'become' (Shakespeare 1892, 2.2.194n).

23 As will be argued, much of what passes for Prospero's magic can be explained by ordinary means, but an exception seems to be the dry and undamaged clothing of the Italian courtiers. Ariel is explicit that 'All but mariners | Plunged in the foaming brine' and yet they received

'On their sustaining garments not a blemish, | But fresher than before' (1.2.211–12, 19–20). Antonio perversely contradicts Gonzalo when he marvels at their garments being undamaged ('If but one of his pockets could speak, would it not say he lies?' 2.1.70–1) and Gonzalo seems to retract his absolute admiration by saying that his doublet is 'in a sort' (2.1.108), that is only somewhat, as fresh as when he first put it on. And yet, something miraculous seems to have occurred, although the wonder if is not that the clothing remained dry but that it was not ruined by a wetting. The same can at least be said for the costumes of Amphion (Caliban) and Corinea (Ariel-as-sea-nymph) which can hardly have remained dry during the sea-pageant but which were still worth giving to the actors Burbage and Rice 'in liew of their paynes therein' (Wallace 1913).

24  Peggy Muñoz Simonds took the harp to be Orpheus', not Amphion's (Simonds 1995). The obvious problem with this reading is that, charming as it was upon the living ear, there are no stories of Orpheus' music affecting stones.

25  The trajectory of late twentieth-century responses to the play can be traced through the stress placed on this moment. For Frank Kermode it was only an 'apparently unnecessarily perturbation' (Shakespeare 1954, lxxv) whereas by the 1980s it marked 'the first moment when the magician . . . is in danger of losing his control' over the events on the island (Shakespeare 1987, 50), and could even be read as 'the most important scene of the play' (Barker and Hulme 1985, 196).

26  One committed commentator, Martin Clout, maintains that Thrale and Malone were right: see Clout 1987a; Clout 1987b; Clout 1992; Clout 1993–4. The overwhelming contrary evidence is summarized in Mulryne and Shewring 1997.

# References

Apollodorus (1921) *The Library*, James George Frazer (ed. and trans.), Vol. 1: Books 1–3.9, The Loeb Classical Library, London: Heinemann.

Aristotle (1910) *The Works*, David Ross (ed.), Vol. 4: HISTORY OF ANIMALS: *Historia Animalium*, 12 vols, London: Oxford University Press.

Aristotle (1930) *The Works*, David Ross (ed.), Vol. 2: PHILOSOPHY OF NATURE: *Physica*; *De Caelo*; *De Generatione et Corruptione*, 12 vols, London: Oxford University Press.

Baran, Paul (1964) 'On Distributed Communications Networks', *Institute of Electrical and Electronic Engineers Transactions on Communications* 12: 1–9.

Barker, Francis and Peter Hulme (1985) 'Nymphs and Reapers Heavily Vanish: The Discursive Con-texts of *The Tempest*', in *Alternative Shakespeares*, John Drakakis (ed.), New Accents, London: Routledge, 191–205.

Bate, Jonathan (1990) 'Ovid and the Sonnets: Or, Did Shakespeare Feel the Anxiety of Influence?', *Shakespeare Survey* 42: 65–76.

—— (1991) *Romantic Ecology: Wordsworth and the Environmental Tradition*, London: Routledge.

—— (1993) *Shakespeare and Ovid*, Oxford: Clarendon Press.

—— (2000) *The Song of the Earth*, London: Picador.

Belsey, Catherine (1985) 'Disrupting Sexual Difference: Meaning and Gender in the Comedies', in *Alternative Shakespeares*, John Drakakis (ed.), New Accents, London: Routledge, 166–90.

—— (1999) *Shakespeare and the Loss of Eden*, Basingstoke: Macmillan.

Bentham, Jeremy (1789) *An Introduction to the Principles of Morals and Legislation*, London: T. Payne and Son.

Berry, Herbert (1987) *Shakespeare's Playhouses*, New York: AMS.

Blake, William (1789) *Songs of Innocence and of Experience, Shewing the Two Contrary States of the Human Soul*, London: William Blake.

Blumenberg, Hans (1997) *Shipwreck with Spectator: Paradigm of a Metaphor for Existence*, Steven Rendall (trans.), Cambridge MA: The Massachusetts Institute of Technology Press.

Bowerbank, Sylvia (2004) *Speaking for Nature: Women and Ecologies of Early Modern England*, Baltimore MD: Johns Hopkins University Press.

Bramwell, Anna (1989) *Ecology in the Twentieth Century: A History*, New Haven CT: Yale University Press.

Branch, Michael P., Rochelle Johnson, Daniel Patterson, and Scott Slovic (eds) (1998) *Reading the Earth: New Directions in the Study of Literature and Environment*, Moscow ID: University of Idaho Press.

Bray, Alan (1982) *Homosexuality in Renaissance England*, London: Gay Men's Press.

Brecht, Bertolt (1964) *Brecht on Theatre*, John Willett (ed. and trans.), London: Methuen.

Brooks, Cleanth (1947) *The Well Wrought Urn: Studies in the Structure of Poetry*, New York: Reynal and Hitchcock.

Brown, Michael and John May (1989) *The Greenpeace Story*, London: Dorling Kindersley.

Brown, Paul (1985) '"This Thing of Darkness I Acknowlege Mine": *The Tempest* and the Discourse of Colonialism', *Political Shakespeare: New Essays in Cultural Materialism*, Jonathan Dollimore and Alan Sinfield (eds), Manchester: Manchester University Press, 48–71.

Bullough, Geoffrey (1973) *Narrative and Dramatic Sources of Shakespeare*, Vol. 7: Major Tragedies: *Hamlet; Othello; King Lear; Macbeth*, 8 vols, London: Routledge & Kegan Paul.

Bullough, Geoffrey (1975) *Narrative and Dramatic Sources of Shakespeare*, Vol. 8: Romances: *Cymbeline; The Winter's Tale; The Tempest*, 8 vols, London: Routledge & Kegan Paul.

Butler, Charles (1609) *The Feminine Monarchie or a Treatise Concerning Bees, and the Due Ordering of Them*, STC 4192, Oxford: Joseph Barnes.

Butlin, R. A. (1976) 'Land and People, Circa 1600', in *A New History of Ireland*, 3: Early Modern Ireland 1534–1681, T. W. Moody, F. X. Martin and F. J. Byrne (eds), Oxford: Oxford University Press, 142–67.

Callaghan, Dympna (ed.) (2000) *Shakespeare Without Women*, Accents on Shakespeare, London: Routledge.

Campbell, Lily B. (1947) *Shakespeare's 'Histories': Mirrors of Elizabethan Policy*, San Marino CA: Huntington Library.

Capell, Edward and John Collins (1779–80a) *Notes and Various Readings to Shakespeare*, Vol. 1: *All's Well That Ends Well; Antony and Cleopatra; As You Like It; The Comedy of Errors; Coriolanus; Cymbeline; Hamlet; 1 Henry IV; 2 Henry IV; Henry V; 1 Henry VI; 2 Henry VI; 3 Henry VI; Henry VIII; Julius Caesar; King John; King Lear; Love's Labour's Lost*, London: Henry Hughs.

—— (1779–80b) *Notes and Various Readings to Shakespeare*, Vol. 2: *Macbeth*; *Measure for Measure*; *The Merchant of Venice*; *The Merry Wives of Windsor*; *A Midsummer Night's Dream*; *Much Ado About Nothing*; *Othello*; *Richard II*; *Richard III*; *Romeo and Juliet*; *The Taming of the Shrew*; *The Tempest*; *Timon of Athens*; *Titus Andronicus*; *Troilus and Cressida*; *Twelfth Night*; *The Two Gentlemen of Verona*; *The Winter's Tale*, London: Henry Hughs.

Chambers, E. K. (1923) *The Elizabethan Stage*, Vol. 2, 4 vols, Oxford: Clarendon.

—— (1924–5) '"The Disintegration of Shakespeare": The British Academy Annual Shakespeare Lecture Read 12 May 1924', *Proceedings of the British Academy* 11: 89–108.

—— (1930) *William Shakespeare: A Study of Facts and Problems*, Vol. 2, 2 vols, Oxford: Clarendon Press.

Chapman, George (1612) *The Widdowes Teares a Comedie*, STC 4994 BEPD 301, London: [W. Stansby] for J. Browne.

Clarke, Arthur C. (1972) *Report on Planet Three, and Other Speculations*, London: Gollancz.

Clout, Martin (1987a) 'Appendix 2: Notes on the Reconstructed Globe', in *'The Shape of the Globe' and 'The Interior of the Globe': Reports on Seminars Held on 29 March 1983 and 12 April 1986*, Ronnie Mulryne and Margaret Shewring (eds), The Renaissance Drama Newsletter Supplements, 8, Coventry: University of Warwick Graduate School of Renaissance Studies, 94–5.

—— (1987b) *The Globe That Shakespeare Knew: A Critique of the Replica Reconstruction of the First Globe Theatre By the International Shakespeare Globe Centre and a Proposal for as Authentic a Reconstruction as is Possible from Contemporary Evidence*, Battle, East Sussex, UK: Martin S. Clout.

—— (1992) 'The Evaluation and Scheduling of the Globe Theatre Estate', *London Archaeologist* 6(15): 407–14.

—— (1993–4) 'Hester Thrale and the Globe Theatre', *The New Rambler* 9: 34–50.

Coghill, Nevill (1958) 'Six Points of Stage-craft in *The Winter's Tale*', *Shakespeare Survey* 11: 31–41.

Collingwood, R. G. (1945) *The Idea of Nature*, Oxford: Clarendon Press.

Crosby, Joseph (1986) *One Touch of Shakespeare: Letters of Joseph Crosby to Joseph Parker Norris, 1875–1878*, John W. Velz and Frances N. Teague (eds), Washington DC: Folger Shakespeare Library.

Culler, Jonathan (1975) *Structuralist Poetics*, London: Routledge & Kegan Paul.

Dawkins, Richard (1976) *The Selfish Gene*, Oxford: Oxford University Press.

—— (1986) *The Blind Watchmaker*, Harlow: Longman.

De Grazia, Margreta (1991) *Shakespeare Verbatim: The Reproduction of Authenticity and the 1790 Apparatus*, Oxford: Clarendon.

Dennett, Daniel C. (1995) *Darwin's Dangerous Idea*, London: Penguin.

—— (2003) *Freedom Evolves*, London: Penguin.

Dent, R. W. (1981) *Shakespeare's Proverbial Language: An Index*, Berkeley CA: University of California Press.

Dickens, Charles (1850) *The Personal History of David Copperfield*, illustrations by H. K. Browne, London: Bradbury and Evans.

—— (1854) *Hard Times: For These Times*, London: Bradbury and Evans.

Dillon, Janette (2000) *Theatre, Court and City, 1595–1610: Drama and Social Space in London*, Cambridge: Cambridge University Press.

Dollimore, Jonathan (1984) *Radical Tragedy: Religion, Ideology and Power in the Drama of Shakespeare and His Contemporaries*, Hemel Hempstead: Harvester Wheatsheaf.

Duncan-Jones, Katherine (2001) *Ungentle Shakespeare*, The Arden Shakespeare, London: Thomson Learning.

Eagleton, Terry (1983) *Literary Theory: An Introduction*, Oxford: Basil Blackwell.

—— (1990) *William Shakespeare*. Rereading Literature. Oxford: Basil Blackwell.

Egan, Gabriel (1997) 'Ariel's Costume in the Original Staging of *The Tempest*', *Theatre Notebook* 51: 62–72.

—— (2004) *Shakespeare and Marx*, Oxford Shakespeare Topics, Oxford: Oxford University Press.

—— (2005) 'Platonism and Bathos in Shakespeare and Other Early Modern Drama', *Refiguring Mimesis: Representation in Early Modern Literature*, Jonathan Holmes and Adrian Streete (eds), Hatfield: University of Hertfordshire Press, 59–78.

Empson, William (1930) *Seven Types of Ambiguity*, London: Chatto & Windus.

Felperin, Howard (1990) *The Uses of the Canon: Elizabethan Literature and Contemporary Theory*, Oxford: Clarendon.

Fitzpatrick, Joan (2005) *Food in Shakespeare*, Aldershot: Ashgate.

Foakes, R. A. and R. T. Rickert (eds) (1961) *Henslowe's Diary, Edited with Supplementary Material, Introduction and Notes*, Cambridge: Cambridge University Press.

Ford, John (1997) *'Tis Pity She's a Whore*, Derek Roper (ed.), Revels Student Editions, Manchester: Manchester University Press.

Fudge, Erica (2000) *Perceiving Animals: Humans and Beasts in Early Modern English Culture*, Basingstoke: Macmillan.

—— 'How a Man Differs from a Dog', *History Today* 53(6): 38–44.

Garnier, Robert (1595) *The Tragedie of Antonie*, Mary Herbert (Countess of Pembroke) (trans.), STC 11623 BEPD 108b, London: P[eter] S[hort] for William Ponsonby.

Gibbons, Brian (1996) 'The Question of Place', *Cahiers Élisabéthains* 50: 33–43.

Godlovitch, Stanley, Rosalind Godlovitch and John Harris (eds) (1971) *Animals, Men and Morals: An Enquiry Into the Maltreatment of Non-humans*, London: Gollancz.

186   References

Grady, Hugh (1991) *The Modernist Shakespeare: Critical Texts in a Material World*, Oxford: Clarendon Press.

Grafton, Richard (1569) *A Chronicle at Large . . . of the Affayres of Englande from the Creation of the Worlde, Vnto the First Yere of Queene Elizabeth*, STC 12147, London: Henry Denham for Richard Tottle and Humphrey Toye.

Granville-Barker, Harley (1927) *Prefaces to Shakespeare*, Vol. 1: Introduction, *Love's Labour's Lost, Julius Caesar, King Lear*, London: Sidgwick & Jackson.

Greenblatt, Stephen (1985) 'Invisible Bullets: Renaissance Authority and Its Subversion, *Henry IV* and *Henry V*', in *Political Shakespeare: New Essays in Cultural Materialism*, Jonathan Dollimore and Alan Sinfield (eds), Manchester: Manchester University Press, 18–47.

—— (2004) *Will in the World: How Shakespeare Became Shakespeare*, London: Random House.

Greene, Robert (1588) *Pandosto: The Triumph of Time*, STC 12285, London: Thomas Orwin for Thomas Cadman.

Greg, W. W. (ed.) (1907) *Henslowe Papers: Being Documents Supplementary to Henslowe's Diary*, London: Bullen.

Gurr, Andrew (1977) '*Henry V* and the Bees' Commonwealth', *Shakespeare Survey* 30: 61–72.

—— (1988) 'Money or Audiences: The Impact of Shakespeare's Globe', *Theatre Notebook* 42: 3–14.

—— (1989) '*The Tempest*'s Tempest at Blackfriars', *Shakespeare Survey* 41: 91–102.

—— (1999) 'Who is Lovewit? What is he?' in *Ben Jonson and Theatre: Performance, Practice and Theory*, Richard Cave, Elizabeth Schafer, and Brian Woolland (eds), London: Routledge, 5–19.

Haffenden, John (2005) *William Empson*, Vol. 1: Among the Mandarins, 2 vols, Oxford: Oxford University Press.

Hammond, Antony (1987) ' "It Must be Your Imagination Then": The Prologue and the Plural Text in *Henry V* and Elsewhere', in *'Fanned and Winnowed Opinions': Shakespearean Essays Presented to Harold Jenkins*, John W. Mahon and Thomas A. Pendleton (eds), London: Methuen, 133–50.

Harrison, Thomas P. (1910) 'A Note on *The Tempest*', *Modern Language Notes* 25: 8–9.

—— (1943) 'A Note on *The Tempest*: A Sequel', *Modern Language Notes* 58: 422–6.

Hazlitt, William (1817) *Characters of Shakespear's Plays*, London: C. H. Raynell.

Heffernan, Carol Falvo (1995) *The Melancholy Muse: Chaucer, Shakespeare and Early Medicine*, Duquesne Studies: Language and Literature Series, 19, Pittsburgh PA: Duquesne University Press.

Henry, Prince of Wales (1610) *Londons Love, to the Royal Prince Henrie, Meeting Him at His Returne from Richmonde. [By A. Munday]*, STC 13159, London: E. Allde for N. Fosbrooke.

Hine, William L. (1995) 'Inertia and Scientific Law in Sixteenth-century Commentaries on Lucretius', *Renaissance Quarterly* 48: 728–41.

Hofstadter, Douglas R. (1980) *Gödel, Escher, Bach: An Eternal Golden Braid*, Harmondsworth: Penguin.

Holinshed, Raphael (1587) *The First and Second Volumes of the Chronicles. (The Third Volume.) Newlie Augmented and Continued By J. Hooker Alias Vowell Gent. and Others. (A. Fleming; F. Thin [I.e. Thynne; and J. Stow])*, STC 13569, Vol. 1, 3 vols, London: [H. Denham,] (at the expenses of J. Harison, G. Bishop, R. Newberie, H. Denham, and T. Woodcock.

Holland, Henry (1606) *The Historie of Adam: The Four-fold State of Man, Well Formed in His Creation, Deformed in His Corruption, Reformed in Grace, and Perfected in Glory*, STC 13587, edited and completed by Edward Topsell, London: T[homas] E[ast] for Thomas Man.

Holland, Peter (1995) 'The Shapeliness of *The Tempest*', *Essays in Criticism* 45: 208–29.

—— (1997) *English Shakespeares: Shakespeare on the English Stage in the 1990s*, Cambridge: Cambridge University Press.

Hopkins, Lisa (1997) 'Neighbourhood in *Henry V*', in *Shakespeare and Ireland: History, Politics, Culture*, Mark Thornton Burnett and Ramona Wray (eds), Basingstoke: Macmillan, 9–26.

Hornblower, Simon and Antony Spawforth (eds) (1996) *The Oxford Classical Dictionary*, 3rd edition, Oxford: Clarendon.

Hosley, Richard (1975) 'The Playhouses', *The Revels History of Drama in English*, 3: 1576–1613, Clifford Leech and T. W. Craik (eds), London: Methuen, 119–235.

Hunt, Alan (1996) *Governance of the Consuming Passions: A History of Sumptuary Law*, Basingstoke: Macmillan.

Hunter, Robert (1979) *The Greenpeace Chronicle*, London: Pan.

Jardine, Lisa (1983) *Still Harping on Daughters: Women and Drama in the Age of Shakespeare*, Hemel Hempstead: Harvester Wheatsheaf.

Jardine, Mick (1999) 'Jonson as Shakespeare's Other', in *Ben Jonson and the Theatre: Performance, Practice and Theory*, Richard Cave, Elizabeth Schafer, and Brian Woolland (eds), London: Routledge, 104–15.

Jensen, Michael P. (2003–4) 'Talking Books with: Jonathan Bate', *Shakespeare Newsletter* 53: 113–14.

Jonson, Ben (1616) *The Workes of Benjamin Jonson*, STC 14751, London: William Stansby.

Jusserand, J. J. (1916) *With Americans of Past and Present Days*, London: T. Fisher Unwin.

Kastan, David Scott (1999) *Shakespeare After Theory*, New York: Routledge.

Keats, John (1820) Lamia, Isabella, The Eve of Saint Agnes, *and Other Poems*, London: Taylor and Hessey.

Kingsley-Smith, Jane (2003) *Shakespeare's Drama of Exile*, Palgrave Shakespeare Studies, Basingstoke: Palgrave Macmillan.

Kirk, Gwyn (1997) 'Standing on Solid Ground: A Materialist Ecological Feminism', in *Material Feminist: A Reader in Class, Difference, and Women's*

*Lives*, Rosemary Hennessy and Chrys Ingraham (eds), New York: Routledge, 345–63.

Knights, L. C. (1933) *How Many Children Had Lady Macbeth?*, Cambridge: Gordon Fraser.

Knowles, Richard (2002) 'How Shakespeare Knew *King Leir*', *Shakespeare Survey* 55: 12–35.

Knutson, Roslyn Lander (2001) *Playing Companies and Commerce in Shakespeare's Time*, Cambridge: Cambridge University Press.

Kristeva, Julia (1984) *Desire in Language*, Oxford: Basil Blackwell.

Laertius, Diogenes (1891) *The Lives and Opinions of Eminent Philosophers*, C. D. Yonge (trans.), Bohn's Classical Library, London: George Bell.

Laroque, François (1984) 'A New Ovidian Source for the Statue Scene in *The Winter's Tale*', *Notes and Queries* 229: 215–17.

Lefebvre, Henri (1991) *The Production of Space*, Donald Nicholson-Smith (trans.), Oxford: Blackwell.

Lesser, Zachary (2004) *Renaissance Drama and the Politics of Publication: Readings in the English Book Trade*, Cambridge: Cambridge University Press.

Lovelock, James E. (1972) 'Gaia as Seen Through the Atmosphere', *Atmospheric Environment* 6: 579–80.

—— (1983) 'Daisy World: A Cybernetic Proof of the Gaia Hypothesis', *Coevolution Quarterly* 38: 66–72.

Lovelock, James E. and Lynn Margulis (1974a) 'Atmospheric Homeostasis by and for the Biosphere: The Gaia Hypothesis', *Tellus* 26: 2–9.

—— (1974b) 'Biological Modulation of the Earth's Atmosphere', *Icarus* 21: 471–89.

Lucretius Carus, Titus (1924) *De Rerum Natura*, W. H. D. Rouse (trans.), The Loeb Classical Library, London: Heinemann.

Lyne, Raphael (2000) 'Ovid, Golding, and the "Rough Magic" of *The Tempest*', in *Shakespeare's Ovid: The* Metamorphoses *in the Plays and Poems*, A. B. Taylor (ed.), Cambridge: Cambridge University Press, 150–64.

McCombie, Frank (1981) 'Garlands in *Hamlet* and *King Lear*', *Notes and Queries* 226: 132–4.

McCracken, Eileen (1959) 'The Woodlands of Ireland Circa 1600', *Irish Historical Studies* 11: 271–96.

McGuire, Philip (1994) *Shakespeare: The Jacobean Plays*, English Dramatists, Basingstoke: Macmillan.

McNeill, John (2000) *Something New Under the Sun: An Environmental History of the Twentieth-century World*, London: Penguin.

Marlowe, Christopher (1604) *The Tragicall History of D[octor] Faustus*, STC 17429 BEPD 205a, London: Valentine Simmes for Thomas Bushell.

—— (1616) *The Tragicall History of the Life and Death of Doctor Faustus*, STC 17432 BEPD 205d, London: for John Wright.

Marx, Karl (1954) *Capital: A Critical Analysis of Capitalist Production*, Frederick Engels (ed.), Vol. 1, 3 vols, London: Lawrence & Wishart.

—— (1967) 'PhD Thesis (University of Jena): "The Difference between the Democritean and the Epicurean Philosophy of Nature"', in *Activity in Marx's Philosophy*, Norman D. Livergood (ed.), The Hague: Martinus Nijhoff, 57–109.

—— (1977) *Economic and Philosophical Manuscripts of 1844*, London: Lawrence & Wishart.

Marx, Karl and Frederick Engels (1940) *The German Ideology, Parts 1 and 3*, The Marxist-Leninist Library, 17, London: Lawrence & Wishart.

—— (1974) *The German Ideology*, C. J. Arthur (ed.), London: Lawrence & Wishart.

Meadows, Donella H., Dennis L. Meadows, Jorgen Randers, and William W. Behrens III (1972) *The Limits to Growth: A Report for the Club of Rome's Project on the Predicament of Mankind*, London: Earth Island.

Mehren, Joan von (1994) *Minerva and the Muse: A Life of Margaret Fuller*, Amherst MA: University of Massachusetts Press.

Mellor, Mary (1996) 'Ecofeminism and Ecosocialism: Dilemmas of Essentialism and Materialism', in *The Greening of Marxism*, Ted Benton (ed.), Democracy and Ecology, New York: Guildford Press, 251–67.

Merton, Robert King (1965) *On the Shoulders of Giants: A Shandean Postscript*, New York: Free Press.

Milton, John (1966) *Poetical Works*, Douglas Bush (ed.), London: Oxford University Press.

Morgann, Maurice (1777) *An Essay on the Dramatic Character of Sir John Falstaff*, London: T. Davies.

Mullaney, Steven (1988) *The Place of the Stage: License, Play, and Power in Renaissance England*, London: University of Chicago Press.

Mulryne, J. R. and Margaret Shewring (eds) (1997) *Shakespeare's Globe Rebuilt*, Cambridge: Cambridge University Press.

Murdoch, Iris (1973) *The Bell*, London: Chatto & Windus.

Nanda, Meera (1997) '"History is What Hurts": A Materialist Feminist Perspective on the Green Revolution and Its Ecofeminist Critics', in *Material Feminist: A Reader in Class, Difference, and Women's Lives*, Rosemary Hennessy and Chrys Ingraham (eds), New York: Routledge, 364–94.

Orrell, John (1980) 'Peter Street at the Fortune and the Globe', *Shakespeare Survey* 33: 139–51.

Ovid (1567) *The Xv Bookes of . . . Metamorphosis, Translated Oute of Latin Into English Meeter By Arthur Golding*, STC 18956, London: William Seres.

—— (1916a) *Metamorphoses*, Frank Justus Miller (trans.), Vol. 1: Books 1–8, 2 vols, The Loeb Classical Library, London: Heinemann.

—— (1916b) *Metamorphoses*, Frank Justus Miller (trans.), Vol. 2: Books 9–15, 2 vols, The Loeb Classical Library, London: Heinemann.

Paster, Gail Kern (2004) *Humoring the Body: Emotions and the Shakespearean Stage*, Chicago IL: University of Chicago Press.

Phillips, Bill (2004) 'The Rape of Mother Earth in Seventeenth Century English Poetry: An Ecofeminist Interpretation', in *Atlantis: Revista de la Asociacion Espanola de Estudios Anglo-Norteamericanos* 26: 49–60.

Piozzi, Hester (1910) *Dr Johnson's Mrs Thrale: Autobiography, Letters, and Literary Remains*, A. Hayward and J. H. Lobban (eds), Edinburgh: T. N. Foulis.

Plato (1871) *The Dialogues, Translated in English with Analyses and Introductions*, Benjamin Jowett (ed. and trans.), Vol. 1: *Charmides, Lysis, Laches, Protagoras, Euthydemus, Ion, Meno, Euthyphro, Apology, Crito, Phaedo, Symposium, Phaedrus, Cratylus*, 4 vols, Oxford: Clarendon Press.

Quarshie, Hugh (1999) *Second Thoughts About* Othello, International Shakespeare Association Occasional Papers, 7, Chipping Campden: International Shakespeare Association.

Rawls, John (1971) *A Theory of Justice*, Cambridge MA: Harvard University Press.

Rhodes, Richard (1986) *The Making of the Atomic Bomb*, New York: Simon & Schuster.

Rudd, Niall (2000) 'Pyramus and Thisbe in Shakespeare and Ovid', in *Shakespeare's Ovid: The* Metamorphoses *in the Plays and Poems*, A. B. Taylor (ed.), Cambridge: Cambridge University Press, 113–25.

Rueckert, William (1978) 'Literature and Ecology: An Experiment in Ecocriticism', *Iowa Review* 9(1): 71–86.

Rutland, Duke of (1905) *The Manuscripts of His Grace the Duke of Rutland, G. C. B., Preserved at Belvoir Castle*, Vol. 4, 5 vols, London: Historical Manuscripts Commission.

Saenger, Michael Baird (1995) 'The Costumes of Caliban and Ariel Qua Sea-nymph', *Notes and Queries* 240: 334–6.

Schleiner, Winifred (1980) 'Jaques and the Melancholy Stag', *English Language Notes* 17: 175–9.

Segrè, Emilio (1970) *Enrico Fermi, Physicist*, Chicago IL: University of Chicago Press.

Shakespeare, William (1597) *[Richard 3] The Tragedy of King Richard the Third*, STC 22314 (Q1) BEPD 142a, London: Valentine Simmes [and Peter Short] for Andrew Wise.

—— (1916b)(1608) *[King Lear] M. William Shak-speare: His True Chronicle Historie of the Life and Death of King Lear and His Three Daughters*, STC 22292 BEPD 265a (Q1), London: [Nicholas Okes] for Nathaniel Butter.

—— (1623) *Mr. William Shakespeares Comedies, Histories, & Tragedies. Published According to the True Originall Copies*, STC 22273 (F1), London: Isaac Jaggard and Edward Blount.

—— (1723) *The Works*, Alexander Pope (ed.), Vol. 3: *King Lear; King John; Richard 2; 1 Henry 4; 2 Henry 4; Henry 5*, 6 vols, London: Jacob Tonson.

—— (1725) *The Works*, Alexander Pope (ed.), Vol. 1: Preface; *The Tempest; A Midsummer Night's Dream; The Two Gentlemen of Verona; The Merry Wives of Windsor; Measure for Measure; The Comedy of Errors; Much Ado About Nothing*, 6 vols, London: Jacob Tonson.

—— (1733a) *The Works*, Lewis Theobald (ed.), Vol. 4: *King Henry V; 1st Part of King Henry VI; 2nd Part of King Henry VI; 3rd Part of King*

*Henry VI; King Richard III*, 7 vols, London: A. Bettesworth, C. Hitch, J. Tonson, F. Clay, W. Feales, and R. Wellington.

—— (1733b) *The Works*, Lewis Theobald (ed.), Vol. 6: *Coriolanus*; *Julius Caesar*; *Antony and Cleopatra*; *Cymbeline*, 7 vols, London: A. Bettesworth, C. Hitch, J. Tonson, F. Clay, W. Feales, and R. Wellington.

—— (1747a) *The Works of Shakespear*, William Warburton (ed.), Vol. 4: *Richard II*; *1 Henry IV*; *2 Henry IV*; *Henry V*; *1 Henry VI*, 8 vols, London: J. and P. Knapton and S. Birt.

—— (1747b) *The Works of Shakespear*, William Warburton (ed.), Vol. 6: *King Lear*; *Timon of Athens*; *Titus Andronicus*; *Macbeth*; *Coriolanus*, 8 vols, London: J. and P. Knapton and S. Birt.

—— (1765) *The Plays*, Samuel Johnson (ed.), Vol. 4: *The Life and Death of Richard the Second*; *The First Part of King Henry the Fourth*; *The Second Part of King Henry the Fourth*; *The Life of King Henry the Fifth*; *The First Part of King Henry the Sixth*, 8 vols, London: J. and R. Tonson [etc.].

—— (1778a) *The Plays*, George Steevens (ed.), Vol. 6: *King Henry V*; *King Henry VI Part I*; *King Henry VI Part II*, *King Henry VI Part III*, 10 vols, London: C. Bathurst [and] W. Strahan [etc.].

—— (1778b) *The Plays*, George Steevens (ed.), Vol. 9: *Troilus and Cressida*; *Cymbeline*; *King Lear*, 10 vols, London: C. Bathurst [and] W. Strahan [etc.].

—— (1780) *Supplement to the Edition of Shakespeare's Plays Published in 1778 By Samuel Johnson and George Steevens*, Edmond Malone (ed.), Vol. 1: Advertisement; Additional Observations; *Venus and Adonis*; *The Rape of Lucrece*; *Sonnets*; *The Passionate Pilgrim*; *A Lover's Complaint*, 2 vols, London: C. Bathurst [and] W. Strahan [etc.].

—— (1821) *The Plays and Poems*, Edmond Malone and James Boswell (eds), Vol. 17: *Henry IV Part II*; *Henry V*, 21 vols, London: F. C. and Rivington [etc.].

—— (1892) *The Tempest*, Horace Howard Furness (ed.), New Variorum, 9, Philadelphia PA: Lippincott.

—— (1898) *Coriolanus*, E. K. Chambers (ed.), The Warwick Shakespeare, London: Blackie.

—— (1928) *Coriolanus*, The New Variorum, Philadelphia PA: Lippincott.

—— (1946) *Sixteen Plays:* The Tempest; Much Ado About Nothing; A Midsummer Night's Dream; The Merchant of Venice; As You Like It; Twelfth Night; Richard 2; 1 Henry 4; Henry 5; Romeo and Juliet; Julius Caesar; Macbeth; Hamlet; King Lear; Othello; Antony and Cleopatra, George Lyman Kittredge (ed.), Boston MA: Ginn.

—— (1954) *The Tempest*, Frank Kermode (ed.), The Arden Shakespeare, London: Methuen.

—— (1975) *As You Like It*, Agnes Latham (ed.), The Arden Shakespeare, London: Methuen.

—— (1977) *Antony and Cleopatra*, Emrys Jones (ed.), New Penguin Shakespeare, London: Penguin.

—— (1982) *Henry V*, Gary Taylor (ed.), The Oxford Shakespeare, Oxford: Oxford University Press.

—— (1986) *The Complete Works*, Stanley Wells, Gary Taylor, John Jowett, and William Montgomery (eds), Oxford: Oxford University Press.

—— (1987) *The Tempest*, Stephen Orgel (ed.), The Oxford Shakespeare, Oxford: Oxford University Press.

—— (1993) *As You Like It*, Alan Brissenden (ed.), The Oxford Shakespeare, Oxford: Oxford University Press.

—— (1994a) *Anthony and Cleopatra*, Michael Neill (ed.), The Oxford Shakespeare, Oxford: Oxford University Press.

—— (1994b) *Coriolanus*, R. B. Parker (ed.), The Oxford Shakespeare, Oxford: Oxford University Press.

—— (1995) *Antony and Cleopatra*, John Wilders (ed.), The Arden Shakespeare, London: Routledge.

—— (1997) *As You Like It*, John F. Andrews (ed.), The Everyman Shakespeare, London: J. M. Dent.

—— (2000a) *King Lear*, Stanley Wells (ed.), The Oxford Shakespeare, Oxford: Oxford University Press.

—— (2000b) *The Tempest*, Christine Dymkowski (ed.), Shakepeare in Production, Cambridge: Cambridge University Press.

Shelley, Percy Bysshe (1840) *Essays, Letters from Abroad, Translations and Fragments*, Mary Shelley (ed.), Vol. 1, 2 vols, London: Edward Moxon.

Sidney, Philip (1595) *The Defence of Poesie*, STC 22535, London: [Thomas Creede] for William Ponsonby.

Simonds, Peggy Muñoz (1995) '"Sweet Power of Music": The Political Magic of "The Miraculous Harp" in Shakespeare's *The Tempest*', *Comparative Drama* 29: 61–90.

—— (1998) '"My Charms Crack Not": The Alchemical Structure of *The Tempest*', *Comparative Drama* 32: 538–70.

Singer, Peter (1973) '"Animal Liberation": Review of Stanley Godlovitch, Rosalind Godlovitch, and John Harris, Editors *Animals, Men and Morals* (New York: Taplinger, 1971)', *New York Review of Books* 20(3): 17–21.

Singer, Peter (1975) *Animal Liberation: A New Ethics for Our Treatment of Animals*, New York: New York Review.

—— (1979) *Practical Ethics*, Cambridge: Cambridge University Press.

Smith, Irwin (1952) 'Theatre Into Globe', *Shakespeare Quarterly* 3: 113–20.

Snow, C. P. (1959) *The Two Cultures and the Scientific Revolution: The Rede Lecture 1959*, Cambridge: Cambridge University Press.

Sokal, Alan and Jean Bricmont (1998) *Intellectual Impostures: Postmodern Philosophers' Abuse of Science*, London: Profile.

Sokol, B. J. (1995) *Art and Illusion in* The Winter's Tale, Manchester: Manchester University Press.

—— (2003) *A Brave New World of Knowledge: Shakespeare's* The Tempest *and Early Modern Epistemology*, Madison NJ: Fairleigh Dickinson University Press.

Soper, Kate (1996) 'Feminism, Ecosocialism, and the Conceptualization of Nature', in *The Greening of Marxism*, Ted Benton (ed.), Democracy and Ecology, New York: Guildford Press, 268–71.

Speed, John (1612) *The Theatre of the Empire of Great Britaine: Presenting an Exact Geography of of the Kingdomes of England, Scotland, Ireland*, STC 23041, London: [William Hall] to be sold by John Sudbury and George Humble.

Spurgeon, Caroline F. E. (1931) *Shakespeare's Iterative Imagery: (1) as Undersong (2) as Touchstone in His Work*, Annual Shakespeare Lectures at Oxford, Oxford: Oxford University Press.

Stephenson, Tom (1989) *Forbidden Land: The Struggle for Access to Mountain and Moorland*, Ann Holt (ed.), Manchester: Manchester University Press.

Sterne, Laurence (1760) *The Life and Opinions of Tristram Shandy*, second edition, Vol. 1, 9 vols, London: R. and J. Dodsley.

Swift, Jonathan (1721) *The Bubble: A Poem*, London: Benjamin Tooke sold by J. Roberts.

Taylor, Charles (1989) *Sources of the Self: Making of the Modern Identity*, Cambridge MA: Harvard University Press.

Taylor, Gary (1983) '*King Lear*: The Date and Authorship of the Folio Version', *The Division of the Kingdoms: Shakespeare's Two Versions of* King Lear, Gary Taylor and Michael Warren (eds), Oxford Shakespeare Studies, Oxford: Clarendon, 351–468.

Taylor, Gary and Michael Warren (eds) (1983), *The Division of the Kingdoms: Shakespeare's Two Versions of* King Lear, Oxford: Clarendon Press.

Thomas, Keith (1983) *Man and the Natural World: Changing Attitudes in England 1500–1800*, London: Penguin.

Thomson, Leslie (1999) 'The Meaning of *Thunder and Lightning*: Stage Directions and Audience Expectations', *Early Theatre* 2: 11–24.

Tillyard, E. M. W. (1943) *The Elizabethan World Picture*, London: Chatto & Windus.

Topsell, Edward (1607) *The Historie of Foure-footed Beastes*, STC 24123, London: William Jaggard.

—— (1608) *The Historie of Serpents*, STC 24124, London: William Jaggard.

Wallace, C. W. (1913) 'A London Pageant of Shakespeare's Time: New Information from Old Records', 28 March, *The Times*, 6.

Wear, Andrew (1992) 'Making Sense of Health and the Environment in Early Modern England', in *Medicine in Society: Historical Essays*, Andrew Wear (ed.), Cambridge: Cambridge University Press, 119–47.

Wells, Robin Headlam (2000) *Shakespeare on Masculinity*, Cambridge: Cambridge University Press.

Wells, Stanley, Gary Taylor, John Jowett, and William Montgomery (1987) *William Shakespeare: A Textual Companion*, Oxford: Oxford University Press.

White Junior, Lynn (1967) 'The Historical Roots of Our Ecological Crisis', 10 March (Number 3767), *Science* 155: 1203–7.

Wiener, Norbert (1950) *The Human Use of Human Beings: Cybernetics and Society*, London: Eyre & Spottiswoode.

Wiggins, Martin (2000) *Shakespeare and the Drama of His Time*, Oxford Shakespeare Topics, Oxford: Oxford University Press.

Williams, Raymond (1958) *Culture and Society, 1780–1950*, London: Chatto & Windus.

—— (1973) *The Country and the City*, London: Chatto & Windus.

—— (1976) *Keywords*, London: Croom Helm.

Wordsworth, William and Samuel Taylor Coleridge (1800) *Lyrical Ballads, with Other Poems*, second edition, Vol. 1, 2 vols, London: T. N. Longman and O. Rees.

# Index

Nazism 54, 90
Neill, Michael 109, 112, 114, 118
Neptune (Roman mythology) 154, 162, 164
New Age movement 3, 30
New Criticism 9, 26–9, 33, 177
New England (USA) 40
New Exchange (London) 49
New Hampshire (USA) 40
New Orleans 3
New Shakspeare Society 11
New York (USA) 45
Newton, Isaac, *Opticks* 148; *Principia Mathematica*: 22, 25–6, 116, 148, 170–1, 173–4; his work on alchemy 148
Nile river 109–10, 111–13, 117, 131
Noah (of Genesis) 61, 105–6, 130, 131, 165
Northern Ireland Civil Rights movement 18
nuclear weapons *see* atomic weapons
'Nuke-Away', atomic-spillage cleaning product humans lack 178

Oppenheimer, J. Robert 17
organic unity in art 8–14, 26–9
Orgel, Stephen 152, 153, 162, 166
Orpheus (Greek mythology) 181
*Othello* 8, 31–2, 63, 135, 178
Ovid, *Metamorphoses* 111–12, 130–1, 149, 158, 168–9
ozone hole 22–3

Paris (France) uprising 18
Paris Garden, Liberty of 47
Paster, Gail Kern 97–8, 175
pastoralism 35, 39–40; and exile 95–6, 104–5, 106
Pauling, Linus 173
Philadelphia (USA) 4
Philistines 62

Piozzi, Hester 172–3, 181
Plato 114; *The Republic* 36–7; *Symposium* 110
playhouses, location of 45–8, 151–2, 153–4; *see also* Blackfriars, Liberty of, and playhouse, Globe playhouse, Rose playhouse, Theatre, playhouse called the, and Fortune playhouse
Plutarch 112
Pope, Alexander, his edition of Shakespeare 5–6, 11, 12–13, 37, 82
postmodernism 28, 30, 175
predation 103
prophecy 83–9, 136–7, 150
Proserpina (Greek mythology) 125–6
Protestantism 69, 93
Pyrrha and Deucalion, Greek myth of 61–2, 130–1
Pythagoras 116–17

Quarshie, Hugh, *Second Thoughts about* Othello 31
queer theory/gay studies 34, 44, 175

racism 3, 20–1, 30–1
Ramblers' Association 40
Rand Corporation 18
Rawls, John, *Theory of Justice* 53
Rice, John, actor 152, 163, 181
*Richard 2* 68, 69, 82–4, 86, 87, 89–90, 95, 138, 139, 150, 155, 178–9
*Richard 3* 180
Richards, I. A. 177
Romantic poets 34, 35–9, 43, 148
Rome (Italy) 52, 54, 57, 61, 64
*Romeo and Juliet* 146
Rose playhouse 96
Rousseau, Jean-Jacques, *Discourse on the Origin of Inequality* 53; *The Social Contract* 53